Assessment in Art Therapy

Assessment in Art Therapy gives a unique insight into the diverse contemporary practices that constitute assessment in art therapy, providing an overview of the different approaches employed in Britain and the USA today. This professional handbook comprises three parts. 'Sitting Beside' explores the discursive and the relational in art therapy assessments with adults and children in different settings. 'Snapshots from the Field' presents a series of short, practice-based reports which describe art therapists working in private practice, secure settings and community mental health centres. 'A More Distant Calculation' consists of chapters that describe the development and use of different kinds of art-based assessment procedures developed on both sides of the Atlantic, as well as different kinds of research about art therapy assessment. Both students and practitioners alike will benefit from the wealth of experience presented in this book, which demonstrates how art therapists think about assessment; the difficulties that arise in art therapy assessment; and the importance of developing the theory and practice of art therapy assessment, whilst taking into account the changing demands of systems and institutions.

Andrea Gilroy is Head of the Department of Professional and Community Education at Goldsmiths, University of London.

Robin Tipple is Associate Tutor in Art Psychotherapy at Goldsmiths, University of London.

Christopher Brown is an Art Therapist with Hertfordshire Partnership NHS Foundation Trust and Associate Tutor in Art Psychotherapy at Goldsmiths, University of London.

'This book is a timely addition to the literature particularly in the current climate of 'evidence-based practice' and how decisions regarding referral and assessment of art therapy are reached. Understanding suitability and recommendation to different treatment approaches within the context of a multidisciplinary team is an essential component of the discrete activity of the art therapist and how patients can find their way to access this type of ongoing treatment approach. Using theoretical approaches, formal testing procedures and illustrated clinical examples, the chapters offer a variety of consideration to the different ways of thinking which contribute to understanding the complex activity of what happens at the first encounter between art therapist and patient.'

Tessa Dalley, Association of Child Psychotherapists, Honorary Member of British Association of Art Therapists, Member of Health Professions Council (HPC)

Assessment in Art Therapy

Edited by
Andrea Gilroy, Robin Tipple and
Christopher Brown

Routledge
Taylor & Francis Group

LONDON AND NEW YORK

First published 2012
by Routledge
27 Church Road, Hove, East Sussex BN3 2FA

Simultaneously published in the USA and Canada
by Routledge
711 Third Avenue, New York NY 10017

Routledge is an imprint of the Taylor & Francis Group, an Informa business

British Library Cataloguing in Publication Data
A catalogue record for this book is available from the British Library

Library of Congress Cataloging-in-Publication Data
Assessment in art therapy / edited by Andrea Gilroy, Robin Tipple, and Christopher Brown.
     p. cm.
   Includes bibliographical references and index.
   ISBN 978–0–415–56794–7 (hardback)—ISBN 978–0–415–56796–1 (pbk)   1. Art therapy—Evaluation.   I. Gilroy, Andrea, 1949–
II. Tipple, Robin.   III. Brown, Christopher.
   RC489.A7A88 2012
   616.89′1656–dc23   2011026729

ISBN: 978–0–415–56794–7 (hbk)
ISBN: 978–0–415–56796–1 (pbk)
ISBN: 978–0–203–14044–4 (ebk)

Typeset in Times by RefineCatch Limited, Bungay, Suffolk

Paperback cover design by Andrew Ward
Cover image: *Untitled collage* by Robin Tipple

Contents

Illustrations

Plates

Situated between pp. 100 and 101

Contributors

Rebecca Arnold is an art therapist/educator who currently resides in Allentown, Pennsylvania. She works in various clinical settings with individuals admitted for inpatient psychiatric and behavioral health services and is an adjunct art therapy professor for both undergraduate and graduate art therapy students.

Donna Betts is a professor at George Washington University, Washington, DC, where she teaches assessment procedures and research. She is involved in a collaborative autism study, is pursuing research at the Smithsonian Institution and continues her research on assessment which includes development of the International Art Therapy Research Database (IATRD; www.arttherapy research.com).

Christopher Brown is an art therapist working in adult mental health in the NHS and teaching on the MA Art Psychotherapy at Goldsmiths, University of London. He is also on the Editorial Board of *Art Therapy Online* (ATOL) and a member of the Tavistock Society of Psychotherapists and Allied Professionals.

Caroline Case is an analytical art therapist in private practice and a child and adolescent psychotherapist at the Knowle Clinic, Bristol. She is known through her many publications in art therapy and psychotherapy journals and through books. For example she is co-author of *The Handbook of Art Therapy* (1992) and recently published *Imagining Animals: Art, Psychotherapy and Primitive States of Mind* (2005) which explores work with hard to reach children.

Martin Cody trained in sculpture in the late 1970s and as an art therapist in 1985. He has recently retired from the NHS having worked in adult psychiatry and therapeutic community settings in Middlesex and Birmingham.

Philippa Cronin is an art therapist with many years of experience of working with forensic patients in prison and currently as Head of Arts Therapies in an NHS adult forensic psychiatry service. She is currently in training as an adult psychoanalytic psychotherapist and has a private art therapy supervisory practice.

Arnell Etherington is an art therapy educator who co-ordinates the Masters of Art Therapy programme at the University of Notre Dame de Damur in San Francisco where she is currently Dean of Art. She has worked in private practice for many years.

Linda Gantt is an eminent art therapist and researcher, currently the Executive Director of the Trauma Recovery Institute (TRI) in Morgantown, WV. She has many publications to her credit and has developed the Formal Elements Art Therapy Scale (FEATS). She has served as the President of the American Art Therapy Association.

Andrea Gilroy is an experienced art therapy educator and researcher, currently Reader in Art Psychotherapy and Head of the Department of Professional and Community Education at Goldsmiths, University of London. Her many publications include *Art Therapy, Research and Evidence-Based Practice* (2006) and *Art Therapy Research in Practice* (2011).

David Henley is an experienced art therapist and educator who has lectured, taught and written extensively on many aspects of art therapy. For many years he has worked with children who have different kinds of disability. He has also taught graduate art therapy students at Long Island University.

Myra Levick developed the first graduate training program in art therapy at Hahnemann/Drexel University, Philadelphia. She was a founder and first president of the American Art Therapy Association and is Editor-in-Chief Emeritus of the *Arts in Psychotherapy*. Now retired, she has founded the South Florida Art Psychotherapy Institute where she continues to consult, teach and supervise.

Marian Liebmann currently works in the Bristol Inner City Mental Health Team. She is also a visiting lecturer at Bristol University and City of Bath College. She has published several books and papers on art therapy, including *Art Therapy with Groups*, *Art Therapy with Offenders* and *Art Therapy in Conflict Resolution*.

Laura V. Loumeau-May teaches Art, Diagnosis and Assessment and other courses at Caldwell College. She specializes in psychiatry, including six years at Mount Sinai Medical Center, New York, and bereavement, through Valley Home Care since 1995. In 2002 an ABC-TV Primetime segment focused on her work with children of 9/11 victims.

Andrew Marshall-Tierney has 25 years experience as an art therapist in adult mental health, mostly in community settings and currently in a low secure unit. He is also Senior Lecturer on the MA Art Therapy course at the University of Hertfordshire.

John McCulloch is an experienced art therapist who provides art therapy for adults with learning disabilities and mental health problems in a number of specialist NHS units in Scotland. This includes work with adults who require short admissions to assessment and treatment services.

Shaun McNiff is an experienced artist, therapist and researcher, currently Dean of Arts at Lesley University, Massachusetts. Past President of the American Association of Art Therapists he has published widely, his many publications include *Art as Medicine* and *Art-Based Research*.

Jane Saotome is a HPC registered art therapist and artist with many years experience working in NHS adult and adolescent mental health settings. She currently works in a therapeutic day service for young people with complex mental health, emotional and behavioural difficulties. She is a visiting lecturer on the MA Art Therapy course at Roehampton University.

Kim Thomas trained as a painter/collage maker, then discovered art therapy, qualifying in the early 1980s. She has many years experience working in adult mental health primarily in the NHS, offering both group and individual art psychotherapy for community and acute inpatient settings.

Robin Tipple works in the NHS with children and young people who have developmental disorders and teaches on the MA in Art Psychotherapy at Goldsmiths, University of London. He has written about art therapy with adults who have learning difficulties and the art therapist's contribution to multidisciplinary assessment.

Introduction

Andrea Gilroy, Robin Tipple and Christopher Brown

This book explores the different practices that constitute assessment in art therapy. Our interest began at a conference hosted by the Scottish Arts Therapies Forum in Edinburgh in March 2008. 'Sharing Best Practice in Assessment in the Arts Therapies' saw a lack of clarity emerge about what exactly assessment is – of what, for whom and how? – coupled with a confusing variety of theories and practices. Set alongside a notable absence of a literature in Britain and a contrasting presence of literature in the USA, art therapy assessment seemed ripe for exploration.

As the book developed it became apparent that art therapy assessment was embedded in different discourses and practices. The aims of assessment were variable: to assist in establishing a diagnosis; to determine the suitability of clients for treatment; and to evaluate progress and outcome. Research and practice could also be linked to the development and use of particular techniques, tools and formal procedures which lay claim to validity and so contributed to professional credibility. This led us to think about why and how these discourses and practices have developed and to consider the social, cultural and political contexts in which they exist.

Understanding the etymology of the word 'assessment' helped us to think about this diversity. 'Assessment' comes from the Latin '*assidere*' which means to 'sit beside' or 'assist in the deliberations of a judge'; this suggests a tension at the heart of art therapy assessment. Is the task to 'sit beside' a prospective new client and provide an environment in which a therapeutic relationship and art-making can begin, or is it a situation that requires judgements to be made about diagnosis, psychopathology, suitability and treatment goals? Other tensions relate to the different discourses within which assessment operates – medical, psychotherapeutic and aesthetic – between practices that are regarded as underpinned by science or by art, and between the rational, the imaginary and the symbolic.

Our aim in this book is to explore these discourses and to capture the diversity of practice in art therapy assessments and so keep the tensions alive in a creative way. Thus, we have not distilled art therapy assessment into guidelines and criteria for practitioners' use; rather we seek to challenge the 'either/or' characterisations of art therapy assessments. We have sought to bring together art therapists who represent different points of view and also cast a wider net through a call, via professional associations and other networks, for short, practice-based reports of art therapy assessments. We were surprised and delighted at the huge range of responses we received from art therapists on both sides of the Atlantic and would like to thank all those who responded so generously, many of whom we unfortunately had to turn down. These responses taught us that the diversity of practice was even greater than we had imagined. Indeed, editing this book has shown us that art therapists do not reflect the stereotypes of 'American' and 'British' practice: American art therapists do not always use art-based tests to assist diagnosis and do attend to unconscious processes; British art therapists do not always seek a psychodynamic formulation and do contribute to diagnostic decisions.

Systems, institutions and people

There are, however, some fundamental differences between American and British systems of mental health care which influence the discourses and practices of assessment in art therapy. The USA has private health insurance for almost everyone, whereas the UK has a National Health Service (NHS) which is free at the point of access, independent of the ability to pay. Health insurance companies in America operate a system of managed care, this being a term 'used to describe a variety of techniques intended to reduce the cost of providing benefits and improve the quality of care' (Wikipedia accessed 22/9/2009). Proponents argue that it increases efficiency and leads to cost-effective treatments; detractors feel that it creates a divide between a target-driven culture and the best interests of patients. Managed care is nearly ubiquitous with 90 per cent of insured Americans enrolled in plans based upon its techniques (ibid.).

It is perhaps not surprising that the model of managed care is now being adopted in Britain in a system that has become over-centralised, inefficient and expensive to run. This has led to a proliferation of government initiatives, management consultants and constant reorganisation, each successive change bringing managed care more fully into the NHS. The UK government's latest paper on the NHS, *Equity and Excellence: Liberating the NHS* (DoH, 2010), privileges patient choice and the measurement of clinical outcomes. This begs a question: as our health care systems become similar, might our practices do the same?

There are, however, differences in art therapists' professional organisations, for example, in their training and entry requirements and thus who art therapists are. In the USA art therapists' first degree may be art, psychology or nursing, whereas in the UK it is usually art. There are also differences in educational and ethical requirements. The ethical principles of the American Art Therapy Association (AATA) direct art therapists to 'develop and use assessment methods to better understand and serve the needs of their clients' (2009: 3). AATA also requires art therapists who use 'standardised assessment instruments' to familiarise themselves with their reliability and validity; practitioners should be competent in their use through appropriate training and supervised practice.

The Health Professions Council (HPC) in Britain provides *Standards of Proficiency for Arts Therapists* (2007) and requires art therapists to 'undertake and record a thorough, sensitive and detailed assessment, using appropriate techniques and equipment'. It is also expected that a 'range of investigation, as appropriate' is undertaken in order to 'observe and record client's responses and assess the implications for diagnosis and intervention'. Art therapists should therefore be able to 'conduct appropriate diagnostic or monitoring procedures'. In contrast, the British Association of Art Therapists (BAAT) offers a statement on diagnosis (2007) which states that the function of assessment is 'to offer therapy'. Whilst there is a recognition that art therapists 'may work alongside medical colleagues who perform diagnosis', in BAAT's view the art therapist 'is not directly involved'. There is, however, a caveat in an acknowledgement that there 'may be useful considerations from the art therapy formulations and hypothesis which may inform or modify the process of diagnosis' (BAAT, 2007).

Added to the requirements of health care systems and professional bodies are the demands of institutions. These vary considerably within the different systems as well as across them. Institutions affect the way in which art therapists formulate their practices and much is dependent on the dominant discourses of the institution. Practice may depend on whether the setting is sympathetic to a psychodynamic approach or aligned to medical, neurological or cognitive approaches. Services and practices are also affected by the presence or absence of physical spaces that enable therapeutic relationships to develop and art-making to flourish, and whether a service's focus is on group and/or individual therapy or on care packages that require only brief work.

The art therapists' personal preferences in relation to theory and practice also contribute to their approach to assessment. Their relationship with other professionals, and the value given to their work, can shape their practice as well. Some prefer to use a particular structure or replicable procedure; others might stress a cognitive approach or be client-centred in their interactions. Some practice with a clear psychotherapeutic intent, interpretation and understanding of the transference being vital to their work; others may or may not include art-making in their assessments. Yet others stress an engagement with art-making; creativity and spontaneity may be foregrounded or the preference might be for art as a communicative medium.

Hierarchical and power relations affect the assessment too. In this way clients could be regarded as the target of practices that begin at a systemic level and work towards them. Here reference is made to health care systems and professional organisations; these impact on institutions and their practices, affecting the person of the therapist and how they construct their work. All of this impacts on the client in the assessment situation. Clients in turn also influence institutional practices, this time in an outward movement – for example the violent client will affect the disposition of the therapist and create the demand for a secure setting.

Division or diversity?

It is clear that national systems, professional training and regulatory requirements, local institutions and different approaches to treatment all place demands and constraints on the assessment practices of art therapists. Add to this the differences in the clinical practice of art therapy in general, in both America and Britain that have been discussed by several authors. Practice in the UK has been described as overly reliant on British psychoanalytic theory and reluctant to incorporate cognitive, humanistic and family approaches and to use theme-based art directives (Hagood, 1994).

Commentators on US practice refer to an apparent polarisation between a diagnostic use of art and art-making as inherently healing via spiritual and studio-based traditions (Woddis, 1986; Byrne, 1987; Gilroy and Skaife, 1997). More recently, Spring (2007) has explored points of similarity and difference in art therapy, juxtaposing US and UK authors in order to create a 'transatlantic dialogue'. The diverse cultural roots from which the authors speak highlight how some American practices are located in a faith in art's healing power whilst others are embedded in managed care, operate within the discourses of medicine and research, or draw on an active approach to groups and work with short-term goals. In contrast, British art therapy is characterised by a focus on interpersonal interaction which unfolds over time and the social construction and impact of different illnesses. Collectively the impression is of different languages being used to describe the use of art in treatment, languages that have their origins in quite different cultures.

Moving from the generalities of American and British art therapy practice to one aspect in particular, assessment, presents a challenge. Generally speaking, the stories thus far of American and British art therapy assessment are very different. In Britain, an art therapy assessment may or may not include exploration of a client's willingness to use art, whether by verbal exploration or an actual engagement with art-making. Psychodynamically orientated art therapists may search for a capacity for relationship, represented through linking, reflection and feeling, contrasting these capacities with cutting off, concrete thinking and dissociation. The existence of hope might be distinguished from resentment about the prospect of an undesired therapy. Some consideration is likely to be given to risk: of breakdown, self-harm, acting out and violence to others. These require a formulation and an account of psychopathology, this being the point at which an art therapy assessment can assist with diagnosis. The likely outcome may also be considered. In America, art-based tests may be used to diagnose psychopathology, generate information about developmental level and evaluate therapeutic progress or outcome; these may or may not determine the treatment approach, inform a focus or goal for art therapy and could aid the work of multidisciplinary teams. These instruments measure clients' responses to particular drawing tasks and require art materials to be limited so that test formats and practices are repeatable and laboratory conditions can be adhered to. This is not the whole story, however, as American art therapy assessments can also be interpretive and embedded in relationship, or might focus exclusively on the client's engagement with art.

How can such diversity be managed in a book like this? Early on we experienced the difference in American and British assessment practice. Our British contributors understood their brief to write about 'art therapy assessment' to refer to an exploration of their first encounter with a prospective client. Some of our American contributors understood their brief differently, 'assessment' referring to the initial meeting and the subsequent evaluation of treatment. However, the range of assessment practices that were then described did not always reflect a transatlantic divide.

The landscape of British art therapy assessment can now be seen to include the use of specific criteria to determine suitability (Marshall-Tierney, Chapter 7), the development of an art-based tool (Thomas and Cody, Chapter 8) and the clear identification of art therapy treatment goals (Liebmann, Report 6). It can also be seen that US assessment practices include the observation of art production over time (McNiff, Chapter 5), portfolio examination (Loumeau-May, Report 7) and the interrogation of institutional discourses that frame the understanding of art in its social context (Henley, Chapter 3).

Mapping the book

In order to describe a continuum of art therapy assessments we have divided the book into three parts. It begins with chapters that explore the discursive and the relational in art therapy assessments before moving to a series of short, practice-based reports and ending with chapters that describe the development and use of different kinds of art-based assessment procedures on both sides of the Atlantic.

Part I sets the scene for the unfolding of discourses that focus on different aspects of context, relationship and art-making. Andrea Gilroy (Chapter 1) explores art therapy assessments within the political context and diagnostic framework of evidence-based practice (EBP). She identifies a series of principles, attitudes and criteria that are embedded in the British literature on art therapy assessment and suggests how the evidence base might be developed. The influence of different institutional contexts and multidisciplinary teams on the art in art therapy assessments are discussed by David Henley (Chapter 3) and Robin Tipple (Chapter 6). Henley presents his assessment of a sexually abused child within an ongoing evaluation of art therapy, questioning the scientific approach to assessment and describing a vigorous multidisciplinary team discussion. He argues for a pluralistic, postmodern and inclusive approach to art therapy assessment. Tipple describes an assessment of a child on the autistic spectrum, placing art production in its social context and using post-structuralist theory to argue that assessment, conducted within the practices of an institution, produce subjects and subjectivities.

Shaun McNiff (Chapter 5) situates looking at the artistic process and art object as the primary focus of his assessments, his interest being in spontaneous expression. He argues that this method embraces a deeper means of evaluation with outcomes that are as valid as scientific testing. Caroline Case (Chapter 4) and Christopher Brown (Chapter 2) both conduct their assessments within a psychodynamic frame. Case's approach to the assessment of children makes use of images, interactions with the environment and reflections on countertransference phenomena, aiming to construct an account of the child's internal world in relation to their family's social world and to contribute to the multidisciplinary team's assessment. Brown frames his assessment of adult outpatients as a crucial moment of choice for both patient and therapist. He suggests that the need to find things out in an assessment may not sit comfortably beside the culture of managed care in the modern workplace and could lead to tension and conflict for art therapists who take a psychodynamic approach to assessment.

Part II presents the reader with a variety of brief practice reports showing what art therapists actually do in their assessments. Rebecca Arnold (Report 2) and Pip Cronin (Report 4) both describe assessment in secure settings. Arnold describes an acute, inpatient secure unit where she is required to provide a formal assessment of individuals within 72 hours of admission, a key element being assessing the risk of harm to self or others. Cronin works in a forensic secure unit and also seeks to understand and manage risk, drawing on British object relations theory to make a formulation that informs about the patient's internal world. John McCulloch (Report 3) describes his input to a multidisciplinary assessment in a learning disability inpatient unit. He outlines the difficulties of understanding mental health problems in this client population and how he accesses the emotions underlying his client's behaviour. Marian Liebmann (Report 6) works in a community mental health team where her assessments have a gate-keeping function for art therapy and priority is given to establishing motivation and therapeutic goals. Jane Saotome (Report 5), Arnell Etherington (Report 1), and Laura Loumeau-May (Report 7) describe their assessments of children and young people. They represent different approaches and contexts: from a first encounter with a boy in a public sector day service for difficult to engage adolescents where the task is to determine if the young person is willing and able to engage in any meaningful exchange (Saotome); to an initial and ongoing assessment in private practice of a young autistic boy that works with the relationship and uses art-based tools (Etherington); and a service that provides support for bereaved children and young people where free drawings, family drawings and formal assessments all have a role to play in determining suitability and evaluating progress (Loumeau-May).

The chapters in Part III describe different approaches to the development of formal procedures and assessment criteria in art therapy assessments. Donna Betts (Chapter 11) debates the value and use of art-based tools and urges art therapists to desist from 'testing' but continue assessing, drawing on positive psychology to give a rounded account of the whole person. Myra Levick (Chapter 9) and Linda Gantt (Chapter 10) both describe how they developed their respective assessment tools. Levick's, situated within the history of art-based assessments in the USA, seeks to assess psychopathology, based on the work of Anna Freud. Gantt's is a standardised measure which evaluates the formal elements in a drawing, linked to specific disorders and to changes in drawings over time. Andrew Marshall-Tierney (Chapter 7) and Kim Thomas and Martin Cody (Chapter 8) describe the different structures and criteria they have developed in their art therapy assessments. Marshall-Tierney links his assessments with performance art and outlines his criteria for saying 'yes', 'no' and 'maybe' in response to his clients' spontaneous interactions with him and the art materials, while Thomas and Cody describe a series of art-based exercises which are evaluated and matched to the available art therapy services.

We wanted to keep alive the discussion about the diversity of practice and discourse in art therapy assessment and so asked our contributors a series of questions about the key issues that have emerged in both the writing and editing of this book. Their responses and our reflections form the concluding remarks.

References

AATA (2009) *Ethical Principles for Art Therapists*. American Art Therapy Association, Inc. Available at: www.americanarttherapyassociation.org

BAAT (2007) *British Association of Art Therapists (BAAT) Statement on Art Therapy and Diagnosis*. BAAT Council, May 2007. London: BAAT. www.baat.org.

Byrne, P. (1987) 'Letter from LA', *Inscape*, Summer: 30–32.

Department of Health (DoH, 2010) *Equity and Excellence: Liberating the NHS*. London: DoH.

Gilroy, A. and Skaife, S. (1997) 'Taking the pulse of American art therapy', *Inscape*, 2 (2): 57–64.

Hagood, M. (1994) 'Letter to Inscape', *Inscape*, 2 (2): 55–57.

Health Professions Council (HPC, 2007) *Standards of Proficiency for Arts Therapists*. London: HPC. Available at: www.hpt-uk.org

Spring, D. (2007) *Art in Treatment. Transatlantic Dialogue*. Springfield, IL: Charles C. Thomas.

Woddis, J. (1986) 'Judging by appearances', *Arts in Psychotherapy*, 13: 147–149.

Part I

Sitting beside

Chapter 1

What's best for whom?

Exploring the evidence base for assessment in art therapy

Andrea Gilroy

How do art therapists assess clients for art therapy? What are the criteria for deciding whether a client should enter individual art therapy, join an art therapy group or attend an open studio? Are there different assessment practices for different client populations and does diagnosis have a role to play? In this chapter I explore how art therapists have described their assessment practices and consider how this relates to 'what's best for whom'. I begin with reviews of the British literature on assessment for art therapy, exploring the underlying principles and attitudes that influence practice before identifying specific factors which indicate suitability for art therapy. I go on to consider the use of art-based assessments in the USA and outline strategies for developing the evidence base for art therapy assessments.

But first, what does 'assessment' mean? Assessment comes from the Latin '*assidere*' meaning 'to sit beside' or 'assist in the office of a judge'. It also has legal overtones, referring as it does to the estimation of a person's assets for the purposes of taxation (www.merriam-webster.com). This suggests, as Holmes (1995) points out, two aspects of clinical assessment, one suggesting an empathic response and the other a more distant calculation. Holmes calls this a 'dual function' (p. 28) of subjectivity and objectivity. I think this is a tension, one that sits at the heart of the assessment process and is central to thinking about the evidence base for assessment in art therapy.

Second, what do we mean by an 'evidence base'? This refers to the paradigm that is evidence-based practice (EBP). This comprises a cycle of activities which seek to ensure that every clinical practice is based on rigorous research so that everyone is working according to what the 'best evidence' suggests are the most clinically effective and cost-efficient ways. This is achieved through research findings being pooled, critically appraised and assigned to a hierarchy of levels that represent the nature of the research and hence the 'strength' of the evidence it provides. The 'evidence' is then distilled into recommendations and guidelines that inform policy, provision and practice and from which standards of delivery can be determined; everything is then audited. The whole process identifies gaps not only in research but also in knowledge; this leads to further research and so the cycle continues (see Gilroy, 2006, for further discussion). What then, is the evidence base for assessment in art therapy?

Absence (of evidence) and presence (of knowledge)

Assessment is often mentioned in the British art therapy literature, sometimes accompanied by brief vignettes of practice (e.g. Wood, 1986; Case and Dalley, 1992/2006; Liebmann, 1994; Gale and Matthews, 1998; Rees, 1998; McNeilly, 2000; Edwards, 2004), but despite the ubiquitous nature of assessment in art therapy, there are just two research-based papers (Evans and Dubowski, 2001; Tipple, 2003). However, there are also two academically rigorous papers (Case, 1998; Dudley, 2004) and a clinical guideline (Brooker *et al.*, 2007) which can also be considered as 'evidence': the former because they are situated within a well-sourced, critical context, are focused, relevant and directly applicable to practice; the latter because, although not primary research (i.e. an empirical study), it appraises and develops existing material and draws on the opinions of experts, practitioners and service users and so is a form of secondary research.

The evidence base for art therapy assessment in Britain is therefore rather thin, i.e. within the frameworks of orthodox EBP which requires large scale randomised controlled trials at best and other kinds of quantitative research at least. Here it must be acknowledged that there are other kinds of research and different kinds of evidence (Gilroy, 2006), and that the absence of evidence neither infers the ineffectiveness of an intervention nor equates with an absence of knowledge (Parry and Richardson, 1996; Richardson, 2001). It is also important to recognise that art therapists have an enormous amount of tacit knowledge and clinical experience of assessment. Our challenge is to access and articulate this in ways that contribute to our evidence base and do so in ways that make sense to the discipline.

In my view, assessment is critical to the construction of the evidence base for art therapy. Why? McNeilly (2000) gives an indication in his paper on failure in group analytic art therapy when he says that successful therapy depends on a thorough assessment of, and appropriate selection for, the right kind of therapy for every client. If an assessment is wrong then the subsequent therapy can 'be like trying to fit a square peg into a round hole' (p. 148). This makes the all-important link, as far as EBP is concerned, between the individual client, their particular difficulties and an assessment that identifies what is likely to be the most clinically effective treatment. With this in mind I have reviewed both the research literature and the more general literature on art therapy assessment in Britain and pooled the main points.

Principles and attitudes to art therapy assessment in the UK

A series of underlying principles and attitudes can be discerned in the literature which characterise the psychodynamic nature of art therapy assessment in Britain. This concurs with the survey findings of Crawford *et al.* (2010) which discovered that most British art therapists (60 per cent) describe their practice as being psychodynamically oriented; others espouse an eclectic approach (14 per cent) or use mostly cognitive methods (10 per cent). Nonetheless there seem to be general, mostly practical, points of principle that frame art therapy assessments, as can be seen in Box 1.1. Note that referrals are usually to a service, can be team based or discipline specific and that explanation and an experience of what art therapy involves is included in the assessment process. It seems, however, that very few clients are not offered art therapy: Dudley (2004), for example, says that her service takes on 98 per cent of those referred (p. 22).

The literature also indicates a particular attitude that British art therapists take towards their clients, as can be seen in Box 1.2. This shows that art therapists in the UK are, generally speaking, oriented towards the 'sitting beside' approach to assessment that concurs with their psychodynamic orientation, i.e. rather than an objective, diagnostically oriented function. Some explicitly situate their assessment practices within a psychodynamic framework, others do so implicitly. Several estimate their clients' potential for engagement with art and with a meaning-making process; many aim to generate a 'psychodynamic formulation' of their clients' problems, this being a tripartite construction which addresses the client's 'current life situation, the early infantile relations and the transference relationship' (Hinshelwood, 1995: 155).

Richardson (2004) points out that if the underlying principle of practice is psychodynamic, an assessment is not about identifying what is wrong with the

---

Box 1.1   General points of principle

- Referrals are usually generic and to an art therapy service (Dudley, 2004; Brooker *et al.*, 2007).
- Assessment can be for art therapy alone (Case, 1998; Dudley, 2004) or be part of a team-based assessment (Gale and Matthews, 1998; Tipple, 2003).
- Assessment should be separate from therapy itself (Case and Dalley, 1992/2006; Case, 1998; Dudley, 2004; Edwards, 2004; Brooker *et al.*, 2007).
- Assessment can occur in a single session or a series over 2–8 weeks (Case and Dalley, 1992/2006; Case, 1998; Rees, 1998; Evans and Dubowski, 2001; Tipple, 2003; Brooker *et al.*, 2007).
- Assessment should be in the same room as the therapy (Case and Dalley, 1992/2006; Evans and Dubowski, 2001; Dudley, 2004; Brooker *et al.*, 2007).
- Art materials should be at least be available and at best be used (Case and Dalley, 1992/2006; Case, 1998; Gale and Matthews, 1998; Rees, 1998; Evans and Dubowski, 2001; Tipple, 2003; Dudley, 2004; Edwards, 2004; Brooker *et al.*, 2007).
- Assessment includes an explanation about art therapy (Case and Dalley, 1992/2006; Brooker *et al.*, 2007).

Box 1.2   Attitudinal indicators

- Art therapy assessments are not concerned with diagnosis (Case, 1998; Dudley, 2004).
- Art therapy assessments offer something different from those of other psychiatric/psychological therapies (Case, 1998; Evans and Dubowski, 2001; Dudley, 2004).
- Background information/diagnosis from referrer/multidisciplinary team should be noted but 'put aside' (Case and Dalley, 1992/2006; Case, 1998; Dudley, 2004).
- Art therapy assessment aims at a 'dynamic formulation'/'art psychotherapy formulation' of the problem/s (Case and Dalley, 1992/2006; Dudley, 2004).
- The assessor aims to learn about the person, their experiences and their social context (Dudley, 2004; Edwards, 2004; Brooker *et al.*, 2007).
- The assessor aims to learn about the person's 'art history' (Wood, 1986).
- Assessment is exploratory and aims for the client to feel understood (Case and Dalley, 1992/2006; Case, 1998).
- Assessment aims to establish a rapport between client and art therapist (Case and Dalley, 1992/2006; Evans and Dubowski, 2001).
- The therapeutic relationship begins in the assessment, inferring assessor and therapist are the same (Case and Dalley, 1992/2006; Evans and Dubowski, 2001; Dudley, 2004).
- Assessment is a mutual, collaborative process (Case and Dalley, 1992/2006; Case, 1998; Gale and Matthews, 1998; Tipple, 2003; Dudley, 2004; Edwards, 2004; Brooker *et al.*, 2007).

---

patient but about gaining an understanding of someone's experiences and therapeutic needs in a way that cannot be captured in a diagnostic category. Assessment is key to clarifying the therapist's task but, as he says, many factors influence the outcomes of psychotherapy independent of diagnosis and regardless of the nature of the therapy itself. Richardson suggests that the importance of diagnosis is reduced for an intervention like psychotherapy which has been shown to be helpful for a number of diagnostic groups, but therein lies a tension because, as he goes on to say, EBP requires that evidence of treatments' effectiveness is established in relation to particular conditions. Despite psychotherapists' concerns about diagnosis and the inferred link with psychiatry's 'illness model' of human distress, the consensus is that: 'If the evidence or the treatments we offer is sorted according to the "conditions" for which those treatments are designed, then an evidence-based approach to healthcare requires accurate identification of the condition to be treated' (Richardson, 2004: xiv).

It is therefore interesting to note that the two British art therapy researchers (Evans and Dubowski, 2001; Tipple, 2003) consider diagnosis a key part of their task but take an intersubjective approach to their assessment of people on the autistic spectrum. Tipple's purpose is to 'describe individual children through observation of their interaction with the art materials and with the therapist' (p. 48). His assessments have a simple, clearly defined structure with periods of self-directed activity, turn-taking with the therapist and directed activity, all of which contribute to a multidisciplinary assessment and a differential diagnosis that leads to recommendations for future assessment and management (see also Chapter 6). Evans and Dubowski (2001) describe very detailed, minute-by-minute analysis of video-recorded meetings that attend to issues such as spontaneity, attunement, interaction, behaviour and so on, plus, interestingly I think, an esti- mation of the autistic child's awareness of and sensitivity to objects, people and to the environment – that is to the 'vitality affects' of hardness, softness, colour and texture that Stern (1985) describes. The extraordinary degree of detail in their video analysis captures fleeting communications from which therapeutic strate- gies are devised for each individual. Here a particular kind of assessment is central to the subsequent, highly tailored art therapy intervention. These researchers make explicit links between their clients' difficulties, particular factors within their assessment process, diagnosis and treatment recommendations in the way that EBP requires.

However, most British authors are oriented towards more generic, psycho- dynamically based art therapy assessments that are applicable to all client popula- tions, although it must be acknowledged that the current literature may not represent the range of practice that Crawford et al. (2010) describe. Nonetheless suitability criteria can be discerned (see Box 1.3) which focus on clients' capacity

---

Box 1.3 Suitability criteria

- Capacity for relationship (Case and Dalley, 1992/2006; Case, 1998; Evans and Dubowski, 2001; Tipple, 2003; Dudley, 2004).
- Psychological mindedness, i.e. response to transference interpretations (Case, 1998; Dudley, 2004).
- Developmental stage (Case and Dalley, 1992/2006; Rees, 1998; Evans and Dubowski, 2001).
- Difficulties are to do with the internal world (Case and Dalley, 1992/2006; Case, 1998).
- Motivation for change, 'a small spark of hope' (Case, 1998).
- Capacity for art-making and symbolic/metaphorical thinking about images/objects (Case and Dalley, 1992/2006; Case, 1998; Evans and Dubowski, 2001; Tipple, 2003; Dudley, 2004).

for relationship and change and for thinking psychologically and metaphorically. This situates practice within a psychodynamic frame that does not address the 'distant calculation' of diagnosis.

A series of questions thus frame the assessment encounter, foremost amongst which is:

- Is art therapy a suitable form of treatment for this individual?

If the answer is 'yes', others follow:

- What are the aims/goals of art therapy with this client?
- Which form of art therapy should be offered?
- Which art therapist should work with this client?
- When, where, how often and for how long should art therapy be offered?

Circumstances that might support or sabotage the therapy may also have to be considered:

- Will there be emotional support from family, parents, friends, carers?
- Will there be practical support, e.g. financial, transport, time-keeping?

The British literature describes another sequence within the assessment itself: an introduction to the therapist, to art therapy, to the room and to the art materials; a narrativising by the client of their experiences and difficulties; perhaps an engagement with art-making; and some thinking about the artworks and how both the work and the feelings generated by it, within and between the assessor and the client, relate to the client's story. There follows a formulation by the therapist about the nature and origin of the client's presenting problems which may or may not be discussed with him or her, and discussion between both parties about whether or not art therapy is suitable and, if so, which approach might be best. If not, what are the alternatives? Further information and negotiation of the contract, or onward referral, conclude the assessment.

Generally speaking, British authors are not explicit about which clients with what diagnoses, problems or conditions are suitable for art therapy, nor have they specified who might benefit from a particular treatment approach. Apart from Tipple (2003) and Evans and Dubowski (2001), neither have they (until now, see Marshall-Tierney, Chapter 7; Thomas and Cody, Chapter 8) outlined standardised or systematic assessment procedures. Instead authors, and inferentially practitioners too, have focused on the unique and 'subtle interaction between two "strangers" ' (Ghaffari and Caparrotta, 2004: 73) that occurs in psychodynamically based assessments. In terms of constructing an evidence base for effective and efficient art therapy assessments that require the diagnostic clustering of people and their problems which many art therapists resist, there is much work to do.

What's different about art therapy assessment?

Ghaffari and Caparrotta (2004) identify two generic suitability factors for a psychological intervention: a motivation for change and the capacity to form a therapeutic relationship. They also identify specific tasks in a psychotherapy assessment, namely the identification of problems, articulating a psychodynamic formulation of the difficulties, ascertaining the suitability of the intervention for the person and deciding which modality, where and by whom, can the person be helped best (pp. 27–28). There is significant synergy here with the principles and suitability criteria underlying British art therapy assessments that affirm its psychodynamic orientation. Some assert that an art therapy assessment offers something different from other kinds of psychological assessment (e.g. Dudley, 2004). What, apart from the availability of, and engagement with, art material might this be? Crawford et al.'s (2010) respondents do not mention any assessment criteria linked to art, focusing on motivation to attend and a capacity for change, thought and reflection. However, if the art therapy specific items are drawn out from Boxes 1.1 and 1.2 (pp. 13–14), particularly from research, something interesting emerges (see Box 1.4).

These speak to the significance of context, place and materiality. Why and how are these significant in an art therapy assessment? Evans and Dubowski (2001) offer us the significance of the client's sensory responses to objects, people and place and to the associated 'vitality affects': hardness, softness, colours and textures. Wood (1986) suggests that the assessor should also learn about the person's 'art history'. This caught my attention not only in terms of how to ease clients past any initial discomfort with art-making but also in terms of facilitating play. Play is, as Winnicott (1971) reminds us, central to therapy. Art therapy enables the potential for, and development of, play to be assessed in a very practical, material, tangible and different way through art. An ability to use metaphor, imagination and symbolic thinking can also be addressed through the process of making some 'thing' (Case and Dalley 1992/2006; Dudley, 2004), as can the capacity for making meaning collaboratively with the therapist about an object, as well as about a thought or feeling, in a way that enables a trial interpretation to be made. This represents a particular kind of visual, material, sensual and phenomenological assessment that

---

Box 1.4 Art therapy specific factors

- Assessment should be in the same room as the therapy (Case and Dalley, 1992/2006; Dudley, 2004).
- Art materials should be at least be available and at best be used (Case and Dalley, 1992/2006; Case, 1998; Dudley, 2004; Edwards, 2004).
- Client participation in ward-based, open art psychotherapy groups can serve as an informal assessment for longer term group or individual art therapy (Brooker et al., 2007).

could usefully be elaborated and researched as the different and specific approach to assessment, and to treatment, which art therapy offers. This leads us to explore the American literature on art-based assessments.

A more distant calculation?

Art-based assessments are not usually part of art therapy practice in Britain but have been widely debated and researched in the USA. Perhaps this derives from the American 'managed care' system of private, insurance-led health care which (a) requires a diagnosis before treatment; and (b) links diagnosis with specific treatment plans. It may also be influenced by practitioners' wish to offer something different in their assessments so they can survive in the health care marketplace, as inferred by Gantt's (2004) suggestion that the development of art-based assessments should be guided by a number of questions, one of which was: 'What are we assessing that other related fields are not or cannot?' (p. 25). Surviving in the EBP marketplace is important to practitioners on both sides of the Atlantic, hence the importance of articulating and theorising the unique properties of an art therapy assessment.

How have American art therapists approached the development of an evidence base to their practice? Art-based assessments have been the subject of fierce debate: some art therapists passionately advocate their use, others equally passionately oppose them. Betts (2006, Chapter 11 this volume), in her overview of this debate, says that art therapists use art-based assessments 'to determine a client's level of functioning; formulate treatment objectives; assess client's strengths; gain a deeper understanding of a client's presenting problems; and evaluate a client's progress' (p. 422). This indicates that these assessments – also called instruments, tests and tools – are used not only as part of the 'entry process' into art therapy but also to evaluate therapy at the beginning, middle and end. It seems to me that here the focus is on gathering information, often with the distant, objective, explicitly diagnostic function that contrasts with the 'sitting beside' approach which many British and some American art therapists prefer (see Henley, Chapter 3; McNiff, Chapter 5).

Lots of research, sometimes descriptive but often the controlled, comparative studies that EBP requires, has been done in the USA about different kinds of 'drawing procedures'. These usually focus on the production of a particular image with specific art materials. They range from Cohen's Diagnostic Drawing Series (DDS) to the Ulman Personality Assessment Procedure (see Thayer Cox *et al.*, 2000). Psychological states, cognitive skills and developmental levels are measured, greater understanding of clients' presenting problems is sought and the goals of art therapy are formulated. This practice and research operates within a framework that is about the administration of a test and so is clearly situated within the distant, objective, diagnostic function of assessment.

Given the amount of attention paid to art-based assessments in the US literature, I was interested to read that a survey of AATA's members (Elkins *et al.*, 2003) found that only 31 per cent of respondents included assessments and tests in their practice. Some wonder why these procedures continue to be popular because theoretical and philosophical problems abound and, more importantly, because the evidence base that supports them has been seriously called into question in terms of its validity and reliability (Kaplan, 2003; Gantt, 2004; Betts, 2006, Chapter 11 this volume).

Some American art therapists argue for a middle ground. This involves research that gathers enormous databases of drawings and then tries to describe and rate their 'global qualities' so that norms can be established regarding 'age and gender, as well as socioeconomic, educational, cultural and ethic group membership' (Gantt, 2004: 24). Here I refer to art-based assessments like Gantt and Tabone's Formal Elements Art Therapy Scale (FEATS, 1998; see also Chapter 10 this volume). This looks at the *form* of a drawing – in this instance of a person picking an apple off a tree – not the content. The purpose is 'primarily gathering information to formulate an art therapy treatment plan – not to construct a differential diagnosis' (Kaplan, 2003: 29). However, comparative studies have indicated that the FEATS is useful in diagnosis for example, of substance disorders (Rockwell and Dunham, 2006) and attention deficit hyperactivity disorder (ADHD; Munley, 2002).

These 'global' art-based assessments have highlighted that research on the developmental characteristics of children and adolescents' art work has not developed significantly since Lowenfeld in the 1940s (Kaplan, 2003; Gantt, 2004). This was thrown into relief by Hagood's (2003) research which showed that features thought to be associated with sexual abuse in children's drawings were actually associated with their cognitive development. Gantt developed this when she asked the question:

> How do people draw in their 70s, 80s or 90s who have no significant psychiatric or physical problems? Is there a 'late style' . . .? We simply do not know. And we will not know until we collect and rate thousands of drawings.
>
> (2004: 25)

I suspect that a developmental chronology of drawing across the lifespan would indeed be useful to the development of the evidence base of art therapy assessments.

It is interesting also to note the links being made in some American literature between art-based assessments, the selection of a particular kind of art therapy and its outcome. For example, Francis *et al.* (2003) describe an assessment that involved substance misusers in making a 'bird's nest drawing', their argument being that it is easier for clients to draw birds in their nest rather than their family and that what emerges will, within the framework of attachment theory and other research about theory and different art therapy approaches to substance misuse, inform the assessor about treatment aims and strategies. What is key here, so it seems to me, is that the assessment 'tool' matches the client group and the particular therapeutic approach and that both reflect organisational and systemic needs. McLeod (2001) reminds us that the way we research and write about therapy is 'a political act' (p. 72); so too is practice. No matter where in the world, researchers and practitioners are engaged through their work in political acts, ones that reflect the highly competitive health care marketplace in which we all exist and one where the main currency for us all is the evidence base.

Strategies for developing the evidence base

I have described elsewhere (Gilroy, 2006) how Parry and Richardson (1996) devised standards through which a discipline can demonstrate that it is evidence based. Clinical guidelines are key. This leads me to think that one of the first things art therapists could do to develop the evidence base for art therapy assessment (in the UK) is to replicate Parry's (2001) seminal guideline about referral and selection for psychotherapy in the British National Health Service. This was specifically developed for professionals who refer to the psychological therapies in order 'to aid decisions about which forms of psychological therapy are most appropriate for which patients' (p. 3). It describes different kinds of psychotherapy and matches approach with what the cumulative research suggests would generate the best outcomes for different client populations. Parry emphasises that the guideline is based on critical appraisal and systematic review of the research literature, but adds that when developing the guideline they 'used structured methods to ascertain expert consensus on treatment choice' (p. 3). The result is a series of General Principles and Recommendations about particular therapies for particular problems, each principle and recommendation being rated from A–D according to the strength of the evidence that supports it. Examples include recommendations about treatment length, suitability and patient preference.

Brooker et al.'s guideline (2007) was modelled on Parry's and aimed to guide art therapists in various aspects of their work with people prone to psychotic states. Like Parry we undertook a critical appraisal and systematic review of all the relevant literature which graded it according to its relative strength. For example, findings from the first randomised controlled trial of group art therapy with people diagnosed as schizophrenic (Richardson et al., 2007) led to a recommendation about the referral process and equity which ensured 'that these potential clients are aware of, and can easily access, the Art Psychotherapy services that are available to them' (Brooker et al., 2007: 43). Another drew on local practitioners' views that clients prone to psychotic states were likely to be acute inpatients and suggested that 'client participation in ward-based, open Art Psychotherapy groups can serve as part of the initial, informal discussion and assessment for longer-term group or individual Art Psychotherapy' (p. 44).

We also drew on the knowledge and experience of two 'expert panels': one of art therapists experienced with this client population, nominated by the (then) BAAT Council, and another of local service users. It is worth highlighting here that the process of developing clinical guidelines can be a collaborative procedure which enables users' voices to be heard (Gilroy, 2006). In Brooker et al. (2007) user views were significant, for example, with regard to consent to art therapy that was truly informed and to the importance of a brief and timely assessment of those returning to a service, especially when their health was deteriorating (p. 45).

Users also made recommendations related to language and, inferentially, to art therapists' approach to assessment:

> Art Psychotherapists should use descriptive rather than diagnostic language in the assessment and ensure that clients' experiences and circumstances are articulated in the client's language.
>
> Diagnostic language need not be entirely excluded from an assessment as it may be useful for the client. Art Psychotherapists should be transparent about any diagnosis they, or anyone else, has given.
>
> (Brooker *et al.*, 2007: 46)

The narrative accompanying these recommendations suggests that the client's language should be used to articulate their problems, thus ensuring that links are maintained between the person, their social context and the origins of their distress. However, it adds: 'Whilst users were in broad agreement with this recommendation they thought that the language of diagnosis could also be helpful' (pp. 46–47). According to service users, the 'sitting beside' function that many British art therapists prefer could usefully incorporate transparent and collaborative thinking about the more 'objective' function of assessment embodied in diagnosis. Could 'sitting beside', when appropriate, therefore 'sit alongside' thinking about diagnosis?

The views of the two expert panels, together with local practitioners' tacit knowledge, filled the gaps in our literature about art therapy with people prone to psychotic states and made a contribution to thinking about what constitutes best practice. This, I suggest, is how the gaps in our present evidence base on assessment could be addressed in the short term.

Selection and outcomes

Earlier I outlined criteria that art therapists in the UK explicitly or implicitly use to select clients who are, generally speaking, thought suitable for psychodynamically based art therapy. However, when it comes to selection of clients for a particular art therapy approach – which, in this context, I take to mean studio-based work, individual art therapy or group art therapy – the literature has only the briefest of comments to make, there being little description and no research. There is some disagreement about who is suitable for what, and indeed whether developing criteria for such a thing is even possible (Edwards, 2004: 78). While it may be neither possible nor desirable to devise criteria that are universally applicable, I think it would be helpful to generate guidelines that guide, not prescribe, which art therapy approach is suitable for whom and so begin to articulate the link between referral, assessment, selection for art therapy, treatment approach and outcome.

Several art therapists have offered general opinions about selection for individual, group and studio-based art therapy that could be built upon (see Box 1.5). These criteria are very general and not associated with diagnosis. This, of course,

Box 1.5   Suitability for art therapy: individual, group, open studio

Individual art therapy indicated for:

- internalised problems, difficulty articulating feelings, speech/language difficulties, depressed, too confused, withdrawn or vulnerable for a group (Case and Dalley, 1992/2006; Edwards, 2004).
- particularly vulnerable, seriously at risk (Brooker *et al.*, 2007).
- disruptive or hostile behaviour makes them unsuitable for a group (Brooker *et al.*, 2007).

Contraindicated for:

- problems with intimacy of one to one (Edwards, 2004).

Group art therapy indicated for:

- interpersonal problems, relationship difficulties, developmental problems, neurotic/character problems; anxieties/inhibitions; those with ego strength; ability to differentiate between inner/outer realities; capacity for relationship with therapist and a group; aware of vulnerabilities (Case and Dalley, 1992/2006).
- people who are isolated, lack confidence (Brooker *et al.*, 2007).
- wish to explore interpersonal relationships (Dudley, 2004).
- social problems, problems with intimacy of one to one (Edwards, 2004).

Contraindicated for:

- severe and complex problems, psychopathy, hyperactivity (mania), severe LDs, problems with intimacy, limited tolerance of others, inability to share therapist's attention (Case and Dalley, 1992/2006).
- narcissistic personality, severe personality disorder, people with low self-esteem, adults abused as children, those with severe trauma (McNeilly, 2000).

Open studio indicated for:

- highly disturbed clients, especially in acute settings (Edwards, 2004; Brooker *et al.*, 2007).
- focus on art-making, in need of support and encouragement (Case and Dalley, 1992/2006; Dudley, 2004).

is problematic as far as EBP is concerned, but different kinds of art therapy *are* offered to different client populations in different settings, as I discovered when I reviewed the evidence base for art therapy practice (Gilroy, 2006). Thus we could, quite legitimately and I think relatively painlessly – and without resorting to *DSM-IV* (American Psychratric Association, 2000) or *ICD-10* (World Health Organization, 2004) – begin to assess and select clients from different populations and/or with different 'conditions' for different kinds of art therapy with specific assessment criteria in mind. This could relate not only to how we conduct assessments but also to recommendations about different art therapy approaches, i.e. in relation to thinking about whether group, individual or studio-based art therapy is best for a particular individual.

For example, there are two identifiable approaches in the literature about art therapy with adult clients who have been abused or suffered trauma: one uses art to 'go right into' the trauma (McClelland, 1992, 1993), another 'witnesses' trauma in a 'non-invasive' way (Schaverien, 1998). Short-term individual approaches seem effective for these clients (e.g. Peacock, 1991) and self-monitoring through art outside sessions is empowering (Brooke, 1995). Thus an assessment could consider whether it would be helpful for the person to discuss their artwork or better for the art therapist to simply witness the trauma visually, and whether or not he or she could self-monitor.

Turning to the literature on art therapy with children, specifically those diagnosed with ADHD, structured approaches seem to be indicated for group and individual art therapy that enables the self-management of behaviour (Henley, 1998, 1999). Changing art activities, games and physical place also seem to improve these children's social skills, self-control and self-esteem. Assessment could therefore address their suitability for group or individual art therapy and for different kinds of activities in sessions. Art therapy with children who have been sexually abused again indicates different approaches: time-structured art therapy groups seem to reduce post traumatic stress disorder (PTSD), anxiety and dissociation (Brown and Latimer, 2001; Buckland and Murphy, 2001) and a group that combines art therapy with cognitive analytic therapy seems to enable the processing of emotional responses and restores capacity for thought (Brown and Latimer, 2001). Long-term individual art therapy enables containment and management of the sensual properties of art materials and mess-making which leads to emotional and cognitive development and repair (Prokofiev, 2011). Assessment of these children could therefore consider their need for containment and to 'evacuate' material in long-term, dynamically oriented individual art therapy, or whether emotional responses can be accessed and thought about in manageable ways in a short-term, structured group.

Thus the literature is beginning to articulate and suggest different art therapy approaches that 'work' with different client groups. This could be elaborated through clinical consensus procedures that access the tacit knowledge of experienced practitioners and through collaboration with service users, both of whom are critical to guideline development in the absence of research.

Research

I have left research until last because it takes time and often requires funding and so has to be part of a medium to long-term strategy for developing art therapy's evidence base. Remembering that both research and writing are political acts, I would suggest that the first thing art therapists need to do is document our assessments in research-based case studies, both descriptively and visually. These would be what Denscombe has described as 'single example<s> of a broader class of things' (1998: 36) that are specific about the referral, the setting and the client population. These could be linked to the treatment approach and its outcome. Clusters of such descriptive, inductive research can lead to comparative studies, and so the evidence base is built.

Second, I think we should take close, careful and long looks at the art works (Gilroy, 2008) made in art therapy assessments and see what they tell us. Visual and phenomenological research methods are, I suggest, inherently sympathetic to the 'sitting beside' function of an art therapy assessment.

Third, I think art therapists should tune their antennae to noticing which clients seem to benefit from which approaches, as well as who does not, and then deduce backwards, as it were, about how this might be assessed. This came to mind having read about inductive research on assessment for cognitive behavioural therapy (CBT) (Segal *et al.*, 1995). The authors describe noticing over time that some of their clients benefited more from the 20 sessions of CBT they offered than others. They decided to investigate this with an eye to identifying which kind of patient would respond best. They began by exploring what they describe as 'soft' sources, i.e. therapists' intuition and impressions of patients who had difficulty with their approach; this indicated that people who had problems with endings did not do well with a short-term treatment. They also noticed that particular kinds of 'patient presentation', regardless of diagnosis, were linked to a greater ease with CBT and that those with depression and anxiety seemed to benefit the most. From this Segal *et al.* devised an assessment that explored clients' perceptions of short-term work and which included trial CBT interventions. Inductive qualitative research such as this, of groups or 'cohorts' of clients with particular 'conditions' which draw on practitioner observation and description, have much to offer art therapy.

The development of an evidence base for art therapy assessments, whilst being systematic and specific to a particular approach, context and client population, need not be constrained by diagnostic criteria nor by research methods. Rather it can take a pluralistic approach, investigating how best to assess for different approaches to clinical work with different client populations.

Conclusion

Whilst art therapy remains without a critical mass of research I suggest that practitioners draw on other forms of evidence and develop clinical guidelines, accessing the tacit knowledge of 'expert' and local art therapists and drawing on the views of service users. Guidelines could address best practice in the referral process, suitability for art therapy per se and identify selection criteria for group, individual and studio-based art therapy, providing useful information for referrers, practitioners and clients alike.

It may be that 'sitting beside' clients in a psychodynamically oriented assessment and the 'more distant calculation' linked to diagnosis and treatment plans have become polarised in the art therapy literatures on either side of the Atlantic. We may agree that diagnosis is by no means central to psychological understanding and to beginning a relationship, but researchers, clients and therapists alike suggest that the transparent articulation and identification of problems or 'conditions' or diagnoses can and does happen in art therapy and psychotherapy assessments and that this can be helpful to all concerned. Categorising and clustering illnesses, problems and behaviours are central to EBP and to current systems of mental health care. Indeed, British art therapists will have to think about how to assess within a new NHS that has single points of entry, a system which looks likely to require that art therapy assessments are directly linked to diagnostic clusters, care pathways and treatment packages, similar to the 'managed care' system in the USA. This may be uncomfortable but, as art therapy's evidence base expands and different treatment approaches are found to work better for some clients than for others, practitioners may find themselves able to integrate the sitting beside approach to art therapy assessment with a more distant calculation.

References

American Psychiatric Association (2000) *Diagnostic and Statistical Manual of Mental Disorders: DSM-IV-TR*. Washington, DC: American Psychiatric Association.

Betts, D. (2006) 'Art therapy assessments and rating instruments: do they measure up?', *Arts in Psychotherapy*, 33: 422–434.

Brooke, S. (1995) 'Art therapy: an approach to working with sexual abuse survivors', *Arts in Psychotherapy*, 22 (5): 447–466.

Brooker, J., Cullum, M., Gilroy, A., McCombe, B., Mahony, J., Ringrose, K., *et al.* (2007) *The Use of Art Work in Art Psychotherapy with People Prone to Psychotic States. An Evidence-Based Clinical Practice Guideline*. London: Goldsmiths, University of London. Available at: http://eprints.gold.ac.uk/112/

Brown, A. and Latimer, M. (2001) 'Between images and thoughts: an art psychotherapy group for sexually abused children', in J. Murphy (ed.) *Art Therapy with Young Survivors of Sexual Abuse: Lost for Words*. London and New York: Routledge.

Buckland, R. and Murphy, J. (2001) 'Jumping over it: group therapy with young girls', in J. Murphy (ed.) *Art Therapy with Young Survivors of Sexual Abuse: Lost for Words*. London and New York: Routledge.

Case, C. (1998) 'Brief encounters. Thinking about images in assessment', *Inscape*, 3 (2): 26–33.

Case, C. and Dalley, T. (1992/2006) *The Handbook of Art Therapy*. London and New York: Routledge.

Crawford, M., Debate, J. and Patterson, S. (2010) 'Provision and practice of art therapy: a survey of art therapists in the NHS'. Unpublished paper.

Denscombe, M. (1998) *The Good Research Guide for Small Scale Social Research Projects*. Buckingham: Open University Press.

Dudley, J. (2004) 'Art psychotherapy and the use of psychiatric diagnosis. Assessment for art psychotherapy', *Inscape*, 9 (1): 14–25.

Edwards, D. (2004) *Art Therapy*. London: Sage.

Elkins, D., Stovall, K. and Malchiodi, C. (2003) 'American Art Therapy Association Inc.: 2001–2002 membership survey report', *Art Therapy. Journal of the American Art Therapy Association*, 20 (1): 28–34.

Evans, K. and Dubowski, J. (2001) *Art Therapy with Children on the Autistic Spectrum*. London: Jessica Kingsley Publishers.

Francis, D., Kaiser, D. and Deaver, S. (2003) 'Representations of attachment security in the Bird's Nest Drawings of clients with substance abuse disorders', *Art Therapy. Journal of the American Art Therapy Association*, 20 (3): 125–137.

Gale, C. and Matthews, R. (1998) 'Journey in joint working. Some reflections on an experience of arts therapies collaboration', in M. Rees, (ed) *Drawing on Difference. Art Therapy with People who have Learning Difficulties*. London and New York: Routledge.

Gantt, L. (2004) 'The case for formal art therapy assessments', *Art Therapy. Journal of the American Art Therapy Association*, 21 (1): 18–29.

Gantt, L. and Tabone, C. (1998) *Formal Elements Art Therapy Scale: The Rating Manual*. Morgantown, WV: Gargoyle Press.

Ghaffari, K. and Caparrotta, L. (2004) *The Function of Assessment Within Psychological Therapies*. London: Karnac Books.

Gilroy, A. (2006) *Art Therapy, Research and Evidence-Based Practice*. London: Sage.

Gilroy, A. (2008) 'Taking a long look at art', *International Journal of Art and Design*, 27 (3): 251–263. Also available at: http://eprints-gro.gold.ac.uk/113/

Hagood, M. (2003) 'The use of the Naglieri Draw-a-Person test of cognitive development: a study with clinical and research implications for art therapists working with children', *Art Therapy. Journal of the American Art Therapy Association*, 20 (2): 67–76.

Henley, D. (1998) 'Art therapy in a socialization program for children with attention deficit hyperactivity disorder', *American Journal of Art Therapy*, 37: 2–12.

Henley, D. (1999) 'Facilitating socialization with a therapeutic camp setting for children with attention deficits utilizing the expressive therapies', *American Journal of Art Therapy*, 38: 40–50.

Hinshelwood, R. (1995) 'Psychodynamic formulation in assessment for psychoanalytic psychotherapy', in C. Mace (ed.) *The Art and Science of Assessment in Psychotherapy*. London and New York: Routledge.

Holmes, J. (1995) 'How I assess for psychoanalytic psychotherapy', in C. Mace (ed.) *The Art and Science of Assessment in Psychotherapy*. London and New York: Routledge.

Kaplan, F. (2003) 'Art-based assessments', in C. Malchiodi (ed.) *Handbook of Art Therapy*. New York: Guilford Press.

Liebmann, M. (1994) *Art Therapy with Offenders*. London: Jessica Kingsley Publishers.

McClelland, S. (1992) 'Brief art therapy in acute states', in D. Waller and A. Gilroy (eds) *Art Therapy. A Handbook*. Buckingham: Open University Press.

McClelland, S. (1993) 'The art of science with clients: beginning collaborative inquiry in process work, art therapy and acute states', in H. Payne (ed.) *Handbook of Inquiry in the Arts Therapies: One River, Many Currents*. London: Jessica Kingsley Publishers.

McLeod, J. (2001) *Qualitative Research in Counselling and Psychotherapy*. London: Sage.

McNeilly, G. (2000) 'Failure in group analytic art therapy', in A. Gilroy and G. McNeilly (eds) *The Changing Shape of Art Therapy*. London: Jessica Kingsley Publishers.

Munley, M. (2002) 'Comparing the PPAT drawings of boys with AD/HD and age-matched controls using the Formal Elements Art Therapy Scale', *Art Therapy. Journal of the American Art Therapy Association*, 19 (2): 69–76.

Parry, G. (2001) *Treatment Choice in Psychological Therapies. Evidence Based Clinical Practice Guideline*. London: Department of Health.

Parry, G. and Richardson, A. (1996) *NHS Psychotherapy Services in England: Review of Strategic Policy*. Wetherby: NHS Executive.

Peacock, M. (1991) 'A personal construct approach to art therapy in the treatment of post sexual abuse trauma', *American Journal of Art Therapy*, 29: 100–109.

Prokofiev, F. (2011) '"I've been longing and longing for more and more of this": researching art therapy in the treatment of children with developmental deficits', in A. Gilroy (ed.) *Art Therapy Research in Practice*. Oxford: Peter Lang.

Rees, M. (ed.) (1998) *Drawing on Difference. Art therapy with People who have Learning Difficulties*. London and New York: Routledge.

Richardson, P. (2001) 'Evidence-based practice and the psychodynamic psychotherapies', in C. Mace, S. Moorey and B. Roberts (eds) *Evidence in the Psychological Therapies*. Hove, UK: Brunner-Routledge.

Richardson, P. (2004) 'Foreword', in K. Ghaffari and L. Caparrotta. *The Function of Assessment Within Psychological Therapies*. London: Karnac Books.

Richardson, P., Evans, C., Jones, K., Rowe, A. and Stevens, P. (2007) 'An exploratory randomised controlled trial of group art therapy as an adjunctive treatment in severe mental illness', *Journal of Mental Health*, 16: 483–491.

Rockwell, P. and Dunham, M. (2006) 'The utility of the Formal Elements Art Therapy Scale in assessment for substance use disorder', *Art Therapy. Journal of the American Art Therapy Association*, 23 (3): 104–111.

Schaverien, J. (1998) 'Inheritance: Jewish identity, art psychotherapy workshops and the legacy of the Holocaust', in D. Doktor (ed.) *Arts Therapies and Clients with Eating Disorders: Fragile Board*. London: Jessica Kingsley Publishers.

Segal, Z., Swallow, S., Bizzini, L. and Weber Rouget, B. (1995) 'How we assess for short-term cognitive-behaviour therapy', in C. Mace (ed.) *The Art and Science of Assessment in Psychotherapy*. London and New York: Routledge.

Stern, D. (1985) *The Interpersonal World of the Infant*. New York: Basic Books.

Thayer Cox, C., Agell, G., Cohen, B. and Gantt, L. (2000) 'Are you assessing what I'm assessing? Let's take a look!' *American Journal of Art Therapy*, 39: 48–67.

Tipple, R. (2003) 'The interpretation of children's artwork in a paediatric disability setting', *Inscape*, 8 (2): 48–59.

Winnicott, D. (1971) *Playing and Reality*. Harmondsworth: Penguin.

Wood, C. (1986) 'Milk white panic', *Inscape*, Winter: 2–7.

World Health Organization (2004) *International Statistical Classification of Diseases and Health Related Problems: ICD-10*. Geneva: World Health Organization.

Chapter 2

Assessment

What does it mean?

Christopher Brown

Introduction

The thinking on assessment for art therapy outlined below has been developed over many years of art therapy practice with adult mental health in the National Health Service (NHS) and through my experience of supervising other art therapists and trainees. I suggest that the assessment encounter is a crucial moment of choice and decision making for both patient and therapist where things need to be found out before going any further. This pragmatic need to find things out may be in conflict with an ideology of allowing a more open space like a traditional art therapy studio model where things unfold through art-making processes. Various teachers and supervisors who have used psychoanalytic concepts in their thinking about clinical work have informed my own orientation as an art therapist. I entered the profession at a time when the shift from a studio-based, art-making model to a more psychodynamic model was gathering momentum. This shift involved moving away from being a facilitator offering a safe space with a choice of art materials to a more interpersonal engagement along traditional psychotherapy lines. With this comes a certain tension about privileging one kind of engagement over another in an assessment, such as fostering a response to the art medium or checking out the response to interpretations. However, at some point in an assessment there has to be some evaluation of the material that emerges in order to make a formulation, based on attributing meaning to the material, which can then be used to decide if it matches the approach to treatment. This applies whatever medium is used for expression. In this chapter I will draw upon literature from psychotherapy as well as art therapy to outline in more detail some questions about this match that can usefully be held in the art therapist's mind during the assessment, which can then inform a decision on whether to offer treatment or not.

Choice or decision making?

In the historical context of art therapy and its relationship with psychiatry, choice, and the sense of freedom this brings, has been an important element. Psychiatry has gradually been changing from its traditional position as a rather judgemental and somewhat controlling discipline towards being more flexible and responsive to a patient's individual need (NHS and Community Care Act 1990; DoH, 2005). Along with social and political changes in mental health care this has led to a rather different idea about choice. I have sometimes had the impression that a scenario exists where assessment is avoided and replaced by the therapist offering the patient a range of treatment options to chose from. It is as if the transaction is akin to buying a new car or television and deciding what model to choose. This consumer analogy is particularly relevant in the current climate of change in the NHS. Morante (2008) has addressed this issue. He says: 'The British government's decision to make patient choice central to the way healthcare and treatment are delivered in the NHS in England and Wales is rooted in the current social context with its emphasis on consumer choice and promises of simple and fast solutions to complex problems' (p. 286).

The consumerist society is driven by market forces. In the context of health care provision the market sells the idea of empowerment through wonder drugs and fast track cures that may appeal to patients at a time when they feel most vulnerable and dependent (Morante, 2008). The idea that choice is a function of a consumer transaction may give a false impression about entitlement to treatment and obscure the more fundamental importance of what the choice is really about. In other words, does the patient know what it is they are choosing? What really constitutes informed consent? I will return to these questions later on.

Milton (1997) states: 'I would like to argue that it is not so much for us to say "who is suitable?" (as in fact that is a surprisingly hard thing to do), but for whom would we think psychotherapy, at least in certain settings, was contraindicated, and either harmful or likely to be useless' (p. 52). She leans towards the original ethic of the NHS in suggesting that if someone wants help through psychotherapy, and they understand what it involves, then why should it not be provided? She suggests that it may not be helpful for everybody, potentially placing the assessor in the role of a withholding provider; of having to manage the response from the patient and feel comfortable enough in themselves with this decision.

People come to us with varying degrees of insight and ability to articulate what they want. There can be an expectation of being helped: they may want to be made better, have their problems taken away, or be helped to understand themselves and their difficulties. How do we decide if we can help the person we have in the room with us? Assessment demands that art therapists think about what it is that we actually do in therapeutic treatment. This may challenge our omnipotent fantasies, our self-esteem, our beliefs and assumptions of what is possible. Perhaps it is easier to avoid looking at these aspects of ourselves and at the same time avoid assessment. I am not suggesting that art therapists do not think about what they do and I am aware that it personally took much time and experience to arrive at a theoretical position that enabled me to think more clearly about what I do. I am, however, suggesting that we need to be clear about our model of practice. By identifying and conceptualising what the client brings to the assessment process with what we understand to be the art therapy process, we can begin to think about whether we are likely to be able to help the person in front of us.

Coltart (1987) suggests that the assessment encounter may be a momentous day in the person's life as it holds the hope of embarking on a journey which may be life changing. This is not something to be undertaken lightly and requires serious and thoughtful consideration. Clinical practice in art therapy is varied and how one approaches this task depends on the nature of the treatment on offer, which will be informed by the therapist's theoretical orientation and the context in which it takes place.

Most patients being referred to art therapy in the British NHS will have been through some kind of previous assessment, perhaps with the aim of making a psychiatric diagnosis. Thus, in the context of providing a specialist art therapy service, assessment is always assessment for treatment; the assessment therefore needs to be calibrated to the treatment. For example, on an acute inpatient setting the assessment criterion for an open group might simply be whether the patient can tolerate being in a room with others without becoming too disruptive. However, in individual outpatient art therapy the criteria may be more complex. This will be the focus of my enquiry.

Framing assessment

It seems to be not uncommon across the range of art therapy practices to find assessment blurring into treatment without any real sense of the patient's suitability other than their engagement in a process. This issue was recognised by Case (1998), which suggests that it may be a rather ubiquitous phenomenon. I wonder why this might be and what is being avoided when blurring occurs. Is it due to an unease about putting things into words, as suggested by Case (1998); a reaction against psychiatric diagnosis and reluctance to take on a judgemental role, as suggested by Dudley (2004); or, as I have suggested, that it requires a coherent articulation (in one's own mind at least) of what treatment can and cannot do? Case and Dalley (2006) have this to say about assessment:

> The art therapist assesses aspects of the client's situation, bearing in mind the background to the referral and the amount of detail she already knows. She will explain the assessment procedure – perhaps four sessions which will be followed by a review meeting and feedback of the assessment. At the review, an agreement to enter into treatment will be made with client and therapist.
>
> (p. 190)

I find it interesting that the possibility of not entering treatment is omitted. Later on, an example of assessment of a child is given where the therapist's formulation appears to be that he is already engaged in working on his difficulties and should therefore continue. Whilst not wishing to disagree with or criticise clinical judgement, this highlights the way in which assessment and treatment can run into each other.

Case (1998) argues for assessment to be seen as a discrete piece of work. She presents a case study of a 14-year-old boy whom she assessed over three sessions but in the end did not offer treatment because environmental factors made it unsustainable. She comments: 'It is disappointing when the possibilities of therapy that one can envisage through the creation of images in a brief encounter do not come to fruition' (p. 32). Here we can see the pull to continue engagement and the painful reality of needing to step back and think about the wider picture in order to recommend a different outcome. It is perhaps easier to do this if there are clear boundaries, both in the therapist's mind and in the external setting, that frame the assessment and provide a contained space in which thinking can take place.

This moment of choice about whether or not to offer treatment is quite a responsibility. Saying no can be difficult when under pressure to say yes. This may come from other professionals but the greater difficulty may be a feeling that the art therapist cannot turn the patient away. A brief vignette illustrates some of these issues.

Vignette one

The patient was a young man with a history of depression who had both previous and current involvement with NHS mental health services. He had recently emerged from a five-year court battle against his ex-employer and was referred to psychotherapy by his psychiatrist following a report from the court psychologist who recommended it to help him process this experience. The psychotherapist, who assessed him over two meetings, became concerned about a very paranoid and persecutory layer in the patient's mind, but thought this would be manageable if treatment involved the use of art as an intermediary object.

He was referred and seen for another assessment by an art therapist. In this meeting the patient made it clear that he did not want exploratory therapy but wanted something that would make him feel better. He was allocated to a different art therapist for treatment who discussed the case in supervision before seeing him. The supervisor suggested time-limited treatment of 25 sessions with the court case as a focus. The art therapist 'forgot' this suggestion and during treatment got drawn into a position of believing he needed more exploratory work. Further supervision enabled recovery from this position and a return to the original focus.

I think that we can see a number of things happening here. The court psychologist thinks the patient needs help. The psychotherapist probes the patient's defences and finds a psychotic part of his personality; he sees danger but does not say no. The assessing art therapist does not establish a reason for treatment but offers it anyway. It seems that it is only when it is brought to supervision by another art therapist – the fourth mental health professional involved – that the patient's need can be realistically thought about. Clearly there is something about the patient that evokes a wish to provide help but how this might best be given is difficult to establish. This highlights some of the issues that can make assessment such a challenge for clinicians. I will now look at these in more detail.

Knowing and not knowing

If we frame the assessment as a discrete function that takes place in the initial meeting with the patient rather than being a process which extends over time and blurs into treatment, how then do we discover what we need to know before being able to make an informed decision about whether or not to offer art therapy? Do we rely on a system of classification and try to fit the difficulties presented into a category, be this psychiatric or psychodynamic, or not? If not, how do we define what we have got in the room with us, i.e. what kind of person are we dealing with? Intuition can play a big part in this, as can a willingness to engage in the process of art-making. There may be a belief in the healing power of art that informs the therapist's thinking about what is happening during the process of meeting the person for the first time. In fact, it is this conceptual framework of the treatment, whatever that may consist of, that can inform the therapist about what needs to happen in the assessment. This takes us to a key issue, articulated by Schaverien (2005): 'The questions that exercise art therapists could be summarised as those regarding whether the healing lies in the art alone or whether it occurs when it is mediated within a therapeutic relationship' (p. 88). The nature of individual practiners' approach to art therapy, along with personal and theoretical concepts of healing, will affect how assessment is approached.

I referred above to how intuition may inform decision making; extending this to the therapist's use of feelings evoked by the patient, i.e. the countertransference, offers another way of informing us about what approach might be suitable. I have written about the treatment of a man with paranoid schizophrenia (Brown, 2008), in which the particular approach taken was informed by countertransference in the assessment:

> When I saw him for an initial meeting his account of his personal situation was imbued with repressed hostility, which seemed to colour his relationships with others. He blamed others for his difficulties and wanted me to agree that he had been treated badly. Afterwards, I remarked to a colleague that he was one of the most deeply unpleasant people I had ever met. Something had been projected into me that left me feeling contaminated in some way.
>
> (p. 15)

I did not want to be on the receiving end of such destructive hatred. Thinking about the way he related to me by reflecting on my countertransference enabled me to make a decision about what would be the most suitable treatment to offer him.

I felt that such toxic material would best be managed by encouraging it to be mediated through the art in a studio-based setting rather than one involving exploration of transference.

Diagnosis is a word that many art therapists consider as pejorative but its Greek roots include the idea of *recognising* as well as knowing. If we recognise that there are conditions for which there are specific, agreed treatment approaches, this can inform the therapist's style of relatedness, the tone of their interventions and the topics of initial focus (McWilliams, 1994). Obvious examples are psychotic and borderline conditions, which require a modified approach to treatment (see Brooker *et al.*, 2007).

The recognition of patterns can be problematic when it becomes part of a categorical view of diagnosis that fixes personality into an illness that can or cannot be cured. Various art therapists, e.g. Wood (1997), Henzell (1997) and Molloy (1997), have explored how such a medical model has influenced art therapists working in psychiatry and has been taken up with specific reference to assessment by Dudley (2004). She suggests that people should be taken as they are and that the initial meeting 'is not a fact finding exercise, but rather the beginning and unfolding of a relationship between the two of you and the art' (Dudley, 2004: 19). Here, it seems to me, the central dilemma for the art therapist is highlighted: to what extent should the need to find out more about the nature of the person's difficulties be privileged over waiting for something to unfold?

Perhaps art therapists are reluctant to take a more active role in decision making that contributes to the blurring between assessment and treatment. This reluctance may have its roots in the artistic training and identity of British art therapists along with a tradition of alternative ways of seeing the human condition that shy away from value judgements and categorisation. In contrast to this, the tradition in psychotherapy has been that those undertaking assessment are likely to have had medical experience in psychiatry and familiarity with diagnostic formulation (Coltart, 1987). This polarisation is perhaps embedded in the historical development of British art therapy in art education and psychiatry and its early alliance with the anti-psychiatry movement (Waller, 1991). Does this inhibit the making of formulations in art therapy assessments?

Psychodynamic assessment

Whilst it is common for art therapists to say that they take a psychodynamic approach to treatment, it may also be used as an umbrella term which covers a variety of practices. Roth and Fonagy (2005), in defining psychodynamic therapy, write: 'Both exploratory and focused treatment have the resolution of unconscious conflict as their goal; unlike cognitive and behavioural psychotherapies, these are not primarily or only concerned with achieving symptomatic change' (p. 7). Gabbard (2005) in describing the major modalities of psychotherapy puts it thus:

The terms psychoanalytic and psychodynamic have increasingly been used synonymously in discussions of psychotherapy. Both psychotherapeutic approaches derive from a set of core principles derived from psychoanalysis. Among these principles are transference, countertransference, resistance, the dynamic unconscious, a developmental lens to view adult experience, and psychic determinism.

(p. 3)

Central to the idea of a dynamic unconscious is anxiety and defences against it. It has been suggested that at the start of any session there should always be two rather frightened people in the room and if not then there is something wrong. In the assessment situation the stakes are high and so is the anxiety. Anxiety may be at a high level for the therapist as well as the patient and 'can make one feel that one has not got enough to offer in oneself and the materials, and can lead to suggestions of what to do, which curtails the open space for the client' (Case, 1998: 28). This conveys a feeling of inadequacy that may push the art therapist into inappropriate action and an idea that things need to be kept open in order to see what the patient does with this. However, there may be disadvantages to holding an open space if this leads to avoidance of the tasks of assessment. Case and Dalley (2006) suggest creating an atmosphere that will help to allay initial anxiety. The art therapy room is seen as a safe space, perhaps to a degree that nothing potentially threatening can be allowed into it. However, there may be advantages in allowing an optimal level of anxiety, as in vignette one, where paranoid anxieties emerged that needed to be thought about by the psychotherapist.

Coltart (1987) makes the point: 'In an assessment interview one has to *work*' (p. 134, her emphasis). I understand this to mean that one needs to take an active part, which will most certainly involve taking risks and being prepared to probe the patient's defences in order to gauge degrees of flexibility or rigidity. Probing defences is an invasive procedure that can upset the patient's psychic equilibrium. Milton (1997) likens it to an invasive medical procedure or investigation that means breaking into the body in some physical way. She goes on to say:

So we have to have a good reason to do a psychological investigation that tends to break into the inner world, piercing defences, and potentially causing mental pain and upset, especially when we have before us a patient who is not in active pain and distress *at that moment*.

(p. 49, her emphasis)

Garelick (1994) describes, through a review of the psychotherapy literature, an historical shift in emphasis from diagnosis to object relations. Hinshelwood (1991) describes a particular way of making a psychodynamic formulation that focuses on three areas of object relations (the current life situation, the early infantile relations and the transference relationship) in order to hypothesise a core object relationship. He says:

The importance of that object-relationship is that it points directly to a core of *pain*, which the patient is attempting to deal with. I find it is important to formulate what might be called *the point of maximum pain*; that is to say the particular pain which is involved in the object relationship. What follows from that are certain other kinds of object relationships used to evade that pain (the defences). We then have a way of ordering the various objects and the various relationships into a coherent narrative.

(1991: 171, his emphasis)

I do not pretend that I am capable of making such a detailed formulation as Hinshelwood proposes, but it does give a clear reason for undertaking an invasive procedure – in order to conceptualise the patient's difficulties and in the process to show the patient something of what treatment might involve. The patient needs to know that exploratory therapy will be disturbing and the therapist needs to know how the patient will manage being disturbed. In my view, this is the 'live' version of informed consent. If the patient has had a taste of their defences being challenged, experienced the emergence of anxiety and disturbance (Milton, 1997) and been held through this by the containment of the session and interventions of the therapist, then they are in a good position to make an informed choice. The following vignette illustrates some of these points.

Vignette two

The patient, who I shall call Miss A, was referred by a colleague in the psycho-therapy department who had already done an extensive assessment so I had a good deal of information about her before the initial meeting. The reasons given for the referral to art therapy were Miss A's real difficulties in expressing and processing emotions which were felt to be overwhelming. She had difficulties in putting things into words when feeling pressurised to speak and early developmental difficulties in the areas of attachment and separation; these had resulted in a limited capacity for symbolisation. It was felt that she needed a slower pace and I had a vacancy for individual long-term art therapy. Why not just offer treatment? Coltart (1987) refers to the idea of matching patient and therapist. By this she does not mean twinning like with like, rather that some therapist's capabilities and talents are better suited to some patients than others. This might operate on an intuitive level but could also be framed cognitively as questions: Do I want to embark on an emotionally demanding journey with this person? Do I think she has the resources to participate in such a journey?

Miss A was a young woman with a history of depression, alcohol abuse, self-harm, relationship breakdown, and failed commitment in higher education. Her difficulties had started following the suicide of her older sister some years before. She began our initial meeting by giving me an account of her inability to succeed in anything since her sister's death, adding that she felt guilty about it and haunted by her. On exploration of their relationship it emerged that she had formed a close attachment from an early age but then became distant when her sister became depressed and started self-harming as a teenager. She told me she wished she had made more of an effort to understand her sister's state of mind when she was alive. When I pointed out that her own similar behaviour more recently was perhaps a way of fulfilling this wish, through identification, she acknowledged this and then talked about how distressing her own teenage years had been because of her sister's extreme behaviour.

I suggested a scenario to her as follows: the close attachment in childhood to her sister had been ruptured through the sister's out of control behaviour. This had turned the whole family upside down and, after prolonged traumatic failure to be helped, the sister killed herself and then came back to haunt Miss A. This made sense to her and she immediately said that she did sometimes feel angry towards her sister but then feels guilty. I suddenly felt I had found out all I needed to know: that I could help her get in touch with the underlying difficult feelings. The match was made.

After a period of silence, I asked when she first became aware of how ambitious she was. She gave an account of academic success at school and her wish to be the first in her family to go to university. On further exploration it became clear that her wish to succeed was a way to gain father's approval and affection. When I made the link to the hidden feelings of rivalry and competition she told me she felt her sister had been much closer to father than herself. Although she had not thought about things in this way before, she thought it was possible there was something in it. At this point I felt confident to offer her treatment, which she accepted.

It was possible for both of us to make a decision based on our experiences in the encounter. I felt that she had met at least some of the criteria of suitability for exploratory therapy, which is expanded upon by Coltart (1987) who lists nine ingredients in what might constitute 'psychological-mindedness' in the context of assessment for psychoanalytic psychotherapy. Some of these are to do with the ability be in touch with feelings yet step back and look at them from a distance, others about being able to elaborate on thoughts and the capacity for free association, all of which are key to an intensive verbal psychotherapy. The psychotherapist clearly did not feel these were sufficiently in evidence with Miss A. Nevertheless, I thought she did show some potential to recognise internal reality and distinguish it from external reality through acknowledgement of her identification with her sister's behaviour. When I presented her with the scenario about the effects of her sister's behaviour she responded by being able to make a link between personal history and present discomfort, i.e. her guilt about angry feelings. My own countertransference, feeling the match was made, was not only informative on a conscious level but also contained the idealisation pertinent to an emerging father transference. She was willing to consider the existence of an unconscious mind when I made her aware of the hidden rivalry and competition. From this I was able to hypothesise a focus for the treatment and feel confident that she had a capacity to respond. I believe she left the meeting with a sense that her difficulties could be understood along with awareness that this process would involve some discomfort.

What happened to the art?

The assessment described in vignette two did not involve the patient in using art materials and therefore I did not find out what use she could make of them. However, she understood that they would be part of the therapy and was willing to use them. Many art therapists like always to use art materials in the assessment process. This may be predicated on the idea that what we do in treatment is different to other forms of psychotherapy because of the creative aspects of the art medium. Creativity is part of the unconscious symbolic process that exists on a spectrum of fluid and fixed meaning. The context in which I work means that the people referred to me are likely to be inhibited in their capacity to use symbolisation to freely express themselves because so much is fixed in the maintenance of psychological illness. It is the movement into a more fluid and therefore creative use of symbolisation that treatment in art therapy aims to develop. What meaning are we looking for in assessment and if we seek it in the art do we find it there? I think we need to be clear and realistic about what an image can and cannot do in an initial meeting. It may take some time before initial anxiety and inhibition lessen sufficiently for an embodied engagement with the art to happen. In other words, in my view it may not be possible to know what use the patient is able to make of the art-making at this early stage.

Conclusion

I have suggested that the need to find things out in an assessment may be in conflict with an ideology of allowing an open space where things can unfold through the art-making process. This may reflect differences between psychodynamic and studio-based models. Hogan (2009) gives an overview of current UK art therapy practice that delineates approaches with varying degrees of concentration on the art and art-making process, which suggests that the ideology of the studio-based model remains widely used. She presents a continuum as 'a fluid way of conceptualising art therapy practice; it depicts practitioners as potentially not locked into a particular way of working' (Hogan, 2009: 29). However, a recent survey of art therapists in the NHS (Crawford, personal communication, 9 August 2010) found that 60 per cent described their theoretical approach as psychodynamic. This may represent a loose use of the term and may also have implications for how a patient is understood during assessment. Ghaffari and Caparrotta (2004) differentiate between suitability for psychological intervention and suitability for a particular model of therapy. The former uses generic factors (motivation to change and working relationship), the latter uses factors hinged on discipline-specific theoretical concepts to formulate an understanding of the patient. If there is not a coherent model, there cannot be a coherent formulation, tasks and goals of treatment remain unclear; assessment blurs into treatment.

Whether this conflict is inherent in art therapy or not, there is potential for a split between an emphasis either on the art in art therapy or the therapy in art therapy. Skaife (2008) has provided a useful discussion on this split. In art therapy assessments the splits seem to be between knowing and not knowing, between categorisation and providing an open space, between art and verbal mediums. I acknowledge that my own approach to assessment veers dangerously close to becoming indistinguishable from a psychotherapy assessment but I currently have no other way of resolving the conflict. It depends on what we feel is going to get us the information we need to be able to make a decision on whether to offer treatment or not. In my own clinical practice I often feel that the art-making can wait until the first session. What can't wait is finding out more about the person coming for the assessment, whether I feel able to work with them and if so how I understand what the treatment is likely to involve for both of us.

I have presented the assessment encounter as a crucial moment of choice. The growth of consumerism, increase in rights and entitlements arising from the Patient's Charter (DoH, 1997) and the incentivisation of the target-driven culture in the NHS have all created a climate of expectation for patient and clinician alike. Choice is important, but without sufficient information it can be difficult to decide what to choose and there are no simple solutions to complex clinical processes. There are advantages to framing assessment as a discrete process (Garelick, 1994) and when this is underpinned with a clear model of what treatment involves it becomes possible to make a choice based on informed decision making. This decision should provide a match between what the therapist has to give (e.g. treatment model) to what the patient needs (e.g. help to modify psychopathology) with a reasonable expectation of a successful outcome.

References

Brooker, J., Cullum, M., Gilroy, A. McCombe, B., Mahony, J., Ringrose, K., *et al.* (2007) *The Use of Art Work in Art Psychotherapy with People who are Prone to Psychotic States: An Evidence-Based Clinical Practice Guideline.* London: Goldsmiths, University of London. Available at: http://eprints.gold.ac.uk/112/.

Brown, C. (2008) 'Very toxic – handle with care. Some aspects of the maternal function in art therapy', *Inscape*, 13 (1): 13–24.

Case, C. (1998) 'Brief encounters: thinking about images in assessment', *Inscape*, 3 (1): 26–33.

Case, C. and Dalley, T. (2006) *The Handbook of Art Therapy*, 2nd edn. London and New York: Routledge.

Coltart, N. (1987) 'Diagnosis and assessment for suitability for psychoanalytical psychotherapy', *British Journal of Psychotherapy*, 4 (2): 127–134.

Department of Health (DoH, 1997) *Patient's Charter.* London: DoH.

Department of Health (DoH, 2005) *New Ways of Working. Final Report from the National Steering Group, co-chaired by National Institute for Mental Health in England and Royal College of Psychiatrists.* London: DoH.

Dudley, J. (2004) 'Art psychotherapy and the use of psychiatric diagnosis: assessment for art psychotherapy', *Inscape*, 9 (1): 14–25.

Gabbard, G. (2005) 'Major modalities: psychoanalytic/psychodynamic', in G. Gabbard, J. Beck and J. Holmes (eds) *Oxford Textbook of Psychotherapy*. Oxford: Oxford University Press.

Garelick, A. (1994) 'Psychotherapy assessment: theory and practice', *Psychoanalytic Psychotherapy*, 8 (2): 101–116.

Ghaffari, K. and Caparrotta, L. (2004) *The Function of Assessment Within Psychological Therapies*. London: Karnac.

Henzell, J. (1997) 'Art, madness and anti-psychiatry: a memoir', in K. Killick and J. Schaverien (eds) *Art, Psychotherapy and Psychosis*. London and New York: Routledge.

Hinshelwood, R. (1991) 'Psychodynamic formulation in assessment for psychotherapy', *British Journal of Psychotherapy*, 8 (2): 166–174.

Hogan, S. (2009) 'The art therapy continuum: a useful tool for envisaging the diversity of practice in British art therapy', *International Journal of Art Therapy (Inscape)* 14 (1): 29–37.

McWilliams, N. (1994) *Psychoanalytic Diagnosis*. New York: Guilford Press.

Milton, J. (1997) 'Why assess? Psychoanalytical assessment in the NHS', *Psychoanalytic Psychotherapy*, 11 (1): 47–58.

Molloy, T. (1997) 'Art psychotherapy and psychiatric rehabilitation', in K. Killick and J. Schaverien (eds) *Art, Psychotherapy and Psychosis*. London and New York: Routledge.

Morante, F. (2008) 'Challenges of patient-led mental health services to psychoanalytic clinicians', *Psychoanalytic Psychotherapy*, 22 (4): 285–303.

Roth, A. and Fonagy, P. (2005) *What Works for Whom? A Critical Review of Psychotherapy Research*, 2nd edn. New York: Guilford Press.

Schaverien, J. (2005) 'Art therapy and art psychotherapy', in G. Gabbard, J. Beck and J. Holmes (eds) *Oxford Textbook of Psychotherapy*. Oxford: Oxford University Press.

Skaife, S. (2008) 'Off-shore: a deconstruction of David Maclagan's and David Mann's *Inscape* papers', *International Journal of Art Therapy*, 13 (2): 44–52.

Waller, D. (1991) *Becoming a Profession: History of Art Therapy*. London and New York: Routledge.

Wood, C. (1997) 'The history of art therapy and psychosis 1938–1995', in K. Killick and J. Schaverien (eds) *Art, Psychotherapy and Psychosis*. London and New York: Routledge.

Chapter 3

Knowing the unknowable

A multidisciplinary approach to postmodern assessment in child art therapy

David Henley

Postmodernism and diversity of perception

In this chapter the tenets of assessment in art therapy will be applied to postmodernism which challenges pivotal assumptions of individual knowledge, objectivity and truth (Gergen, 2001). Postmodernism is aligned with analysis which tolerates ambiguity of meaning and celebrates metaphor and paradox rather than logic. Assessment in this context rejects the hierarchal dominance of any one paradigm in favor of a diversity of paradigms, any of which are employed to best describe a phenomenon according to a multiplicity of perspectives (Carolin, 2001). The author's assessment approach focuses upon the necessity of an interdisciplinary therapeutic team to contribute disparate viewpoints. Postmodernism then disconnects empirical tests or measures as the dominant paradigm and instead practices a form of methodological relativism which is comprised of each team member's professional contribution to the descriptive narrative. Assessment is not bound to any one of the grand narratives that have prevailed as schools of thought such as modernism, existentialism, psychodynamic theory, as well as postmodernism – all may be deconstructed through interdisciplinary discourse (Lyotard, 1993). From a clinical view, this approach refutes the idea that any one clinician or evaluative instrument can reconstruct the inner life of any client or their art – as multiple causation factors are inextricably interwoven and defy easy categorization. To tease apart and then factor in every genetic, relational, and environmental influence, from birth through childhood, is considered a pretentious idea – one that has led to diagnostic labels, overprescribed medications, misguided behavioral consequences, etc. To ensure that no single profession may dominate the child's course of treatment, Anderson (1991) recommends the convening of a 'reflecting' team – one that shares a multiplicity of ideas with an attitude of transparency, positive attribution, curiosity and de-emphasizes the language of pathology.

Assessment as defined in this chapter is most aligned with the naturalistic method of inquiry, in which clinicians spend long periods of time observing and working with the child, family, within his or her school and culture. Kapitan (2007) identifies this as a qualitative approach, requiring repeated controls of observing and interpreting behavior over time and making 'data checks' with clients to calibrate mutual understandings – only then can the therapist move on to the inductive process of discovery and meaning-making. Assessment then is viewed as an ongoing process, occurring during *and* after the therapeutic session. The therapist assesses client need during sessions, then devises interventions which fit the needs of the child at the appropriate moment of time (Henley, 2007). These interventions are then held up for scrutiny by the interdisciplinary team. It is understood that therapeutic work may or may not unearth conclusive outcomes, as each image, utterance or behavior presents only as a piece of a puzzle, requiring a 'slow and careful process of thinking and understanding how the various pieces may or may not fit together' (Dalley, 2007: 64). Dalley's analogy is colored by postmodernism in that the pieces of the puzzle may not coalesce into a unified picture. More often, each fragment offers up its own meaning and may stand on its own as a valid outcome – despite its lack of cohesion (Flax, 1990). Analysis of therapeutic outcomes may at best provide only a descriptive glimpse at the enormity and complexity of the child's expression in therapy. In 25 years of working with children in art therapy, rarely have my professional publications captured the essence of the child despite voluminous notations and the informed analysis of my colleagues. Outcomes remain ambiguous and undigested in their meaning, despite an informed descriptive analysis (Henley, 2004).

Objectivity in assessment

Objectivity, as observed by the phenomenologist Husserl, never exists without the subjective and vice versa (Dallmayr, 1981). Quantitative assessments that are devised to count a behavior under 'controlled' conditions inevitably carry with them personal subjectivity, whether conscious or unconscious, which may inherently bias research findings. For instance, this author's early research on autism and self-injurious head-banging, sought to correlate the child's progressions or regressions with art therapeutic interventions, by counting the frequency and intensity of each injurious incident (Henley, 1986). My thesis supervisor at the time, E. Kramer, pointed out that my research design was far from a tabula rasa, as I was working within an education program with behaviorally oriented staff whose emphasis was focused squarely upon the 'extinguishing of symptoms'. My statistics appeared promising as the child's head-banging had been discernibly reduced by 35 per cent after three months of clay-work. Kramer then asked whether any symptom substitution had occurred as the self-injurious behavior had lessened. I concurred that yes, hyper-masturbatory behavior had been noted in the charts. She asked whether I factored this substitutive behavior into the statistical analysis. The answer was an unqualified no. Factoring yet another self-injurious behavior was deemed not part of the design 'parameters'.

Kramer gently conveyed that my research outcomes were fatally flawed as the *underlying issues* behind the child's need to bang his head remained *masked*. She recalled remarks by the ethologist, Konrad Lorenz: that before one can gain insight by counting behaviors, one needs to *know what it is they are counting* (Kramer, 1983).

Sokal and Bricmont (1998) write that even in the hard science of medicine, it is common knowledge that in exhaustive and repeated scientific studies outcomes routinely negate each other (a pain reliever is deemed effective only to find its long term effects are toxic), leaving the public to wonder how the supposed objective scientific trials were substantiated. The authors write that, from diagnosis to treatment, all data are subject to interpretation and this remains a highly subjective art. Factors often reflect the bias of the doctor's specialization, training orientation or influence of company pharmaceutical studies, even the government's own sanctioning, continues to be heatedly debated. Sokal and Bricmont propose that medical practice be viewed more as a narration of debatable data that invites multiple interpretations rather than arriving at irrefutable fact. Challenged then is whether scientific models of experimentation can be sufficiently objective to determine the validity of theory.

Given the doubts that scientific method can objectify its own findings, this writer calls into question whether art therapy, a field founded itself on the fragments of other highly subjective-based fields, can aspire to adapting tests or measurements, especially to the field of art. The problem of assessing an image with any degree of accuracy or objectivity is particularly vexing. First, there is an overarching acceptance of the idiosyncratic, intuitive and even ineffable nature of the artist's intent and work. Sass (1992) writes that the standard meanings and habitual constructions of reality posed in everyday life do not hold in artistic creation, unless the works are dictated by cultural dogma or religious orthodoxy. In the Modernist tradition rational deliberation and intent were rejected in favor of imagery mined from the dreams, phantasies and other id-derivatives of the unconscious. Hence, assessment is complicated in the face of the rebellious, idiosyncratic, unconscious nature of artistic expression – a task which defies tidy quantification and generalization (MacGregor, 1989; Maclagan, 2001).

Another issue draws upon Freud's original concept of projective identification. Projection invariably distorts interpretive meanings – as identical images read by different individuals are bound to vary, revealing more about the viewer's own perceptions, culture, affect and other life experiences than the artist's intent. Freud's theory of projection has been applied to art interpretation and most recently to art/neuroscience (Onians, 2007). Gombrich (1963) posited that viewers are predisposed to 'finishing' the artist's picture through their own associations brought to consciousness through projective identification. Gombrich cites Leonardo's *Treatise on Painting* as an age-old illustration, as the master observed that even a 'dark stain on the crumbling wall at the local pub could rouse the mind to new inventions' (1960: 183). Sensory impressions reaching the brain are in constant flux and are often altered by fluctuations in the viewer's mind-set or sensory effects such as shifts in context or even lighting. Anyone viewing Rothko's color-field paintings at Tate Modern's naturally lit gallery can attest to the remarkable transformations. A same work may go through many variations as momentary light effects dramatic changes. As cloud cover gives way to periods of sun, natural lighting alone creates an almost a startlingly different work of art. Such protean shifts in appearance may easily influence the viewer's inferences about these amorphous works and would thus shape interpretation accordingly.

Paradigm bias

The author gave an example of paradigm bias during his graduate work on autistic self-injurious behavior in which competing paradigms of my behaviorist colleagues and psychodynamic oriented supervisor were elucidated. The author experienced first hand the confusing and territorial reluctance of disciplines within the sciences and humanities to cross paradigms beyond their theoretical orientation. I later discovered further that paradigm loyalty is rife throughout the contentious field of autism research. For instance, a world authority on autism, Lorna Wing (1976) virulently criticized the equally renowned ethologist of animal behavior, Nicolaas Tinbergen (1972) for crossing over into autism research – a field outside his own. His approach sought correlations between the autistic experience with that of other animal species who display equal extreme shyness. I found his approach seamlessly translated into strategies for developing safety, trust and relatedness in autistic children (Henley, 1989). As a postmodern construct, Tinbergen's strategies shook the foundations of the established canons of the predominant behavioral approaches to autism treatment. He had contributed a fresh perspective to a phenomenon that has continually eluded the prevailing dominant-theory views on causation and inadvertently helped to promote interdisciplinary study.

Art therapy itself is a relatively recent hybrid discipline which, in its adolescence, continues to search for its own identity and validity. It is under pressure to align itself with the perceived dominance of the scientific method to 'prove' its efficacy through claims of measurable progress and 'evidenced-based practice' (Gantt, 1998; Gilroy, 2006). Quantifying, for instance, a baseline of what constitutes 'normality' in children's art may offer greater justification for settings favoring hard data (Deaver, 2009). Pragmatically, art therapists who employ various 'draw-a-person' tests may enjoy greater status or marketability, equal to those who work within the allied medical model. It may also serve to distance itself from those marginal elements of the field construed as new age and are viewed as pseudoscience by those embracing measurable outcomes.

Art therapists must also deal with confusion over the overlapping between allied fields such as occupational therapy, recreational therapy and open-studio therapeutic art programs. These differing paradigms may result in markedly disparate interpretations and thus further confuse or alienate our colleagues in the field. Hence, art therapists must juggle paradigm loyalty, sort out prevailing theoretical orientations and settle on research methodologies which serve the diversity of professional settings where we practice. Postmodernism suggests however, that efforts to unify the field or become aligned with an allied field such as counseling are misguided and counterproductive. Rather, each practitioner must learn to speak in the language of related paradigms without sacrificing the core elements which comprise their own identity. Being a hybrid discipline does not dilute or pervert the intrinsic identity as practiced by each of the field's unique offshoots.

The unbroken chain between past and present

Postmodernism considers all theoretical constructs as a constant recycling of paradigm dominance, loyalty and bias throughout history. Assessment and its competing paradigms come into vogue and evolve, then lose favor or resurge – as this is the nature of academics. This evolution can be traced back again to Freud's earliest clinical formulations and practice. In the late 1890s Freud delved into one of the most complex pathologies which are still vexing contemporary practice – that of childhood sexual abuse. In the 1980s the author also became immersed within this dark world, working with children who had been sexually molested. I shall now attempt to link our respective struggles with assessing sexual trauma and retrace both Freud's and this writer's journey through the lens of postmodernism. The following narratives focus upon both the phenomenon of childhood sexual abuse and its relation to sexual phantasy – issues which remain as muddled today as when they were first clinically described by Freud.

Over one hundred years ago Sigmund Freud first formulated analytical assessments which he then implemented as therapeutic interventions. One case, that of Emma E, involved a woman whose neurosis Freud concluded was based upon her repressed memories of childhood trauma including possible molestation (Freud, 1896/1953). Freud's analysis was made in collaboration with Wilhelm Fliess, who posited that sexual trauma was linked to a psychogenic disturbance of the 'nose' (Masson, 1984a), an assessment so misguided that he actually performed nasal surgery on the patient who nearly bled to death in the process. Freud was duly horrified by this outcome and yet it did not shake his belief in Fliess, he being a lauded medical doctor and confidant. When, in 1905 Freud finally broke with Fliess, he began to agonize over his own belief in seduction theory, suspecting that his patients' reports of premature sexual experiences as young children were perhaps rooted in phantasy. Since its inception in 1893, Freud's theory of childhood seduction has been rejected and defended with the controversy ongoing to this day. Dealing with early sexual exposure, abuse and even sexual slavery in contemporary childhood remain all too common, especially given the internet and expanding global economy.

In contemporary psychology, Masson (1984b, 1984c) defended seduction theory, while others have vociferously repudiated Freud's theory as unfounded and flawed (Esterson, 1998). The theory persists among contemporary psychotherapists, some of whom are accused of misusing its premises, such as the practice of 'planting' false memories of abuse – a controversy linked to feminist ideologies and heatedly debated (Loftus, 1993). Hence, after a hundred years, the assessment of childhood and adult sexuality and its relationship to phantasy seems impervious to a definitive resolution.

How does Freud's historic analysis of Emma E inform postmodern assessment within psychotherapy? Freud's seminal contribution to assessment pedagogy centers on the plurality of interpretations, in which identical phenomena can be interpreted in contradictory terms yet not lose validity, a construct that has placed Freud among the first postmodernists. Freud's appreciation of the diversity of interpretation places him, according to Lowenburg (2001), as a subversive for his time and still thus relevant today. He found that the myriad variables at play were so many and so complex that he enlisted an interdisciplinary coterie of colleagues to help process and weigh their importance. What has remained remarkably unchanged from Freud's era, however, is the diversity of interpretive assessments which differ from profession to profession, paradigm to paradigm.

Revisiting Freud's case

We might deconstruct Freud's dilemma from this postmodern perspective. As occurs to this day, Freud spent years agonizing over the validity of his interpretations, unable to differentiate between his patient's phantasy material and alleged actual trauma. He wrote voluminous supervision letters to Fliess, though this reputable doctor was working from his own antiquated science. Despite Fliess's distorted ideas, one can argue that both he and Freud were practicing alternative healing strategies that were cutting edge for their time, perhaps not unlike contemporary holistic physicians who, despite their detractors, continue to explore the mind–body connection.

The cultural mores of the period in which they were practicing, Victorian Europe, was also a critical co-factor which escaped Freud, as he was still a man of his time. In this culture it was often the norm for middle or upper class women to repress sexual desires and experiences which could become traumatic if overly stimulated. Unaccustomed to the sexual vicissitudes of the female psyche, neither Freud nor his then co-investigator Breuer were prepared for the uprush of previously repressed affect that occurred as their patients' defenses were probed during analysis. The resulting weakened defenses led on occasion to unleashed affection which in turn led to confounding transferences for both men, a terrifying reaction which drove Breuer from the field altogether (Freud and Breuer, 1895).

Then there is the issue of sexual development in childhood. Child sexuality remains as impressionable and vulnerable as it was in Victorian Vienna, as surely children from present time and onward have been sexually exposed, violated or worse. Adult sexual exploitation of children remains a sensational topic. Witness the rancor over widespread contemporary accusations of sexual abuse among child-care workers. While some charges were factual, others proved baseless. In a case in New Jersey (Rangel, 1988; Talbot, 2001) a child-care teacher was sentenced to 47 years for alleged abuse, and after serving five her conviction was overturned due to 'coercive questioning' by authorities. Despite the use of 'expert witnesses', no one could tell with scientific certainty if abuse was reality or phantasy – an issue that harks back some 300 years when a similar phenomenon occurred in Puritan America – the height of binary thinking. During the Salem witch trials scores of falsely accused women perished during a frightening period of mass hysteria.

The layered complexity of causal mechanisms which faced Freud was considerable. It required that he consider and integrate the patient's adult and childhood psychosexual issues, her cultural-based repressions, socio-economic status and physiological conditions and Freud's own emotional transferences. These factors all remain relevant to the present. In the following vignette, I shall shadow Freud's journey into a contemporary case where sexual activity in children is deconstructed under the guise of interdisciplinary inquiry.

Connections to contemporary child sexual activity

The author shall now attempt to connect the complexity of assessment issues with which Freud had grappled, that of alleged sexual abuse and seduction phantasy. The account centers on a 10-year-old deaf child whom I shall refer to as M. She came from an impoverished Caribbean family who had immigrated to the States with a large extended family when she was eight years old. They left after she purportedly had a sexual relationship with a 22-year-old uncle, for which he was prosecuted and jailed. She was thus at risk of further sexual involvement. A predisposing factor for sexual activity was her medical hormonal condition termed Central Precocious Puberty (Bonnets, 2005). This condition produced in M premature secondary sexual characteristics such as large breasts which she developed around age eight and perhaps precipitated M's sexual urges such as masturbating, and later on acting seductively towards the boys at the school for the deaf.

As an immigrant deaf child M was both non-verbal and non-lingual in American Sign. Faced with an alien environment she became emotionally withdrawn. Reluctant to interact with those in the school community, M drew readily, creating many figurative works during our two years of art therapy. It became immediately apparent after the first six months that M's art curiously displayed few indications of trauma, as there was no discernable morbid distortion in her art. Though sexual features were duly depicted, they were without exaggeration, indicating that precocious development was for her an assimilated aspect of the body-ego. If we figure developmental theory into the analysis, we observe that M's figures were immature for a ten year old, but were articulated enough to convey a fully formed self-concept which included limited narrative contexts. With regard to content, references to graphic sexual depiction occurred only in five images out of 32 collected. Plate 1 (situated between pp. 100 and 101) is one of the first 'disclosure' drawings, created after a prolonged period of trust building, towards the end of the first year of work.

Assessing any art work should proceed initially without symbolic connotation but as a narrative composed of formal elements such as form and content. To this end, M is depicted standing naked side by side with her uncle, their skin tone a rich Caribbean tan, each smiling broadly. M is rendered with her secondary sexual characteristics exposed, her arm embracing him while he fondles her vulva. This part of the narrative may be deemed significant given that the vaginal area is accentuated by M's choice of a scribble of black, applied with heavy pressure. A bright yellow arrow-like form contributes another striking element which draws in the eye of the viewer. The accentuated use of this bright colour appears to link the two sexually and helps drive the narrative. While the content is libidinous it is also curiously matter of fact. It remains unclear whether this image references earlier abuse or current phantasies, or signified an interweaving of the two.

Next the analysis focuses upon M's behavior during the art process, particularly the nuances of her sign language as a signifier of meaning. After creating Plate 1, M referred to her work and her subject of sexual relations for the first time. When I pointed to 'loaded' elements quizzically (assessing anxiously whether she could handle such a direct intervention), she smiled and began to sign 'sex good'. However, as the long arc of the sign 'good' was formed, at the last possible moment she turned the face of her hand down, forming the word 'bad', perhaps an allusion to her ambivalence. After this sign, she followed it with a long fluid motion forming the word 'and'. Bringing her fingers together to a point then drawing her hand across her face, she paused suspending the sign, elongating it in mid-air 'and. . . . .'. The hand was held in silent repose – an enigmatic pause and silence left us both in a state of silent contemplation and reflection (Epstein, 1995). Was she lost in the warm recall of their gentle embrace, the internal tingling of arousal or the lost intimacy that was eventually stolen from her? Was she troubled by a feeling of stigma, given the vigilance of the school officials? M's ephemeral motion suggests a moment that is intensely personal, mysterious and analytically challenging. Cardinal suggests that at this pivotal point we put aside clinical assessment for the moment, perhaps by penning a haiku poem to best capture its elusive essence (1979). What perhaps would the therapeutic team make of such an anti-clinical reference?

The interdisciplinary team assessment meeting

M's case was brought to the therapeutic team by the author during mid-treatment, whereby the author confessed it was beyond the capacity for any one individual to deconstruct. What are the issues of sexuality in this child as they are linked to aetiology and approach to treatment?

It was the team's leader, a neuropsychologist who first spoke – which itself is perhaps an indicator of his and his field's status on the team. He marveled how she and her abuser were depicted without any hint of guilt or embarrassment. Disturbed most by M's lack of sexual inhibition he quickly pathologized its meaning, analyzing her neuro-hormonal and cognitive deficits. The author then commented that lust in so-called 'normal' individuals may also lead, inexplicably, to a loss of inhibitions, often to great personal and professional consequences. How do we pathologize M's desires when a former US president received oral sex in the Oval office with an inappropriate partner, then shamelessly lied about it to the American people? If not considered sexual abuse, it could be argued that his actions possessed such gravity that he directly brought down his political party and plunged the nation into one of the darkest presidencies for the next decade. This illustrates how sex is acted out at the highest levels of maturation and yet the consequences of such actions vary with the individual's power and status. The former presidential perpetrator was chastised but now enjoys a resurgence of stature while the other, a poor, illiterate uncle of color was simply jailed – this social commentary was met with a disconcerted silence by the team.

Her teacher, who was deaf, changed the course of discussion, pointing out that this child was so lacking in language skills that her capacity for concept formation and metacognition was seriously limited. The teacher's orientation fell clearly within the deaf culture paradigm (Ladd, 2003). This postmodern view rejects the notion that deafness is a pathological condition based upon a 'deficiency' of hearing function. Instead it has been reframed as discrimination against a minority culture, which now asserts its own proud identity. She stated that as a deaf child with special needs, everyone assumed she understood the most elementary teachings that we of the hearing world take for granted, such as the concept of time. For instance, she could not grasp the concept that slavery was no longer practiced, that, for all she knew this disturbing historical event was still a real threat in her culture. The teacher's cultural interpretation asserted that M's lack of sensory input when amongst hearing individuals would have made cause/effect, and interpersonal relations, particularly anticipating the intentions of others, more difficult. The group voiced agreement (perhaps in deference to the teacher) to calm rising tensions within the discussion – that this 'cultural' divide could indeed hamper an appropriate reaction to social cues (including sexual) – and might exacerbate her predisposition to acting on her hormonal urges (Schick, 2005). However, the teacher also added that despite her empathy towards M's sexual history, her mission as an educator was to suppress her symptoms in order to maintain the safety of the other children in her classroom.

The neuropsychologist then introduced the latest concept of the 'theory of mind' and research on 'mirroring neurons'. The latter are specialized neurons which fire when an individual observes the same action taken by another. Mirroring the behavior of the other individual, on a lingual or gestural level, furthers all learning including that of empathy and appropriate social interaction. Mimetic learning and empathic emotional reactions have been shown to 'light up' discrete areas of the brain during functional MRI scanning; hence these centers are being mapped for further research (Decity, 2004). He then deduced that suppressed mirror neurons could account for her incapacity to assimilate the modeling of socially acceptable behaviors. Thus M's incapacity to read intentions, mood states, and desires, her lack of empathy may all be a form of 'mind-blindness' – a marker of autism (Baron-Cohen, 1991). I interjected that the neurology of mirroring was also at the center of attachment and object relations development in which the mutual gaze and comforting tactile sensations are mirrored back and forth between mother and child, cementing the bond between the two (Mahler *et al.*, 1975). The psychologist then light-heartedly referred to Mahler as being 'stuck in the 70's', essentially negating my comment and was received with nervous laughter by the group.

No matter, the social worker also seized upon the disquieting issue of mother/child relations, reporting that during meetings M's mother displayed a marked lack in warmth in their relating and seemed to not appreciate the breadth of M's problems. As a deaf, silent and passive child and a mother who relegated care to a large hearing extended family, one can easily disappear, particularly into the arms of a lascivious uncle, the sex not even noticed. The social worker also stirred the group's sense of political correctness by generalizing that sex between extended family members in the West Indies is more casual and precocious than western norms. As a handicapped child within this group, she would be an even more vulnerable target. She stated that the World Health Organization found that 40 per cent of children in the West Indies have been sexually abused, 60 per cent of them disabled, with 25 per cent by a relative. One minority team member protested this finding regardless of its statistical validity – that the mother's behavior should not automatically infer deficit or pathology but is matter of 'cultural difference' – which white professionals might find abnormal. This topic lapsed into a heated digression that was more political than clinical; again, assessment was taking its emotional toll.

Undeterred, I then reframed this 'dominant cultural bias' point to that of existentialism. I proposed that for M, her uncle may well be the first and last lover she was ever to have. We of the professional, middle class would ensure that this vulnerable disabled child would be 'protected' from further abuse and in the process deprive her of the only love and gratification she would perhaps ever enjoy in her life. Sex is of course destructive for a ten year old, but not according to M's own bodily needs and her cultural norms. Thus one could interpret her image as an existential position – of defining her bid for identity by her relationships and the gratification it provided. As her therapist I welcomed this search for identity through her art, but as a disclaimer also identified with the deaf teacher's concern for modeling appropriate behaviors. This included not inadvertently 'feeding' into or further stimulating her appetites towards sexual arousal through the eliciting of sexually 'loaded' imagery. The degree of permissiveness versus limit setting created a contradictory position. Loosening defenses permitted spontaneous free expression to flourish which is critical to art therapy work. Yet M sometimes became overstimulated during art therapy, during which her drawings could regress and thus lose some of their developmental strength. Again I identified with her teacher that as a former special educator myself I fretted that limitless sexual depiction might stimulate more acting out. Permissiveness could also increase risk of sexualized transferences, as I became cathected as the 'good' father/lover/artist and holder of confidences. I expressed my confusion over these paradigms and asked the team for guidance and consultation on this issue.

Discussion

The team dynamic during this case meeting was courteous but not without its paradigm territoriality and personal sensitivities. Yet each team member had already developed rapport and professional trust, so that each position was greeted with a modicum of respect despite its diversity. Thus, the multiplicity of truths theorem was preserved, albeit in a fragile atmosphere of intellectual freedom. For when issues skirted with cultural or political sensitivity, the discussion became more contentious and personalized. Note again the team member repudiated the WHO as flawed findings despite the empirical statistical evidence. As a woman of color herself, she argued, not without her own transferences, that given the West Indian links to a traumatic history of slavery, prejudice and poverty, she should not lapse into a judgment of the family, particularly the mother. The deaf-culture position was also politically and personally sensitive as the deaf teacher's own experience with prejudice had added intensity to the group dynamic.

The team did reach consensus that M's artistic imagery provided the most helpful picture of this child's inner life. Thus they confirmed the importance of continued art therapy services with this author as primary therapist, with the caveat that I balance creative free expression with guiding appropriate behavior. Other consensual recommendations included total immersion in sign language instruction, therapeutic role play and empathy games, as well as supervised and mediated social engagements. Birth control measures and hormonal therapy would remain in effect. Social work initiatives remained a thorny issue as the team was at a loss as to how to deal with the mother. The social worker's attempts to have her participate in 'bonding' play sessions had previously been met with resistance, considering them a personal attack as a minority and defective mother. The team agreed that any increased pressure for parental counseling might precipitate the mother's refusing to cooperate altogether – which would be catastrophic if M's therapy was to have any efficacy. It seemed the long maligned 'blame the mother' paradigm was too incendiary to be navigated – regardless of the 'datedness' of its theoretical construct.

The art therapist's input

Team protocol dictated that to conclude the conference I sum up my own findings as to whether M's art was an expression of phantasy and/or actual ongoing sexual activity and its relation to her prognosis.

I first reiterated that M's uninhibited and undifferentiated figures did not simply indicate sexual abuse – which had been the team's focus. The form and content of the imagery suggested that M considered her abuser as much a lover. We might plot this relational conundrum to those development phases that interfered with

M's capacity to bond with or differentiate from the mother. This could have left her incapable of developing a fully developed stable sense of self and others later in life (Henley, 2005). I reminded skeptical team members that Bowlby's (1969) formulations on attachment dynamics are in no way antiquated psychoanalytic constructs, but are theorized as biologically driven and instinctually programmed. Perry's (2009) use of neuro-imaging defines how the failure to bond or mothers who are neglectful to their children may adversely affect developing brain systems and in severe cases may result in visible cortical atrophy. Here science can argue the neurological consequences of severe maternal neglect.

M's primitive drive for relational satisfaction may then cast her sexual relations in a more different light. Instead of pursuing sexual gratification in the adult sense, M's relations were more infantile and thus self-stimulatory in nature. Her relations perhaps fulfilled her need for reciprocal sensual tactile stimulation, eliciting feelings where she could be acknowledged as a person, deserved of comfort and love. The image then could be interpreted as a manifestation of emotional wish fulfillment as she searched for an object that provided mutual affection. Sex acts and sex phantasies would then remain subject to primary process impulses, roaming the psyche, in a state as protean and undifferentiated as her distorted sense of time. Her West Indian environment might behaviorally reinforce these impulses as being relativisitically 'normal' and go unnoticed. Given the alleged early abuse and lateness of interventions, it remained an open question as to what degree M might surmount her developmental arrest towards greater creative and maturational growth, an anti-climactic appraisal seemingly accepted by the group.

With these final comments regarding M's guarded prognosis, the team adjourned. As we dispersed one team member wondered aloud that even with all these data and learned viewpoints whether any of us had inched any closer to M's worldview. I found this to be a surprisingly existential, Zen-infused rhetorical question. Several other team members took notice with wistful facial expressions, as well as at least one audible sigh, one that seemed to capture the contemplative yet exhausted mood of our dispersal.

Conclusion

In the dawn of art therapy, pioneer Margaret Naumburg argued convincingly that the creation of the art image fixes in time and space, the artist's ideas and phantasies that might otherwise remain evanescent (1945/1973). It remained the task of the team to bring into focus the realm of possibilities which gave the art its multiplicity of meanings. No one individual, however, laid claim to a hierarchical understanding of the phenomenon. The process and outcome recalled Freud's own agonizing struggles of how sexual urges and phantasy interact between psychic and behavioral states of being. Both cases reflect the paradoxical aspects of sexuality. The western-puritan tinged narratives that have exerted censorship, taboos, double standards, and of course 'scarlet letters' for centuries, contrasts with a culture wildly obsessed with sex from the erotic-saturated media, social promiscuity, everlasting prostitution, and traumatic, under-age abuse. Sex will remain among the most formidable and inevitable instincts which strive for gratification. It is an impulse which will confound human behavior for all time.

As Freud never verified Emma E's abuse, or ascertained the veracity of his patient's assertions, our team may not have fared any better, despite being armed with the latest theories and interventions. Regardless of theory, during therapy we accompany our clients while they navigate the realm of transitional space, where inner needs must reconcile the norms of the dominant cultures in which we must function (Winnicott, 1953). As Freud accomplished with latent dream material and free associations, the art therapist relies upon the created image, which remains a vital residue of individual experience. Yet interpreting this image never became definitive or predictive but only suggestive of possibility. Taking from R. D. Laing's (1960) anti-psychiatry movement of the 1960s, we are reminded that therapy is not an experiment, nor is it meant to reduce its maker to a diagnostic category. This idea holds despite the onward march of 'scientification', with genetics and neuroscience or the other grand paradigms holding sway over those oriented within the withering humanities. However, it is the author's contention that technology can never be programmed to approximate the empathy necessary to access the inner life of the individual. To claim so remains pretentious and illusory. Assessing the art image as a stand-alone answer to interpretive meaning is to become part of that illusion. As Freud pointed out so early on, paradigms must be applied with an awareness of the researcher's own transferences in order to keep inevitable projections flexible. Informed engagement with multiple paradigms may increase the possibility of untangling the web of human identity and experience. As art therapist, my goal then is to be entrusted with a momentary glimpse of the child and to attempt, with humility and reservation, to convey these impressions to others.

References

Anderson, T. (1991) *The Reflecting Team: Dialogues and Dialogues About Dialogues.* New York: Norton.

Baron-Cohen, S. (1991) 'Precursers to a theory of mind: understanding the intentions of others', in A. Whiton (ed.) *Natural Theories of Mind.* Oxford: Oxford University Press.

Bonnets, J. (2005) 'Etiology and age of incidence of precocious puberty in girls', *Journal of Pediatric Endocrinology*, 1: 695–701.

Bowlby, J. (1969) *Attachment, Vol. 1.* New York: Basic Books.

Cardinal, R. (1979) 'Drawing without words', *Comparison*, 10.

Carolin, R. (2001) 'Models and paradigms of art therapy research', *Art Therapy: Journal of the American Art Therapy Association*, 18: 190–205.

Dalley, T. (2007) 'Piecing together the jigsaw puzzle: thinking about the clinical supervision of art therapists working with children and young people', in J. Schaverien and C. Case (eds) *Supervision in Art Psychotherapy.* London and New York: Routledge.

Dallmayr, W. F. (1981) *Twilight of Subjectivity: Contributions to a Post-Individualist Theory*. Amherst, MA: University of Massachusetts Press.

Deaver, S. (2009) 'A normative study of children's drawings', *Art Therapy: Journal of the American Art Therapy Association*, 26 (1): 4–7.

Decity, J. (2004) 'The functional architecture of human empathy', *Behavioral Cognitive Neuroscience Review*, 3: 71–100.

Epstein, M. (1995) *Thoughts Without a Thinker: Psychotherapy From a Buddhist Perspective*. New York: Basic Books.

Esterson, A. (1998) 'Jeffrey Masson and Freud's seduction theory: a new fable based on old myths', *History of Human Sciences*, 11 (1): 1–21.

Flax, J. (1990) *Thinking in Fragments*. Berkeley, CA: University of California Press.

Freud, S. (1896/1953) *The Standard Edition of Complete Psychological Works of Sigmund Freud*, ed. and trans. J. Strachey. London: Hogarth Press.

Freud, S. and Breuer, J. (1895/1936) *Studies in Hysteria*. New York: Nervous and Mental Disease Publication Co.

Gantt, L. (1998) 'A discussion of art therapy as science', *Art Therapy: Journal of the American Art Therapy Association*, 15: 3–12.

Gergen, K. (2001) 'Psychological science in a postmodern context', *American Psychologist*, 56 (10): 803–813.

Gilroy, A. (2006) *Art Therapy Research and Evidence-Based Practice*. London: Sage.

Gombrich, E. (1960) *Art and Illusion*. New York: Phaidon Press.

Gombrich, E. (1963) *Meditations on a Hobby Horse*. New York: Phaidon Press.

Henley, D. (1986) 'Emotional handicaps in low-functioning children: art therapeutic and art education interventions', *Arts in Psychotherapy*, 13 (1): 35–44.

Henley, D. (1989) 'Nadia revisited: a study into the nature of regression in the autistic savant syndrome', *Art Therapy: Journal of the American Art Therapy Association*, 6: 43–56.

Henley, D. (2004) 'The meaningful critique: responding to art from pre-school to postmodernism', *Art Therapy: Journal of the American Art Therapy Association*, 21: 79–87.

Henley, D. (2005) 'Attachment disorders in post-institutionalized children: art therapy approaches to reactivity and detachment', *Arts in Psychotherapy*, 32: 29–46.

Henley, D. (2007) 'Supervisory responses in child art therapy', in J. Schaverien and C. Case (eds) *Supervision in Art Psychotherapy*. London and New York: Routledge.

Kapitan, L. (2007) 'The power of $N=1$: An art therapist's qualities of mind', *Art Therapy: Journal of the American Art Therapy Association*, 24 (3): 1–3.

Kramer, E. (1983) *Unpublished Notes and Criticisms*. New York University.

Ladd, P. (2003) *Understanding Deaf Culture*. Cambridge: Cambridge University Press.

Laing, R. D. (1960) *The Divided Self: An Existential Study of Sanity and Madness*. Harmondsworth: Penguin.

Loftus, E. F. (1993) 'The reality of repressed memories', *American Psychologist*, 48: 518–537.

Lowenburg, P. (2001) 'Freud as cultural subversive', in J. Winer and J. Anderson (eds) *Annual of Psychoanalysis*, 29.

Lyotard, J. F. (1993) 'Lyotard and postmodernism', in M. Sanups (ed.) *An Introductory Guide to Post Structuralism and Postmodernism*. Macon, GA: University of Georgia Press.

MacGregor, J. (1989) *The Discovery of the Art of the Insane*. Princeton, NJ: Princeton University Press.

Maclagan, D. (2001) *Psychological Aesthetics: Painting, Feeling and Making Sense*. London: Jessica Kingsley Publishers.

Mahler, M., Pine, F. and Bergmann, A. (1975) *The Psychological Birth of the Human Infant*. New York: Basic Books.

Masson, J. M. (1984a) *The Complete Letters of Sigmund Freud to Wilhelm Fliess*. Cambridge, MA: Harvard University Press.

Masson, J. M. (1984b) *The Assault On Truth: Freud's Suppression of the Seduction Theory*. New York: Farrar, Strauss and Giroux.

Masson, J. M. (1984c) 'Freud and seduction theory', *Atlantic Monthly*, 253: 33–60.

Naumburg, M. (1945/1973) *Dynamically Oriented Art Therapy*. Chicago: Magnolia Street Publishers.

Onians, J. (2007) *Neuroarthistory*. New Haven, CT: Yale University Press.

Perry, B. (2009) *Maltreated Children: Experience, Brain Development and the Next Generation*. New York: Norton.

Rangel, R. (1988) 'Ex-preschool teacher sentenced to 47 years in sex case in Jersey', *New York Times*, 23rd August.

Sass, L. (1992) *Madness and Modernism*. New York: Basic Books

Schick, B. (2005) 'Language and theory of mind: a study of deaf children', *Child Development*, 78: 376–439

Sokal, A. and Bricmont, J. (1998) *Intellectual Impostures: Postmodern Philosophers', Abuse of Science*. London: Profile Books.

Talbot, M. (2001) 'The Devil in the nursery', *New York Times Magazine*, 7 January, Section 6: 51–59.

Tinbergen, N. (1972) *Autistic Children: New Hope for a Cure*. Oxford: Oxford University Press.

Wing, L. (1976) 'The aetiology of autism: a criticism of Tinbergen's ethological theory', *Journal of Psychological Medicine*, 6 (4): 533–543.

Winnicott, D. W. (1953) 'Transitional objects and transitional phenomena', *International Journal of Psychoanalysis*, 34: 89–97.

Chapter 4

Image and process

Twin exploration in art therapy assessment

Caroline Case

Introduction

This chapter follows a previous article on art therapy assessment, 'Brief Encounters' in which assessment was explored as a discrete piece of work (Case, 1998). In this article the many images available to the art therapist during an assessment were explored. There are those that are made by the child and those formed mentally by the therapist during the encounter. Further to these there is the countertransference response to the child and to the images; the way that past object relations are recreated in the room (Dresser, 1985). Children create other images in the mind's eye; by their physical presence, the way they arrive and by the way they are, non-verbally in the room.

A model of assessment was discussed of meeting with the referrer, other agencies involved and parents to obtain not only a factual history but also a mother's/carer's narrative about her child and family history. The therapist and child usually meet for three individual sessions before meeting again with referrer and parents to feed back. In these sessions the therapy room and the materials are a constant. How the child responds in this situation, the process of making/not making, keeping, transforming, destroying as well as the final image are all sources of information that enable thought about the child. During the assessment, external world circumstances are considered, as well as trying to form a picture of the child's internal world and developmental stage.

This assessment model is using an interactional model as a framework, both in the sense that the interactions between therapist and child mirror other object rela-tions and in the sense that development can be viewed as an interactional dynamic between internal and external factors (Harris and Meltzer, 1976; Wittenberg, 1982; Case, 1998). There needs to be an indication of enough robustness in the child and in the system for therapy to succeed. The parent has to manage the feelings aroused by having to turn to an external source for help. Will this child be able to make use of the sessions, therapist and materials? What kind of parent work will be needed to support the child therapy? Is art therapy the treatment of choice, for therapist, child, and parent? Will practical arrangements work and does the carer have the commitment to bring the child each week?

Assessments can be intense pieces of work. There is sometimes pressure on the therapist to formulate an opinion on the child before they have had time to process impressions. Colleagues and parents may have strong opinions as to whether this child should have individual work. The three sessions that are usually offered may have every sort of potential meaning for the child from intense longing, 'Can I come here every day?', to refusal to come into the room, 'I *don't* want to *be* here, I want to do my school work!' The transference to therapist and institution can be powerful at an assessment.

It would be usual in the UK, when working as a therapist with children, to be working as part of a team. I would see the assessment as potentially contributing to general thinking about the family and child, so that even if individual art therapy sessions do not happen the work will still have been useful. Art therapists working in a child and adolescent mental health service (CAMHS) are members of a multi-disciplinary team offering a range of core therapeutic skills in general family sessions. They are assessing as a contribution to general thinking about the family as well as being referred children for specialist work. The specialist work may be individual, group or family art therapy. It is essential that there is supportive family work in parallel to individual child work. In educational settings and social service settings, part of statutory care, they also work as members of multidisci-plinary teams or are specialists who need to liaise alongside other disciplines working with the children and their families. Children who have been taken into local authority care because their parents have been unable to look after them, known as 'looked after children', will frequently need their therapist to liaise with the wide network that supports them so that the therapy is supported and embedded in the statutory care.

At an assessment there is an interplay between the child's way of presenting and their development, assessment of the family and their context in the external world, and the transference and countertransference, giving a picture of the internal world. This method of assessment focuses particularly on 'open-ended' use of materials which has been discussed by other writers on art therapy (Kramer, 1971; Rubin, 1978; Kramer and Schehr, 1983). This chapter develops ideas in the previous article concentrating particularly on the process of image-making and on the completed image whether or not it is actually 'finished'. Sometimes children are not able to talk and may work silently, or they may not use materials for art-making but are able to play with toys as a means of communication, or they may be completely frozen and will need to be brought to a state of being able to play and eventually to art work in their own time.

I do not use art-based clinical tests or psychological testing, although there are many examples of their use in the literature and in this book (see Levick, Chapter 9; Gantt, Chapter 10; and Betts, Chapter 11). The child and therapist are active participants and either may choose to talk, play or use art materials, or not. The three sessions form a treatment in miniature with a beginning, middle and end session. In previous writing different aspects of this process have been explored focusing on the image- and art-making process in assessment in the various settings of CAMHS, social services and education. These will be briefly reviewed before new clinical work is discussed.

In the *Handbook of Art Therapy* we were interested in the way that working processes and the use of materials might reflect the child's state of mind (Case and Dalley, 2006). Children referred for art therapy may not be communicating through language but through actions and behaviour, some may be traumatised. In this situation, the therapist needs to be able to observe and to think about what is observed. This is an essential tool in the work. Some of my writing in the 1990s focused on silence and anxieties in assessment and the difficulties for those children who were not able to reach out to use materials (Case, 1995). In my supervisory practice it was helpful to encourage therapists to look beyond the actual art image made (if any) and to look at all the imagery present in the room. This led to the first article about the different images available to the therapist in an assessment (Case, 1998). Later writing, when again many of the children on my caseload were traumatised, led to thinking about frozen, silent children and how to bring them into a state of being able to play (Case, 2005a). Some of these traumatised children took an animal form during the assessment, and after as a defence (Case, 2005a).

The reader who is interested in the process of making both in assessment and in treatment may wish to follow these themes through this later writing about clinical material in the 2000s. All these writings contain assessment material which focuses on image and process, trying to develop understanding that is embedded in the art-making process. The use of scissors was explored in the significance of cutting out (Case, 2005a); and on cutting out and sticking down representing an island of experience (Case, 2005b). Traumatised children needing to be drawn into contact, art materials fostering 'first attentiveness', thoughts on fragmentation and each medium allowing expression to a different cut-off part of the child, all formed the basis of later work (Case, 2005a). More recent chapters and articles have looked at: assessment using Winnicott's squiggle game (Case, 2008); on the actualisation of a traumatic situation (Case, 2009); layered pictures and repetitive play in assessment and finally on assessing parental support that might be needed (Case, 2010). The method of assessment described owes much to early models of art therapy which were studio based, healing through art, a form of art therapy respecting the process of art-making and also psychodynamic theory which has working with transference/countertransference responses as a major component of healing. These two threads in the therapy reflect my backgrounds in art therapy and child psychotherapy.

This sustained investigation of art therapy assessment is a form of qualitative research. Its theoretical foundation lies in psychoanalysis and the method is best described as a careful and systematic exploration of the transference (see Meltzer *et al.*, 1975) and the countertransference response to art and art production (Schaverien, 1992). It is premised on the idea that case studies do enable schemas to be constructed which can be assessed in relation to other individual cases and critically examined in relation to clinical experiences (Galatzer-Levy *et al.*, 2000;

Midgley 2004, 2006). In this way the development of theory becomes grounded in practice, through an interplay between observation and understanding. This development of clinical practice is available to all with good supervision generating thoughts and hypotheses and is probably undervalued with the general pressure towards evidence-based practice driven in the UK by the government setting targets in the National Health Service (NHS).

Two cases are used to illustrate this method, both from clinical work with looked after children and/or adopted children which usually forms part of the art therapist's caseload both in a CAMHS service and in social services. In this method of assessment a diagnosis will have been made during initial family sessions, but further assessment will have been indicated either because the work feels stuck and/or the child is puzzling, therefore to add to the original assessment by thinking about the child's inner world; or for suitability for individual work, which may be art therapy, child psychotherapy or play therapy with myself or another member of the team. In this situation an open-ended session without any set tasks is very useful as the child's response to materials, therapist and setting gives insight into attachment relationships, inner world and outer world as well as assessing for future individual work. Other possible outcomes from the assessment might be a suggestion of attachment work with the carer and child, family therapy or linking the child more firmly into the community and giving parental support.

Clinical vignette: thinking about process

The first example explores the child's way of using materials, the process of working, as well as a dual presentation as a six-year-old child and an older child of nine or ten. The process of making and a final image is discussed in relation to helping the network around a looked after child, in this case foster mother and school, think about the child.

Freddy, a looked after child age six, was referred for assessment for individual work because of his angry and aggressive outbursts at school and to his foster parents. He had a history of broken relationships. His father had left and then he was abandoned by his mother towards the end of the first year of his life and taken to live with his paternal grandmother. He knew that his father and mother had had subsequent children with different partners and did not want him. The arrangement with his grandmother had broken down and he had gone back and forth between different family members before becoming a looked after child in his third year. His foster mother wanted to care for him but he presented as an older child as if he had grown out of needing mothering, going into seemingly unpredictable rages. It was difficult for the adults caring for him to see how these were triggered.

Observation in the three art therapy sessions showed that Freddy fluctuated between presenting as a six year old and presenting as an older boy. I began to think that he presented in an older style when he was actually anxious or feeling insecure. He used an older boy's language and posture but there was tension in the room at these times. The tension in the countertransference helped me to understand that he was very insecure in this presentation. An accompanying prickliness in demeanour actually kept adults at bay at the very time that he most needed adult support.

When you enter the therapy room the first object that you come to is the sandtray. Children respond in many ways, for example, they may ignore this, exclaim 'sand' with delight, or stop to touch it. In the first session Freddy dropped immediately before it, almost clasping the end as if he might bury himself in it. He decided to play there and I thought that it was a way of managing anxieties in this new situation, almost as if he had attached himself to the first object available. He made a castle and played with two figures. One was a good knight who battled with a crocodile that became 'an angry dragon'. Whatever the knight did, the 'bad' dragon kept coming back and could not be defeated. It was impossible to control it. Freddy ended the game in a defeated looking way and moved to the paints. The whole image of the little game and almost holding on to the sandtray suggested his position of defence and the huge burden of trying to control his anger and yet his great need for a supportive relationship.

His process of working with the paints may give insight into his difficulties when working at school. He had the outward intention of making 'a nice picture', possibly to please the therapist or to be doing 'the right thing'. He was very tense and anxious that it should 'look right'. However, off the picture surface he used enormous force on the materials. He cleaned the brush by stabbing it almost viciously into the water pot and then squeezed it between paper towels screwing up his face as he did so. In this first session he wanted to paint a blue sky with birds but anxiously tried to draw round bird figures in the animal box as it was so important not to make a mistake. He clearly did not think that his own efforts would be good enough. When he used the paint palette an interest in mixing new colours clashed with a desire to make all into a muddy mess. However, when I commented on this and what a struggle it was to let something new happen, to keep a newly mixed colour and use it, I found that he responded very positively to my interest in what he could make. We had a moment of fun as he made new colours and made up names for them. However, when he wanted to move to doing more drawing and it 'went wrong' it felt quite humiliating for him, not feeling good enough. It was as if he felt shame at being young and a small child. He desperately wanted to be older and present as older to cover up the vulnerable little child that he was, but his drawing, quite appropriate for a six-year-old boy, betrayed his inhabitation of an older boy presentation.

It was hard for this child to be a child without feeling humiliation or shame. Instead he presented as an older child in a rather self-conscious, tense way. Freddy was not able to let himself be in a dependent position to anybody and was therefore hard for his foster carer to mother. Adults had left him in order to be with other adults and to have children with them so at his foster home he created situations where he got in between his foster parents. He was very anxious that he might be left again. In the second session he needed to go to the toilet but it was partly an excuse to check to see that his foster mother was there. Unfortunately, she had decided to 'pop out' to an outside shop to get something. She had been asked to wait in the building for Freddy during his session but I think she did this because he communicates that he does not need her. Freddy came back with me extremely upset after looking into the waiting room and finding it empty and began to knock over and tip out anything he could from boxes. I talked to him about these tipped out feelings that he has inside him when his foster mother is not there and I said that I was sure that she would be back for him at the end of the session. He listened to me and put some things back but the tension in the room was palpable. I talked to him about how little and anxious he feels when he cannot see his foster mother. He struggled with these feelings until the end of the session and was clearly very relieved when his foster mother was there at the end of our time.

His foster carers had mentioned that Freddy was much easier to parent when he was on his own with one of them but repeatedly got into rages and aggressive behaviour if they tried to go out all together. In the last session the image he made suggested that he was struggling with guarding their relationship, because he feared being abandoned. He spent some time struggling with getting ready, lining up paints, pencils and felt tips, washing an already clean palette and the paints. Washing the paints made the hard blocks of paint run into each other which upset him so that they had to keep being washed and the tension in the session grew. His experience was that two people joining together meant that he would be abandoned; this was reflected in his distress when two colours from the palette mixed and 'made a mess'. Eventually he was able to let himself start and painted a rather brooding heavy sun in the sky with rays and sky colour mixed up. Underneath this there is a pencilled house, which was guarded by a policeman in a helmet and a dog. Smoke was coming out of the chimney and there was a portcullis at the door, which was raised and heavy red marks in felt tip on the windows like bars. The house was also coloured in red pencil and the lead pencil lines were heavily reinforced at the sides (see Plate 2 situated between pp. 100 and 101). It had some characteristics of where he lived with his foster family but was also very tall with a lot of floors; this could represent the different homes that he had lived in and a sense of history and impermanence. His past experiences had left him feeling that if he was not 'constantly on guard' his foster parents would leave him, or get together to have another child which would mean again that he would not be wanted. The picture with the higgledy-piggledy structure of the building left me wondering about his history in the possible layers of past homes that have failed. The little figure with the dog was smiling and had huge buttons, suggesting that it was quite young.

From these sessions it was possible to understand some of his difficulties in learning. For instance, it is easier for us to learn if we can bear to make mistakes, if we can accept that we do not know and that someone else can help us learn. If we present as older than we are because we have been put in situations where we have had to struggle alone and feel humiliated when something goes wrong then learning is a negative experience. Freddy also struggled with trying to keep everything nice and to do things right. He had nowhere to safely express his anger at past experiences without risking his present placement. There were some positive moments together when I could see how Freddy responded to understanding and playfulness. This is the kind of hopeful spark of response that is a good indicator for therapy. I will be looking for a response to an intervention that might be the incorporation of something into play, a drawing response, look or comment that is an indicator that the child would find it useful and supportive to come to therapy. The image of his home made a possibility of thinking together about how he felt he had to patrol and guard and the huge fears he had that this placement would break down. It was a surprise to his foster mother that Freddy missed her and was anxious when she was out of the building because he had given her very little indication that she was important to him, usually appearing not to need her.

This open-ended assessment gave much opportunity of feeding back to the network around Freddy and helped in thinking about how he presented as older and independent in order to protect young feelings of dependency and fear of further abandonment. I was also able to offer individual art therapy to Freddy.

Clinical vignette: facts and feelings

In the following section the theme of the assessment of children who have been looked after children is continued as this can form the majority of the art therapist's caseload. The process of art therapy assessment with its entwining of talking, playing and image-making, countertransference response and the forming of images in the therapist's mind is continued together with thinking about the impact and meanings in the final image.

Sebastian had been adopted age five and was referred for assessment for individual work at the age of ten. He had multiple carers in his early life. He had lived abroad in his first two years where he had been abandoned and little is known of his background except that he had been passed from carer to carer as well as living sometimes with adults in a hard drug culture. Sebastian had talked to his adopted parents of very deprived conditions. When he had become a looked after child age two and a half he had been unable to sit up, walk, or been toilet trained. He had had no speech and only fed from a bottle. He was referred because his adopted parents were struggling with a child who was refusing to comply with normal requests, was challenging, destructive of toys, possessions, furniture, and his room. Sebastian had night-time enuresis and had huge rows with his parents about stealing and lying. At school and socially he was struggling to make friends and did not seem to fit into any group but positively he showed good ability at school work and sports.

At the beginning of the first session I felt a huge shock that Sebastian did not look anything like his mother. This might be expected because he is adopted but the strength of my feeling was a communication from him of how he felt that he did not belong. This was a significant feeling as during the first session Sebastian did not make anything or touch the art materials or toys but talked the whole session quite seamlessly about the different 'mothers' and professional carers, social workers and therapists of all sorts that he had had in his life.

Sebastian was thinly huddled in on himself in an anorak, with the hood up, buttoned up to his chin and with his hands inside the sleeves. He looked hunched over like a little old man. When the assessment process had been explained and discussed with Sebastian and his mother, Sebastian visibly relaxed and came out of his outer clothes. Mother left for the waiting room and Sebastian talked about his last therapy which had been for primary age children only, wanting to check out with me that I could work with older boys. He then told me that he had had to travel a long way for his last therapy and had not liked this distance from his mother. This led into talking about the facts of his adoption.

He talked flatly, in a depressed manner, his hands agitated, fiddling with things at times, hunched over. He had been in another country with his mother who had not been able to look after him, left with his father who had not been able to look after him, who had left him with a woman who had not been able to look after him. His mother had gone away, he did not know where, his father had gone away, he did not know where, he had been brought to England and been fostered, and then adopted. I reflected back to him how often adults in his life had left him and that it might make him wonder if there was something about him that made people leave him. He looked gratefully at me and said that he did think that. We talked about the adults that had left him and his adopted parents that loved him and wanted to make a home for him. We discussed how young he had been when this happened and how he may not have words for the feelings he had had but we could try to find words in our work together. He then talked about his temper and how he smashes things but he does not know why and wishes he had not smashed his things afterwards.

We also talked about his wish to be with his real mother who he knows has a baby now, is that his half-sister? He also wished that he had come out of his adopted mother's tummy or had been born from her and not adopted. He then described how he did not fit in at school because he was not from this country but had a father from another country and how he was bullied for being mixed race and adopted. He suddenly asked me if anyone who came here ever curled up in a corner of the room because they did not want to do something? In discussion of this he told me about times when his parents wanted him to do things or he wanted to do things that were not allowed and at these times he 'curled up inside'. During this discussion an image of dental treatment having two possibilities emerged in the conversation, whether to have a new filling or to coat over the troubled area to protect it and not to go inside it. This was an evocative image of his anxieties about whether to explore in therapy.

In the second and third sessions Sebastian, in his words, 'played with clay', enjoying its solid qualities and sense of otherness (Case, 2005a). Talking in the same way, stories of his present life and memories jostled for space in his continuing dialogue. We discussed how his life was remembered by what adult he had been living with at the time. He made a clay head very carefully and this led to a discussion of the film *Honey, I Shrunk the Kids*, because we were so much bigger than the little head. It was significant in this story that the adults cannot hear the little shrunk children and as we explored this he said in a hard way 'do this or do that, they tell you to do things but they cannot hear you'.

In the last session he looked thin and undernourished although he was receiving very good care from concerned parents. He presented physically looking depressed, a combination of a non-vital feel together with a mind struggling to work things out. He could have a sweet wistful look when he smiled. He began to make a tube from thin coils, talking all the time quite seamlessly from one topic to another, often surprising me with his thoughtfulness. He talked about his father and the countries he might have come from, wondering if he might be good at things that people were from that country. He told me more facts about his life that were in a book called 'Sebastian's Life Story' which his adopted mother had shown him. He wished he had up to date information on his half-sister and mother and could write to them and go and find them.

His pot was growing, thin coils without a base, and then he made some thin sticks and some small balls of clay saying that it was 'Sticks and Marbles'. This is a game where there is a tube with holes for sticks to go through on which a group of marbles rest and the players have to take it in turns to withdraw sticks trying not to let any marbles fall to the bottom.

We talked about the tantalising situation of knowing about his mother and sister and imagining how his life might have been if he had stayed with his mother and knowing that his sister had stayed with his mother all the time. This was very painful. He made a lid for the coil tube and wrote the name of the game on it. He now decided to make 'a sort of mattress' for the bottom of the coil pot. I said that it sounded as if the marbles needed a soft landing, somewhere to rest and he said, 'Yes.' I was trying to think about 'sticks and marbles' which gave me an image of something being prodded although in the game it is an unstable floor that has sticks gradually removed and the marbles drop down with a bang, an image of there being no solid ground beneath Sebastian's feet. He showed me how he could push a clay ball around with a stick and I said it felt like he had bits of information about his past history; it got pushed in and rolled around inside and it was hard to know who he felt inside as if. . . . he interrupted me to say, 'Like snooker – the ball goes into a mindless pot.' I said, 'Like a hole into nothing.' There was silence for a moment and I said what a strong and painful image it was of a 'mindless pot'. An image of what it felt like to have these things dropped inside and moving about – as if he cannot stop thinking about them but also does not know if he *is* this piece of information, is defined by it. It is hard to feel who he is apart from these facts. He agreed and made the base to the pot. We then cleared up and discussed the next stage of the assessment which was a joint meeting with parents and parent worker. Following this meeting it was agreed that Sebastian would start individual art therapy with me.

Conclusion

In these two brief accounts, vignettes from the assessment of two boys who were looked after and/or adopted, I have illustrated a method of assessment that is grounded in the meeting of two people in an art therapy room with art materials. There are no set themes and children can choose when and what they want to make with art materials or can play or talk. The therapist works with observation and interaction moving towards trying to understand the child's preoccupations, anxieties and state of mind. The external world of the child and carers and the inner world of the child both contribute towards an assessment of the child's needs.

The art of assessment is in moving fluidly between these different factors. All aspects of art-making, from choosing materials, to the way that they are used, the process of making and the final image unite to give a picture of the child and their object relations. An example has been chosen of a child who found it difficult to talk, Freddy, age six and a child who was actively struggling to find words for his experience, Sebastian, age ten. Image and language both have a capacity, in their different ways, of finding forms and ways of expressing and sharing children's experiences. The making of images may find forms for experience that cannot be put into words and may contribute to generating thoughts between therapist and child about both past experiences and the present situation.

References

Case, C. (1995) 'Silence in progress: on being dumb, empty or silent in therapy', *Inscape*, 1: 26–31.

Case, C. (1998) 'Brief encounters: thinking about images in assessment', *Inscape*, 3 (1): 26–33.

Case, C. (2005a) *Imagining Animals: Art, Psychotherapy and Primitive States of Mind*. London and New York: Routledge.

Case, C. (2005b) 'Observations of children cutting up, cutting out and sticking down', *International Journal of Art Therapy*, 10 (2): 53–63.

Case, C. (2008) 'Playing ball: oscillations within the potential space,' in C. Case and T. Dalley (eds) *Art Therapy with Children: From Infancy to Adolescence*. London and New York: Routledge.

Case, C. (2009) 'Action, enactment and moments of meeting in therapy with children', in D. Mann and V. Cunningham (eds) *The Past in the Present: Therapy Enactment and the Return of Trauma*. London and New York: Routledge.

Case, C. (2010) 'Representations of trauma and memory: layered pictures and repetitive play in art therapy with children'. Online. Available from http://eprints-gojo.gold.ac.uk/atol/home.html. (Accessed 4 August 2010).

Case, C. and Dalley, T. (2006) *The Handbook of Art Therapy*, 2nd edn. London and New York: Routledge.

Dresser, I. (1985) 'The use of transference and counter-transference in assessing emotional disturbance in children', *Psychoanalytic Psychotherapy*, 1 (1): 95–106.

Galatzer-Levy, R., Bachrach, H., Skolnikoff, A. and Waldron, S. (2000) *Does Psychoanalysis Work?* New Haven, CT: Yale University Press.

Harris, M. and Meltzer, D. (1976) *A Psychoanalytic Model of the Child in the Family in the Community*. Geneva: WHO.

Kramer, E. (1971) *Art as Therapy with Children*. London: Elek.

Kramer, E. and Schehr, J. (1983) 'An art therapy evaluation session for children', *American Journal of Art Therapy*, 23: 3–12.

Meltzer, D., Bremner, J., Hoxter, S., Weddell, D. and Wittenberg, I. (1975) *Explorations in Autism: A Psychoanalytic Study*. Strathtay: Clunie Press.

Midgley, N. (2004) 'Sailing between Scylla and Charybdis: incorporating qualitative approaches into child psychotherapy research', *Journal of Child Psychotherapy*, 30 (1): 89–111.

Midgley, N. (2006) 'The "inseparable bond between cure and research": clinical case study as a method of psychoanalytical enquiry', *Journal of Child Psychotherapy*, 32 (2): 122–147.

Rubin, J. (1978) *Child Art Therapy*. New York: Van Nostrand Rheinhold.

Wittenberg, I. (1982) 'Assessment for psychotherapy', *Journal of Child Psychotherapy*, 8 (2): 145–150.

Schaverien, J. (1992) *The Revealing Image – Analytical Art Psychotherapy in Theory and Practice*. London and New York: Routledge

Chapter 5

Art-based methods for art therapy assessment

Shaun McNiff

Pragmatic evaluations of process and product

Assessment is fundamental to everything we do in art therapy. The goal of this chapter will be the identification of empirical methods that can be embraced by all people using art in therapy. The discussion will explore two complementary practices: the assessment of the artistic process and the interpretation of the expressions of images and art objects.

Since these reflections will concentrate on the entire spectrum of experiences within the context of making art in therapy, the orientation can be described as art based. To the extent to which the concept of assessment suggests an effort to objectively determine and communicate psychological states and capabilities it is thoroughly compatible with an artistic orientation to therapy. These appraisals tend to be based on empirical rather than hidden conditions and they may often lend themselves to measurement.

When diagnosis is approached as striving to determine what is occurring during an art therapy session, problems being manifested, things that a person can and cannot do, how to best offer help, and so forth, this term is totally compatible with the pragmatic values and methods of assessment presented here. Although I have always treated diagnosis in an expansive way, synonymous with assessment, it is generally associated with a more circumscribed process of making a judgment and naming a pathological condition rather than attempting to describe the more complicated and expansive landscape of the art therapy experience which includes the practical experiences of making art (McNiff, 2004). Diagnosis thus suggests a singular action whereas assessment looks at the whole range of experiences in art therapy and the resulting artworks, all of which are influenced by interactions between the people involved and the goals of the particular therapeutic setting.

Within art therapy and psychology there has been a history of using art objects to label a particular person's psychological condition and its causes, often according to theoretical constructs at odds with the nature of artistic expression. Those of us who have questioned the validity of approaches to diagnostic art have frequently been called 'non-clinical' and averse to the pathological aspects of the human condition, when we are, ironically, committed to a more precise and valid way of interpreting images in accordance with the tenets of both art and science. Arguably our art-based methods have resulted in more direct and compassionate methods of engaging pathological conditions (McNiff, 2007, 2008a, 2008b). We strive to contemplate the artistic process and objects as completely as possible with the goal of getting closer to them both and more fully appreciating their expressions and communications.

This chapter encourages collaboration with medical science and does not deny the existence of psychopathology. Rather, it is the literal, highly projective and reductive practice of diagnostic labeling based on unreliable psychological assumptions that is contested – attributing artists' psychological states to certain colors, subject matter, styles of expression and compositions that they make: if you paint red you are angry, making big eyes suggests paranoia. These simplistic, speculative and generalized reductions, often made without direct connections to the particular context of creation, have impaired the public perception of art therapy.

Rather than denying that artistic expressions say something significant about the people who make them, I believe that every art work can be viewed as a form of self-presentation with self-portraiture including works rendering a person's physical qualities and more. The self is approached as an ongoing manifestation of a person's relationships with people, places, and nature as well as internal states. It is a creation combining inner and outer experiences (McNiff, 2009). As the novelist Thomas Wolfe declared: 'We are the sum of all the moments of our lives' (1997: 15).

The intention here will be the articulation of an inclusive view of what can be assessed in art therapy and how the process of evaluation is inseparable from every phase of practice. Formal diagnostic assessments are part of what art therapists often do, especially in short-term settings where this might be the primary purpose. Hopefully the principles and methods discussed here will inform these practices and others within the vast range of therapeutic situations and applications beyond the scope of this chapter.

I describe this art-based approach to assessment as empirical and pragmatic because it focuses on what people do in sessions as well as the things they make. The process of creation, making things with art materials in the presence of another person or a group, greatly enriches the assessment context. In relation to this book's focus on the initial art therapy session or sessions, my experience suggests that there can be so much data generated in a single meeting that the assessment process needs to select what will be evaluated in a systematic way.

The principles and methods of the art-based assessment practices discussed in this chapter are relatively consistent in terms of both brief and long-term processes in art therapy. This continuity is in large part due to an overarching orientation to the present moment, where intervals of passing time are relative. Within the context of a very brief period of artistic experience there is the potential to produce extensive data. Our assessment methods need to be guided by methods and goals which help us perceive, interpret, and document what will always be a selective summary of what occurs.

When making assessments during initial art therapy sessions, objectives may range from determining the potential for further participation in artistic activity; the duration of treatment; media preferences for present and future meetings; whether or not individual, group, and/or studio-based approaches are appropriate; and so forth. Whenever possible I try to elicit statements and assessments from the people being served as to their needs, goals, and aspirations. If a person has been referred to art therapy, a number of these questions may have already been addressed. For example, someone might have a history with artistic expression or may have communicated an interest in art therapy, or the absence of verbal communication may make art therapy a preferred option for treatment.

The initial session generally encourages exploratory and spontaneous artistic activities with one or more medium together with addressing resistances, fears, low self-confidence, and other obstructions to expression. We look carefully at the physical qualities of expressions and strive to perceive them as completely as possible from different vantage points, whenever possible in a relaxed manner to lower inhibitions and expand sensory and cognitive acuity. The contemporary value placed on a 'portfolio' of materials as the basis of assessing a person's capability or condition lends itself naturally to art-based evaluations as contrasted to judgments inferred from a single image made during a testing situation. These basic operational principles will invariably generate plentiful information which will then need to be consolidated and summarized in relation to therapeutic goals as described above.

Since the interpretation of imagery is embraced as a primary feature of art therapy practice and assessment, the chapter will explore ways of doing this more accurately, imaginatively and with sensitivity to the actual physical and expressive qualities of the art object and to the process of its creation. I will examine how this practical approach can enrich the assessment process, unifying the community of art therapists, and provide more reliable and consensually validated data for future research.

My colleague Bruce Moon contributes to this inquiry through a discussion that we had on assessment methods. Where my work over the past 40 years has been largely concerned with groups of adults and young children, Moon has been more involved with individual relationships, often with adolescents. Thus our combined experience widens the data for informing practice.

I will conclude with a presentation of features of the art therapy experience that lend themselves to relatively objective observation and description. This chapter attempts to present a philosophy and general guide that will advance application of principles to variable conditions of practice and wide-ranging environments where art therapists work.

Assessment shapes behavior

Contemporary assessment practices in health and educational institutions and the accompanying debates about what can and cannot be measured together with questions about bias and usefulness have much to offer art therapy. The more general assessment discourse underscores how all evaluation methods are predisposed by theoretical frameworks that determine what is to be assessed and how.

The assessment of the most rudimentary behaviors and tangible things in an art therapy session, never mind the highly projective process of trying to determine veiled meanings in an art object, is pervaded by subjectivity. The interpreter brings a perspective to the observation of data in first selecting what to perceive and then determining how to look at it in terms of vantage points, frequency, and so forth. Science has emphasized that even its most empirical methods are never truly objective since observers become part of the systems they attempt to measure and thus alter the physical composition of what is being assessed. If these dynamics are understood and embraced, they can help us establish a more credible and useful approach to assessment in art therapy practice and research.

Art therapists generally set standards and protocols for assessment that address results valued by the professional context where they work. Teams of colleagues will establish the goals of their programs and what will be evaluated to determine how well they are doing in meeting projected outcomes. Often these goals are prescribed to various degrees by external authorities. Individual practitioners also create standards for their sessions and in the context of art therapy it is common and desirable for participants to work together with therapists to establish their own objectives. Agreement is then reached as to how these goals will be assessed. Thus the protocols of art therapy assessment vary in relation to the nature of particular programs and approaches to practice.

Although few will dispute that the discipline of assessment does inform and improve practice, we also know from the realm of institutional evaluation that if an organization begins to assess a behavior as a desired outcome, it will begin to happen. The rule of thumb is that if you want to see a particular result, assess it, which of course applies to the practices of diagnostic art. This can be viewed as the shadow side of assessment, the inherent bias and behavior modifying feature of the process, unavoidable as mentioned above when there is so much potential data for review in every human encounter. But awareness of how assessment shapes behavior can help us approach the discipline mindfully; striving through an ongoing critique of our actions to realize the most complete benefits for others by carefully determining what will be assessed.

Thus I try to establish outcomes that are useful to colleagues in the particular work context and most of all to the people involved in my sessions. In every aspect of my practice, and especially within an initial meeting, the primary objective is to assist the other person in establishing personal intentions. In certain situations it may be helpful to use client satisfaction questionnaires at the end of an initial session to generate feedback and elicit responses about how feelings may have changed as a result of the experience or remained the same. Needless to say, a person's ability or inability to reflect on what just occurred generates considerable information for the evaluation process.

Within art therapy considerable attention is given to artistic images as part of this more general process of self-assessment, guided by the therapist. The making of artistic images is the permeating and distinct quality of the work, so people naturally engage them as an important part of their self-review. As emphasized in *Art as Medicine* (McNiff, 1992) I try to create an atmosphere where the image is approached as a partner, a helper, and guide, intimately related to the artist but autonomous and not a literal printout of the psyche which can be detached from the context of a particular session. When approached in this way, objects are recognized as displaying their own expressive structures and qualities (Arnheim, 1954; McNiff, 1994) which act upon the perceiver. In this respect the art object becomes what I have called a third participant in the relationship between clients and therapists (McNiff, 1981).

Most professional assessment protocols recognize that different kinds of information are gathered in order to make an informed evaluation of a particular problem or situation and that the assessment dialogue occurs in a way that instills confidence in associates from varied disciplines and reasonable observers from the public domain.

This effort to gain consensus as to usefulness and value contrasts to past and present practices within art therapy and psychology where artistic images are sometimes assessed in ways not even universally accepted within the disciplines themselves. Art therapy might consider emulating certain sectors of higher education where assessment activities strive to be inclusive of disciplinary and theoretical differences. In the spirit of consensus we can thus say that it is likely that every person practicing art therapy will affirm both the importance of assessing the process of art-making and including art works within the total assessment portfolio. It is assumed that there will be more agreement with regard to the manner in which we approach the former than the latter. Therefore, while doing our best to solidify commonalities in relation to experiential assessment, further discussion is required with regard to what objects communicate about the people who make them. My sense is that all art therapists will affirm that artworks convey a person's expression, both conscious and non-conscious, and therefore this agreement can be used here and in the discipline at large as a basis for perfecting practice.

How artistic expression furthers understanding

The pursuit of artistic knowing and healing is a primary aim of art therapy (Allen, 1992). Artists understand how the process of creative expression provides access to knowledge and insights that elude more linear ways of knowing. The hand, the body's movement, unplanned gestures, and the more general interaction with materials, colors, shapes, and compositions are modes of thinking and exploration that further certain kinds of problem solving and discovery that are inaccessible to the reasoning mind. Within the visual arts the many media and disciplines of expression available to us (painting, drawing, sculpture, photography, collage, assemblage, digital imagery, environmental construction, performance, and so forth) offer their particular ways of knowing which are the clinical substances and medicines of art therapy practice.

In keeping with the principle of correspondence in world healing traditions, different physical materials may be contemplated or manipulated with the intention of activating corresponding conditions within a person – rocks for firmness and resolve; water for flow and relaxation; and so forth. There are many possibilities for corresponding inner reactions to the qualities of art works that we make or perceive (spontaneity, boldness, balance, and calm) and the materials that we use. Thus the assessment of how to utilize media and the influences they have is a fundamental part of clinical and studio practice (Hyland Moon, 2010).

I have discovered how new artistic media and processes are always expanding therapeutic methods and possibilities. For example, digital photography offers many tools for examining the unique qualities of artistic expression and imagery. We can crop images and do more with details, amplifying qualities that may not otherwise receive careful attention. As I note in *Art-Based Research* (McNiff, 1998) photos can be taken of the different phases of making an image. This documentation can be particularly useful in an initial art therapy session to reinforce change, development, and the incremental movement involved in making an image, all of which generally take place outside conscious perception. Viewing digital images offers a different, not necessarily better, vantage point than standing before the painting. They present what has been lost as well as what persists and document how a painting emerges. In this respect they further conversations about process and complement our tendency in art therapy to interact primarily with the finished image.

We can get to know and develop ourselves, our relationships, and more general sense of experience in more comprehensive ways through varied media and this power is one of the factors that has led to a significant increase in the use of the arts for therapeutic and healing purposes. Although epiphanies and quick flashes of insight commonly occur within all of the arts, the process of gaining a more complete understanding of a particular artistic process and the resulting objects generally requires sustained concentration and reflection together with another person or group. All of the various approaches to art therapy are united in giving attention to creative expressions in this disciplined manner.

We witness one another and reflect on our own expressions with a psychological and artistic concentration intended to further connections to images, materials, and the process of creation. Relationships to art objects tend to be ongoing with the potential of addressing whatever is happening at a given moment. Picasso liked to say that whenever he walked by a particular painting in his home, they had a new conversation.

Prerequisites for discovery within this process include: the suspension of preconceived judgments; the embrace of uncertainty; and the recognition that artistic inquiry is distinguished from analytic science by how its outcomes are not proposed at the beginning of an experiment. Just as artistic expression often happens spontaneously outside the purview of conscious thought and planning, the same applies to our reflections upon art objects. Every phase of art-making, whether within the context of an initial session or over the course of an extended relationship, involves an ongoing process of assessment – making gestures and reflecting on them; responding with more action or knowing when to stop.

I have been heartened by the way attempts to reduce artistic expression to certain pre-existing psychological concepts or biases have been widely questioned by the new mainstream of the art therapy community which is focused on more creative ways of interacting with images and pursuing understanding. In response to the problems of psychological reductionism and labeling in art, many within art therapy totally eschew interpretations by therapists and put all their attention into encouraging participants to interpret their own images. Collaboration toward a more unified professional discipline can be strengthened through the recognition that any attempt to understand the meaning, and better yet meanings, of an artistic image is always an interpretation from a particular vantage point and never an absolute explanation.

If we agree that the responses of therapists to art works are individual creations, we will take a major step forward in terms of psychological validity. This recognition will make it easier for interpretations by therapists and participants in art therapy to stand together, and enable the latter group to freely reflect upon their significance and usefulness. Interpretations of images offered by therapists are thus guided by sensitivity as to the extent to which they are helpful to the other person.

I emphasize how interpretation, which includes artistic activity itself, is our most basic way of understanding and organizing experience. The issue has more to do with the kind of interpretation we value and practice. We might ask how interpretation can become more attuned, psychological, creative, insightful, and useful, as contrasted to the formulaic labeling that has characterized many approaches to the diagnostic use of art. I say to my students, by all means interpret art and use art-making to interpret and know experience! But try to be more sensitive, creative, and thoughtful about the nature of artistic expression.

We also need to be aware of how visual art images express themselves through their various material structures and not via verbal narratives. When we use words to interpret images we are translating these expressions in another modality of communication which at its best establishes a correspondence to visual structures. Talking about an object can also help us see it more completely and share observations with other people. Our verbal responses to images are thus creations within the modality of language, utilizing metaphors, stories, and various narrative structures to establish communications that correspond to what we think and feel when looking at art.

An exchange with Bruce Moon

Bruce Moon, who spent many years working as an art therapist in a hospital setting, has been influential in helping our discipline pay closer attention to the art experience and become more creative in the language used to describe outcomes (1992, 2006, 2007, 2009). His approach to assessment is aligned with the pragmatic methods presented here. Moon shares my concerns about the ethical dimensions of treating images (McNiff, 1991) and my efforts to compare our interactions with them to how we engage people: with respect, compassion, and a desire to learn more about them. He responded to the notion of 'image abuse' raised in *Depth Psychology of Art* (McNiff, 1989) by coining the term 'imagicide' (Moon, 2009), suggesting even more heightened ethical apprehension.

Moon describes how 'artworks are often mysterious and perplexing' and he approaches them 'with a sense of awe and wonder', establishing the basis for a 'respectful conversation with them that honors many possible meanings and connections to a person's life' (Moon, 2007: 4). Metaphor and the process of telling stories, those that he presents in his books and the ones created by the people with whom he works, are primary modes of understanding and communication within Moon's creative practice. He continues by describing how:

> Clients often interpret their works different from how I would. Sometimes this is difficult for me because I want my clients to understand my point and learn from my experiences. But I recognize that in poking around for themselves in metaphors, clients often come up with understandings that are truer, deeper, and more personally significant than anything I could have said. What people realize on their own from metaphors become truths they can harvest for themselves.
>
> (Moon, 2007: 5)

The image as metaphor presents itself as a guide, what the indigenous healer might describe as a familiar spirit, who helps us assess, evaluate, and gain a more complete understanding.

Winnicott (1971) similarly underscored the importance of learning how to step back and let people find meaning for themselves while he strove to establish a creative space that supports the overall process of discovery. He also reported how he sometimes impeded discovery with his 'need to interpret' (p. 86).

In addition to his attenitiveness to metaphor and story, Moon demonstrates in his writings how he is always exploring ways to assess the process of making art more effectively. In a short-term therapeutic setting where diagnosis was a priority he and another art therapist established categories that guided their assessment of a 'patient's sense of self, world view and relationship to others' (1992: 138). These included a documentation of 'Media Characteristics', 'Symbolic Language', and 'Artistic Developmental Level' (pp. 140–142). Moon reinforces my emphasis on the extensive data presented in an art therapy session and how we need to make decisions with our colleagues about what we observe and how we document the work.

In a conversation that I had with Moon he says:

'I think of assessment as a process rather than an event. The great tragedy, in my view, of some recent art therapy literature about assessment is that it becomes clichéd and reductionistic and does not deal with the whole experience. The error is that we have not looked at assessment as a phenomenological process. It has been reduced to – this means that – rather than taking into account how a person moves when making art; what facial expressions they show; how they respond to the art therapist's response to the work. All of this is grist for the mill rather than just looking at the art piece as cadaver, just isolating the product as something to be dissected, as with an autopsy where you take all the life out of it. The other thing you emphasize is the bias of the assessor, that if someone is looking for pathology, they will find it. Assessment is a wonderful thing when it allows art therapists to help clients. It becomes less than helpful when the process of analyzing an artwork takes place in vacuum.'

I respond: 'People offering art diagnoses will no doubt say that they strive to help others', and Moon continues: 'But what they do is analyze art works in a void and this is not a therapeutic process. The whole point of assessment is that it is part of a therapeutic interaction with another person rather a pseudo-scientific exercise.'

'Are the assessments we value grounded in empathy?' I ask.

'Yes,' he replies. 'The purpose of what I call responsive art-making (expression by therapists in response to their clients) is to help you get out of yourself, move beyond your own boundaries to see how the other person feels. It is a vehicle for empathy. I can't be of much help to people unless I get a sense of how they view their own lives. It is a constant process.'

'Empathy does not mean that one adopts the position of another', I answer. 'It suggests an effort to understand another's perspective, or action, by imagining oneself in the same place. It is an important psychological and ethical intelligence, and a key tool of assessment.'

Moon emphasizes how his objective in every form of assessment is always one of advancing the therapeutic process and the person's quality of life:

'The goal of assessment is to improve treatment and to help myself and other staff experience how clients see the world; how they feel about their lives; how they interact with me, the materials; how they handle being with other people in the session and all of this helps us begin to understand the way they function in the world, where they may need help, and most importantly, what their particular strengths are. Unfortunately so many clinical settings use checklists and preformed terminology which are almost always biased toward seeing dysfunction rather than strengths.'

(Personal communication, 21 July 2009)

This exchange with Bruce Moon reinforces how the interpretations of therapists, when and if they occur, are part of a larger effort to help the individual person connect in meaningful ways to their artistic expressions and the more general process of creation and therapy.

Clinical and studio practice: assess, assess and assess

It was clear in my first days and weeks of professional practice as a beginner in art therapy that my primary role was one of first helping people experience the curative affects of artistic expression and then be able to assess the extent to which therapeutic outcomes occurred. I would document my observations and communicate them, when appropriate, to others.

From the start, it seemed that placing primary emphasis on analyzing art works outside sessions, which was common practice throughout the mental health field, resulted in overlooking what was happening in the present moment with people. These procedures lacked what Arnheim called 'the smell of the studio' (1954: 4). I have described how 'depth is on the surface' of our expressions (McNiff, 2009: 140, 164) and how fixations on the past and what is hidden suggest an inability to be open to what is before us, the faces of our expressions.

After every session in my early years of practice, I made detailed notes and entries in people's files. I described how a person handled the various materials, challenges, and tasks of art-making; patterns in behavior and expression; difficulties encountered; levels of motivation; changes in expression and actions in the studio. I described how people made art, their styles, and choices of subject matter, colors, and materials. In general I tried to the best of my ability to describe what was happening with a person in the studio from my perspective. Whenever possible I would also include the participants' own reflections on their experience.

My early studio work gave considerable time to perceiving art works during sessions, talking about them, and interpreting them through other forms of artistic expression – movement, poetry, storytelling, drama. When working with withdrawn people suffering from chronic mental difficulties, the potential for verbal and narrative responses was limited so we focused on activities that furthered perceptual awareness and the articulation of the objective, physical qualities of art works, all of which generated considerable material for assessment. As emphasized throughout this chapter, such extensive data were generated that it became necessary to identify essential elements and behaviors that could be observed and documented over time in keeping with the more general goals of therapy. My selections of data to benchmark were guided by discussions with peers, supervisors, and the people with whom I worked.

In short-term situations, documentation of the phenomena of practice and varied modes of expression enabled me to offer a relatively full assessment of a person's behavior in the studio which was valued by my colleagues whose interactions with people were largely through spoken language. Since I was working in a state hospital, there were people who I was able to engage over extended periods and I could then look with a longitudinal perspective on changes, developments, and consistencies (McNiff, 1981). The process of assessment became a mode of research which led to my first publications documenting how a focus on perceptual qualities in art enhanced more general awareness and stimulated behavior changes (McNiff, 1973, 1974); and how developmental patterns in artistic expression had a corresponding impact on larger spheres of behavior (McNiff, 1975, 1976).

I have found it beneficial, in early and subsequent sessions, to concentrate on the most basic acts of artistic expression – how a person moves with materials and the extent to which there is an ability to sustain gestures and awareness. Can the person move freely on a large surface, or a small one, with drawing or painting materials? Does movement differ in relation to particular media? Is there focus and flow in movement and speech or are these expressions scattered, impulsive, or tightly guarded?

Since perseveration and rigidity were common patterns in the mental hospital studio, my goals were often focused on spontaneity, improvization, and expanding the range of gestures and subject matter. I would typically embrace the most meager initial efforts, and affirm them as starting points that could be varied and expanded. People were encouraged to build upon these first gestures.

As I demonstrated in early publications (McNiff, 1975, 1976, 1981), art therapy is a thoroughly kinetic discipline which can be viewed as a subtle form of movement therapy. People who are greatly intimidated by moving their whole bodies in studio sessions begin to move in what I call a dance on the surface of paper and canvas or in a physical relationship with three-dimensional materials where they might wrestle, bend, and thoroughly transform organic matter. I encourage people to make contact with the ground or floor beneath them while standing before a painting surface or sitting in a chair. With severely withdrawn people as well as with participants in studios for artists and art therapists, I concentrate on the most unlikely movements, acknowledge them, sometimes mirror their expression with my own, and use elemental marks and gestures as a basis for sustained expression.

We assess tension, relaxation, spontaneity, and the ability to breathe naturally when moving. Focusing on the most fundamental aspects of art-making in my experience results in greater psychological depth and insight. The simpler, the deeper, I say (McNiff, 2009). The process can be likened to contemplative practice in that concentration on the most rudimentary actions and breathing tends to expand rather than contract possibilities for expression. We determine the extent to which a person can deal with a simplified approach and become immersed in the experience of the moment. Perceptual awareness and thought, and the ability to articulate what one sees in an art work, are other relatively empirical areas for assessment within the ongoing process of artistic activity.

In my 1981 book *The Arts and Psychotherapy*, I encouraged the assessment of movement qualities in the visual arts and other expressive modalities. I wrote:

> In art therapy there is sometimes too much emphasis on the symbol itself and its relation to the person's past, while the process of creation is overlooked.

The very strength of art therapy, which is the creation of an art object with a fixed and continuous identity within the flux of time and space, can become a detriment.

(p. 127)

Of course I value the symbolic aspects of art therapy but they need to be approached as part of a larger discipline of assessment. In addition to symbolic features, an artistic image displays much more data suggesting what a person is and is not doing.

I described how the mental health field needed to give more attention to the expressions of the body and other 'tangible and objectively manifest behaviors'. We examined polarities of movement – 'spontaneity and restraint . . . social responsiveness and egocentrism . . . precision and randomness, unity and fragmentation, strength and weakness, variation and repetition, imagination and stereotypes' (p. 125). We assessed a person's awareness of the body's movement; the ability to move with others; the capacity to make transitions from one sensory modality to another; consistencies and inconsistencies of expressions in different sense modes – how a person might make a delicate and free drawing while the body's more general movement in space was awkward and rigid. I described how people who are 'completely withdrawn in their speech and movement will express emotions through the visual arts or poetry, and in many cases as speech and movement are restored to their normal levels, the poetry and art will lose their intensity' (p. 127).

This focus on movement was reinforced by my regular use of videotape in art therapy sessions during the formative years of my practice (McNiff and Cook, 1975). It was striking how participants in our groups, more generally prone to withdrawal and a lack of attentiveness, became actively involved in viewing and evaluating themselves during playback sessions. This close involvement in self-assessment tended to happen immediately in the first sessions as contrasted to other aspects of the art-making process that emerged over time. The imagery was tangible and immediate, and perceptually 'new' to the participants who usually showed a degree of involvement not characteristic of their more general behavior when viewing themselves. The medium also provided opportunities for self-assessment over the course of a more expanded relationship. People observing themselves see palpable examples of how their behavior changes – shifts from forceful to more subdued movements, from tight and rigid gestures to more fluid expression, and so forth.

Most of us are much more apt to make changes when we ourselves see difficulties as contrasted to having others call them to our attention. My experience in viewing myself on videotape has had a significant influence on my ongoing self-assessment. I see and hear things about my voice, gestures, and interactions that have a jarring impact as well as more subtle expressions. As with all features of art therapy practice I try to be a co-participant and learner in every phase of practice.

In one of my early studio groups a young man who was severely restricted in his movement was however keenly perceptive of others and the more general studio environment. In his first group session he walked with a stiff shuffle and was not able to hold a brush or pencil. In keeping with my tendency to build upon a person's strengths when they are unable to fully participate in artistic sessions, I encouraged him to respond to video recording of others working when we gathered at the end of the group.

This involvement helped him relax and in the next session he started to paint. I made close-up recordings of his hands moving and he was taken aback by the gracefulness and spontaneity of the gestures and aesthetic quality of the hands interacting with the different materials. Other members of the group affirmed these qualities and the focus on the small motor expressions helped him to move his whole body more freely.

Self-assessment can be empowering and I have encouraged it in every aspect of my practice. In other situations with video recording I will focus on the gradual emanation of the artwork as well as the movements of the artist. The camera documents the phases of creation and the earlier forms of an artwork that are lost as the piece is constructed.

Today with the accessibility of digital recording and editing technology it is a relatively simple process to create videos which illustrate these changes and/or continuities in expression. The assessment of essential movements and bodily gestures during artistic activities has proven to be a primary orientation through every phase of my career. People operating at all levels of autonomy and effectiveness in life can learn so much about their expression by assessing the movements and gestures of the body while making art.

In my studios we also use body movement and other forms of artistic communication to respond to images and as ways of getting closer to their expression. Repeatedly I see how physical and bodily interpretations through spontaneous movement, suggested by an image, help us see it more completely. Movement in this respect becomes a primary vehicle of assessment. The most accurate ways of understanding a person's expression in visual media are not always verbal as described above. Movement expressions also speak a universal language, traveling at the speed of light, which has a visceral effect on viewers, communicating in ways that circumvent many of the obstacles and conventions carried by spoken language.

My practice gives considerable attention to how creative imagination furthers healing and insight. I have found that the method of personifying images has been one of the most effective ways of helping people advance their relationships with artistic expression. When we treat an image as a person, we assume that it has something of significance to express.

What does the image have to say about itself? What insights does it communicate? What does it want us to see or do? This focus on the other, mediated through creative expression and imaginal empathy, accompanied by a relaxation of our pre-existing and habitual attitudes and concepts, helps us access insights not available through more conventional speech.

We might ask the images for help in the assessment process. What do they have to say about what we are doing? How do they evaluate us? What changes have been made? What still needs to occur? How likely is it to happen? What are the obstacles?

I find that it is more reliable and clinically useful to let images speak for themselves in the many languages of artistic expression which we therapists witness and do our best to understand and then communicate our reactions back to the artist. We access a more spontaneous and instinctive sense of what is happening while skirting habitual restraints. It is quite a shift from a supposedly objective diagnostician, looking at an art object apart from an actual session and declaring what is happening inside a person.

In reality artistic images and the process of making them are always a step ahead of the reflecting mind and we do our best to stay closely attuned through an unending process of assessment. Art therapy's ability to physically embody actions and sensibilities is a remarkable asset, and we need to do more to establish empirical methods that help us witness, understand, and make the most of the healing powers of the creative spirit.

References

Allen, P. (1992) 'Artist-in-residence: an alternative to "clinification" for art therapists', *Art Therapy: Journal of the American Art Therapy Association*, 9 (1): 22–29.

Arnheim, R. (1954) *Art and Visual Perception: A Psychology of the Creative Eye*. Berkeley and Los Angeles: University of California Press.

Hyland Moon, C. (ed.) (2010) *Materials and Media in Art Therapy*. London and New York: Routledge.

McNiff, S. (1973) 'A new perspective in group art therapy', *Art Psychotherapy* 1 (3–4): 243–245.

McNiff, S. (1974) 'Organizing visual perception through art', *Academic Therapy Quarterly*, 9 (6): 407–410.

McNiff, S. (1975) 'The case of Anthony: a study in parallel artistic and personal development', *American Journal of Art Therapy*, 14 (4): 126–131.

McNiff, S. (1976) 'The effects of artistic development on personality', *Art Psychotherapy*, 3 (2): 69–76.

McNiff, S. (1981) *The Arts and Psychotherapy*. Springfield, IL: Charles C. Thomas.

McNiff, S. (1989) *Depth Psychology of Art*. Springfield, IL: Charles C. Thomas.

McNiff, S. (1991) 'Ethics and the autonomy of images', *Arts in Psychotherapy*, 18 (4): 277–283.

McNiff, S. (1992) *Art as Medicine: Creating a Therapy of the Imagination*. Boston, MA: Shambhala.

McNiff, S. (1994) 'Rudolf Arnheim: a clinician of images', *Arts in Psychotherapy*, 21 (4): 249–259.

McNiff, S. (1998) *Art-Based Research*. London: Jessica Kingsley Publishers.

McNiff, S. (2004) *Art Heals: How Creativity Cures the Soul*. Boston, MA: Shambhala.

McNiff, S. (2007) 'Empathy with the shadow: engaging and transforming difficulties through art', *Journal of Humanistic Psychology*, 47 (3): 392–399.

McNiff, S. (2008a) 'Creating with the shadow: reflections on Stephen K. Levine's contributions to expressive arts therapy', in E. Levine and P. Antze (eds) *In Praise of Poiesis: The Arts and Human Existence*. Toronto: EGS Press.

McNiff, S. (2008b) 'Creative expression in service of others: reflections on transparency in art therapy practice', in A. Bloomgarden and R. Mennuti (eds) *Psychotherapist Revealed: Therapists Speak about Self-disclosure in Psychotherapy*. London and New York: Routledge.

McNiff, S. (2009) *Integrating the Arts in Therapy: History, Theory, and Practice*. Springfield, IL: Charles C. Thomas.

McNiff, S. and Cook, C. (1975) 'Video art therapy', *Art Psychotherapy*, 2 (1): 55–63.

Moon, B. (1992) *Essentials of Art Therapy Education and Practice*. Springfield, IL: Charles C. Thomas.

Moon, B. (2006) *Ethical Issues in Art Therapy*. Springfield, IL: Charles C. Thomas.

Moon, B. (2007) *The Role of Metaphor in Art Therapy: Theory, Method and Experience*. Springfield, IL: Charles C. Thomas.

Moon, B. (2009) *Existential Art Therapy: The Canvas Mirror*, 3rd edn. Springfield, IL: Charles C. Thomas.

Winnicott, D. W. (1971) *Playing and Reality*. London and New York: Routledge.

Wolfe, T. (1997) *Look Homeward Angel: A Story of the Buried Life*. New York: Scribner.

Chapter 6

The subjects of assessment

Robin Tipple

Introduction

In this chapter I intend to present some research findings, using case material from a discourse analysis of an art therapy assessment with an eight-year-old boy. This analysis of discourse provided me with a fresh understanding of art production and its relation to context, but also facilitated an exploration of the relation of the child and the therapist to assessment practices, thereby leading to a better appreciation of what art therapy can, potentially, contribute to a multidisciplinary assessment which aims at achieving a diagnosis.

Discourses, in the analysis that I am presenting, should be understood as including both the production of texts, speech and non-verbal communication, and social practices, in particular the rituals, ceremony and exchanges that constitute assessment (see Foucault, 1977, 2002; Jaworski and Coupland, 1999). In material terms the research included the examination of video recordings and the transcription of speech, the interpretation of writing and the exploration of visual signs, drawings and three-dimensional objects.

Structuralist and post-structuralist theory was used to ground reflection and interpretation during analysis, especially with regard to the relation between subjects (human subjects, persons) and discourses. Althusser (2001) theorises the social production of subjects in discourses when he presents us with the paradigmatic event of the man who turns in response to the call of a policeman. This turning movement, a moment of recognition which Althusser names as the moment of 'interpellation', places the subject within the social order, the subject thereby becoming a subject for others and subject to ideological discourses and structures, which the turning movement reproduces.

Butler (1997) points out that in Althusser's example some agency on the part of the subject must exist prior to the turning. She accepts that a condition of subordination is necessary in becoming and continuing as a subject. For instance, dependency in the form of an attachment to a good enough caregiver is necessary. However, subjects can shape their subjectivity, through performative iterations, through the repetition and variation of the discursive forms that the subject encounters and which are productive of subjects. For instance, when the child

learns the obligation of please and thank you she also learns to place this obligation on others and learns ways in which she could vary this process to mitigate the
dependent role.

In this chapter 'subject' and 'self' are used interchangeably, although 'self'
could be regarded as a term antagonistic to 'subject' (see Burkitt, 2008) and more
closely related to the body. The self, in this research, is treated as a social and
cultural phenomenon, as a construct that the subject uses to confer meaning on
social practices and achieve 'identification' (see Wetherell, 2008).

Setting

I will now describe the setting and the nature of the assessment that I submitted to
analysis. Chestnut House (a pseudonym) is an NHS (National Health Service)
facility providing multidisciplinary assessments for children and youngsters with
neuro-developmental disorders. The team consists of child and adolescent
psychiatry, clinical psychology, speech and language therapy, occupational
therapy, music and art therapy. Art therapy assessment in this service contributes
to a larger assessment that aims at the provision of a diagnostic opinion, especially
in relation to autism and Asperger's syndrome.

Prior to working at Chestnut House I had developed a psychodynamic approach
to art therapy with learning disabled adults (see Tipple, 1993, 1994). This understanding contrasted with the practices at Chestnut House which were ordered
through medical and cognitive 'sciences', where an aetiology that supports the
search for genetic, biological and behavioural indices was regarded as having
'validity' and 'authority'; here psychodynamic explanation is not encouraged.
Formal assessments that measured an individual's performance against a norm
had status, and when 'informal' assessments such as art or music therapy were
used it was expected that emphasis would be placed upon the disclosure of the
phenomena listed in the diagnostic manuals: for example, impaired social interaction, deviant forms of communication, paucity of imagination, obsessional behaviours and sensory sensitivities.

Despite the dominance of the neurological and cognitive discourses, the team
did value art and music therapy assessments – and this allowed me to approach
the task in a positive frame of mind. Whilst formal assessments use standardised
instruments to obtain measures of development and functioning which can be
rendered into a numerical form, informal assessments rely on description and
interpretation. But informal assessments can encourage choice, initiative and
social interaction, communication and social exchanges that the more directed
and structured assessments might restrict or stifle.

Some of the children and young people referred to the service found direction
difficult and were unwilling to comply with adult imposed tasks; in contrast,
others could not generate ideas without some prompt or structure and found more
open-ended and ambiguous situations too anxiety provoking. Therefore, I decided
to introduce at the beginning of my art therapy assessments a period of choice

where direction was at a minimum and initiative was encouraged. This was followed by a period where direction intervened and choice became more limited but still available; in this period interactions were encouraged. I might then suggest a turn-taking activity, maybe painting together, using the Play-Doh™ together, or joining me in the squiggle game (Winnicott, 1996). On occasions, I also introduced a period where the task was self-evident and where directions were given by the adult, for instance a drawing task might be given. I reasoned that having this shape to the assessment would allow me to maximise the potential of these brief assessments and enable me to comment on the child's response to different situations.

To facilitate a description of social interaction and communication the art therapy assessments at Chestnut House are recorded on video. The assessment lasts for one hour and after the assessment I provide a report for the team and referring agents. All reports are shared with parents and the parents often watch the assessment via a monitor in another room.

Methodology

The methodology of the research entailed the examination and analysis of clinical documents (Atkinson and Coffey, 1997), an analysis of video material aimed at constructing a transcript that emphasised the 'dramaturgical' nature of social interaction (Brisset and Edgley, 1990), and a close examination of art products in order to produce an ostensive description, a description that directs a reader towards what can be seen in a reproduction (Baxandall, 1991). The research produced four case studies and the cases were first presented through the study of the documents held in the clinic's files.

Case material

Brian was referred to the service by a consultant community paediatrician who described Brian as an 'interesting boy with high functioning autism'. Advice was sought concerning the management of behaviour, respite care, and help with transfer to a suitable secondary school. Brian's language development was delayed and although demonstrating an ability to relate to others, a pattern of 'extreme' social withdrawal is reported. Imaginative play is recorded but play is also described as 'strikingly obsessional'.

The educational psychologist says that Brian 'has been known to draw the same picture over 500 times'. The school say that Brian has made 'remarkable progress', but his behaviour is 'very variable'. Brian is reluctant to attend school. He is bossy towards his friends and has never been able to sit on the carpet with the other children and dislikes the playground. When admonished he hides in corners and has hit teachers and threatened others with a knife.

Despite his resistance to school, his resistance to interactions with his peers and his social withdrawal, he is described as being able to 'hold a detailed and intelligent conversation' and 'can be very articulate about feelings and emotions'. Brian is also described as naive, immediately admitting to his part in a fight even though this might be to blame himself.

A questionnaire completed by the school staff is summarised as a list of complaints. Brian is 'constantly restless and fidgety'; he 'constantly fails to finish things'; 'needs reminders'; 'never responds positively to demand of task'; 'frequently destroys own and school property'; 'does not accept responsibility for own actions'; 'constantly needs reassurance for everyday events'; and 'is frequently defiant'.

What is worth noticing is that despite the negative image that the reports convey there are often comments that show Brian providing behaviour that impresses adults, for example, 'can do imaginative play'; 'has friends'; is 'popular'; and has an ability to hold 'intelligent conversations'. Difficulties or problems with social interaction, communication and social imagination are variable. It is not an all-or-nothing presentation that is required for diagnosis. Brian is not described as never interacting with reciprocity, or never being able to communicate or produce imaginative play. Obsessive, ritualistic and repetitive behaviours are not the only behaviours reported. The presence and the use of diagnostic criteria does not imply that adults do not notice and acknowledge other positive or 'normal' behaviours. The subject is not produced as totally autistic, wholly given over to his or her autisticness. Or, to put it another way, whilst autism might be presented as dominating an individual child's life, for example, we gain this impression in the account of Brian at school, there still seems to be a time or occasions when the subject is free from autism, at least from that form of autism which is often presented as destructively pervasive. Here we are reminded of Meltzer's account of autism and his notion of 'autistic states' and 'post autistic mentality' (Meltzer *et al.*, 1975).

As we can see, it is this process of reconciling differences whilst producing a subject child in his or her oppositions, difficulties, developmental delays, powers and abilities that the documents trace. And, we should notice, it is expected that the art therapist, with his report which is written after his assessment, will contribute to this adult-led process.

I shall now present an extract from the transcript (see Key, see Box 6.1, p. 96) and analysis of the video that shows Brian at aged eight years six months, an extract from the very beginning of the art therapy assessment. The assessment begins with the therapist adjusting the camera and walking into view.

Therapist: I'm not going to move it/
Therapist: Now – right/
Brian: [where's] that paper aeroplane/
Therapist: Let me see if I can find it./

The therapist's initial comment is in relation to the camera and he is seeking to reassure Brian. The therapist does in fact move the camera from time to time.

Brian is keen to find the paper aeroplane, the overlap in speech shows him hurrying things on. The therapist finds the paper aeroplane and places it on the table and pushes it towards Brian.

Therapist: Now – are you going to teach me then/

This comment refers to a previous agreement, an agreement that Brian would show the therapist how make an aeroplane. In response to this reminder Brian goes towards the camera and looks directly at the camera puts his thumbs in his ears and wiggles his fingers and sticks his tongue out.

Therapist: Where are you going to sit/
Therapist: Are you going to sit there?/
Brian: Err:: – here! – no I wont sit here I'll stand here – ok/
Therapist: [All right]
Therapist: You teach me how to make one/

Brian places the paper aeroplane down in front of him and looks at the camera.

Brian: E::::asy/
Therapist: Do you want to get a fresh sheet of paper?/
Brian: OK/

Brian is aware that he is subject to the camera's gaze, observed by his parents and professionals in another room. Surveillance is part of the ceremony of the assessment, and in response to this situation Brian produces some ceremonial behaviour of his own. It is a playful gesture which, whilst acknowledging the practice of the adults, asserts his right to disparagement and defiance. He does not physically attack the camera. Brian's behaviour is also an assertion of his independence and after looking at the camera he declares that the task, showing the therapist how to make an aeroplane, is easy, stretching the sound of the word in such a way as to reinforce his confidence and power. The therapist has to take account of the camera as well. He has to demonstrate, to the parents and the other professionals in the assessment team, that his examination is conducted properly and you will notice that after Brian's gesture the therapist asks Brian where he is going to sit. The therapist wants to show that he is attempting to conduct the assessment in an approved manner and endeavours to assert some adult authority here, even if not wholly succeeding, since Brian refuses to sit and emphasises the word 'stand'.

   Following the demonstration Brian, wearing his football shirt and trainer bottoms, directed the therapist in a game of 'football', using a paper aeroplane as a ball, throwing aeroplanes across the room. Brian established the presence of the 'line' and 'goalposts' and he decided the score in disputes. When the questions about the camera were put aside it was possible for both participants, Brian and the therapist, to share in the reverie of the play, to become absorbed in the game. In this sense both participants shaped the shared experience in the imaginary situation. In the play Brian was, when he caught a paper aeroplane, the victorious goal keeper and his victory dances, his gestures and turns provided him with a particular pleasure.

After this play with paper aeroplanes, the period of 'free choice', Brian was encouraged to play 'squiggles' to take turns in producing images from quickly scribbled lines. In the squiggle game Brian reintroduced the theme of football. First he produced an image of the ball going into the back of the net; in response the therapist produced an image of a goalkeeper with the net behind him.

The therapist began the next turn with angled lines attached to an open rectangle (see Figure 6.1). This geometric 'squiggle' was then used by Brian to form the sides of a torso, the bottom of a football shirt, and arms. In this way he produced a figure whose head disappears off the top of the paper. The top of the paper cuts through the figure's head at the level of the eyes and appears to cut his eyes in half, bringing the viewer's attention to these features, and to the grim looking mouth below, a mouth which is surmounted by a heavy moustache. The tunic or shirt has a stripe across the shoulder and down the arms. This line seems to continue the moustache in many ways and again refers us back to the footballer's face. The figure looks startled or in defensive pose, arms at the ready, open eyed. The cropping and the central placing of the figure situates the viewer in close proximity, in the position of one who now meets his opponent at close quarters, very much like the view that the therapist had of Brian during the preceding 'football' game with the paper aeroplanes.

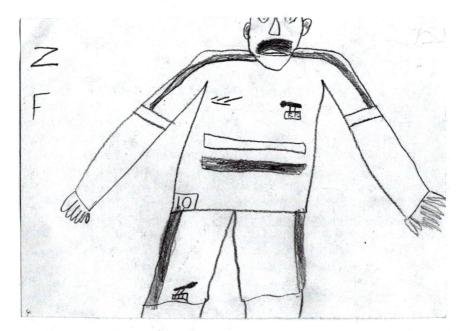

Figure 6.1 Footballer.

Therapist:	Is this the Arsenal goalie/
Brian:	Nope no/
Therapist:	Can't think of his name now/
Brian:	Not Arsenal/
Therapist:	No/
Therapist:	England?/
Brian:	No not English team/
Therapist:	It's not an English goalie/
Brian:	No/

We are back with goalkeepers and a guessing game begins as the therapist shows his interest in Brian's drawing.

Therapist:	*You have a similar shirt on*/

The identity of the figure keeps the therapist guessing.

Brian:	Don't normally have whiskers this man but anyway/
Therapist:	Is it your <u>dad</u>/
Brian:	Yeah/
Therapist:	Yeah/
Brian:	No/
Therapist:	Is it you/
Brian:	No/
Therapist:	Your brother/
Brian:	No it's a man does not have whiskers and he's an adult/

This man, who has whiskers, but doesn't normally, is and isn't his father, and is not his brother, and it isn't Brian himself in the drawing, he remains mysterious. Brian understands the pattern of these kinds of guessing games and enjoys holding the answer.

Therapist:	Right ok so we don't know who it is/
Brian:	I do/
Therapist:	Who is it/
Brian:	Begins with a zee a zed./

The therapist shakes his head. The therapist has tried to guess but has no knowledge of football and fails – his speech diminishes into a shameful silence.

Brian:	It's Zedan/
Therapist:	Zeedan *proves I'm poor at*((almost inaudible))/
Brian:	I don't know about position/
Therapist:	You don't know what position/

Nothing more can be said about the drawing, although the drawing itself is eloquent. Brian has identified the player and himself as one who knows about football. The therapist moves the game on again, trying to regain some initiative and power in the situation. The therapist takes another sheet of paper and places it down in front of Brian.

Therapist: Ok do another one for me/

Brian draws on the paper quickly.

Brian: ((Singing without words))/
Therapist: Looks like you got this one all worked out have yer/
Brian: Umm/

The therapist's comment 'Looks like . . .' suggests he is joining in the competitive spirit. The therapist studies the drawing and turns it.

Therapist: It looks like a crown/
Brian: Give you another/

Brian adds a figure carefully to the edge of the drawing and some looser marks.

Therapist: It's a spike/
Brian: Umm/
Therapist: What is this then is it fire/
Brian: Yeah/
Therapist: Is it hell/
Therapist: *What's this*/

The therapist adds a figure on the left of the picture.

Brian: It's a cat/
Brian: Ah ah ah aaah ((diminishes and trails off))/
Brian: Eh eh/
Therapist: Umm/
Brian: I know what it is/
Brian: It's err the door thing/

This longer sequence of speech and action shows how the picture (Figure 6.2) develops. First Brian draws his 'squiggle', the crown-like shape, confidently, singing. The therapist proposes that Brian has it 'all worked out'. Brian agrees with that interpretation of his singing and action with the pencil. The therapist then studies the ziz-zags or spikes for a little while and ventures an interpretation. The 'crown' is not what Brian intends so he gives more clues, adding the figure falling

Figure 6.2 Hell.

on to the spikes and some looser marks at the bottom left of the picture. This next bit of drawing is understood by the therapist and he now interprets the spikes as fire, his interpretation is endorsed by Brian's 'Yeah'. The therapist enlarges this theme by adding a figure of his own which Brian then has to interpret.

As can be seen there are some marks in the body of the figure that Brian placed on the spikes, towards the top of the thigh and in the chest area, that might indicate clothing, or wounds. Some marks in the circular head probably refer to hair and facial features. To the left of the paper the therapist has quickly sketched in the figure of the devil. He has two large spiky ears and, in between the ears, two horns. He has also been given a mischievous smile or grin, and eyebrows set at an angle to signal his disposition. There is a line for a tail and he is holding out towards the falling figure a trident, which appears to have flames coming off it. The devil's body is hidden in part behind one of the spikes which could be interpreted as spiking him in the genitals! The knees of the devil figure knock together (see Figure 6.2).

If it is hell then the devil should be present but Brian thought that the figure which the therapist drew was a 'cat'. Brian appears to see things differently after further looking. The exchange of sounds in the middle of the verbal interaction, 'Ah ah ah aaah', 'Eh eh' and 'Umm' show adjustment of view and some agreement with the therapist. Nevertheless Brian does not use the word 'devil' or 'hell', instead he labels the image as 'the door thing'. This label appears to refer to the whole picture. The devil, or a representative, is usually shown by the door or entrance to hell, and the figure that Brian drew, the figure that falls on the spiky flames, does appear to be suffering some punishment or torture. Brian doesn't stay with this image much longer, instead he takes up another sheet of paper.

Brian: And then/
Therapist: Who's going to finish up in hell/
Brian: What's this look/

The therapist wanted to explore the idea of hell, but Brian takes the initiative here and directs the therapist's gaze with *his* question towards his fresh production. As we shall see, Brian's image does have some association with hell.

Brian: *Some few cuts there and nose coming up here*/
Therapist: Umm skeleton/
Brian: Umm/
Therapist: Scary/
Brian: Still not scary/
Therapist: Ah hah sword in his head/
Brian: Da de doo de di doo ((singing))/

Brian drops his pencil down on the table and swings his legs. The dropping of the pencil and the leg swinging is a 'look at that' moment. Brian is confident (the singing) that he has done something impressive (Figure 6.3). This drawing was completed without a squiggle from the therapist. The skeleton is placed near to the left edge of the paper, his legs disappear off the bottom of the paper, just cutting off the feet. Brian has used a simple but effective schema to portray a skeleton. From the skull, at an angle, a sword, with quite a broad blade, protrudes. The skull has a rectangular mouth and square jaw with dark eye sockets as might be expected. From the eye socket near to the sword a line runs down to the mouth, suggesting blood or tears. The skeleton faces the viewer directly, his arms held out from his body, the pose is not so different to the goalkeeper pose in Figure 6.1. This time the viewer faces something more dreadful at close quarters.

Therapist: Looks like something that's been found in a graveyard
Therapist: These are quite scary things the devil and skeletons/
              why did he get a sword in his head/
Brian: Sword cut urgh/

The therapist connects the image to the previous image and wants more comment, he appears to be seeking a narrative, but Brian does not have any verbal associations. Instead he rises from his seat and clenches his fist and shakes his right arm at the camera, screwing up his face at the same time as if striking at the camera with

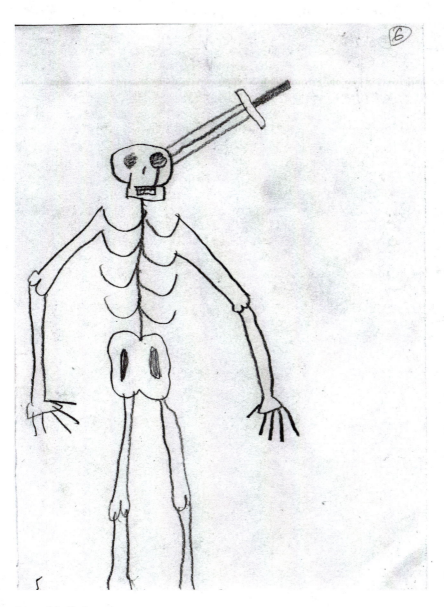

Figure 6.3 Skeleton.

a sword. We could regard the drawing, supported by the gestures, as the visual equiv-alent of a speech act (Austin, 1962). Through the skeleton Brian gives a warning to the observers in the other room. Death, and possibly hell, is intended for Brian's enemies, parents and adults who conduct assessments – speech is redundant here.

A fresh description of assessment

I shall now show the significant relations that the discourse analysis has revealed, first through a representation of the art therapy assessment in a diagrammatic form (Figure 6.4). The outer frame for the assessment is constructed from the documentary analysis. It is the story of difference that adults construct, through their exchanges and report writing. This frame stages the assessment encounter. It presents the therapist with a particular charge and limits what is legitimate and significant to report in relation to the subject child.

Inside this frame an assessment text is developed jointly by the child and the therapist through their exchanges with the outer frame and the practico-inert which enables semiosis to develop. I have used the term 'practico-inert' to refer to the objects and materials available in the assessment space. Sartre (1960) describes the practico-inert as a combination of *praxis* (activity directed towards the future) and the *inert* (matter) that is used to produce a particular object or thing for use, for example, a pencil, the insertion of graphite into a wooden case to enable a user to mark paper. Language is also considered part of this practico-inert in that sounds are inscribed with meaning and are thereby intended for future use (see Cannon, 2005). Of course people can change the meaning of words and the use and meaning of objects, but as my discourse analysis shows meaning is constantly negotiated as interpretations are developed by the participants in the assessment.

Semiosis is the name given to the 'action of signs' (Cobley, 2001), and I have in this chapter concerned myself with 'social semiosis' – especially as described by Peirce (1985) and Hodge and Kress (1988). There are many different signs in

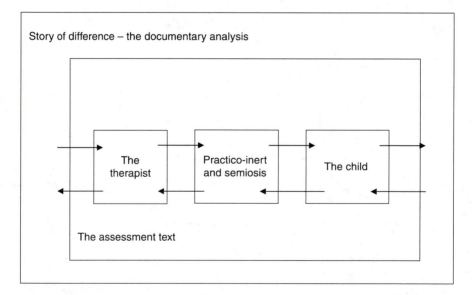

Figure 6.4 Story of difference – the documentary analysis.

use in the assessment setting, some signs are immediate in environmental terms, in that they reside within the practico-inert, but both deliberately, and inadvertently and unconsciously, signs are continuously exchanged and interpreted by participants during the course of the assessment. Signs in use include symbols, as in the use of words; iconic signs, the production of images, for example, which may also carry some symbolic content; and indexical signs, for example, bodily movements such as pointing or presenting an object. However, movements might also include enactments or mimesis, which have a further iconic significance. Signs in combination, and through differences, produce messages (see Hodge and Kress, 1998). Messages, represented by the arrows in Figure 6.4, circulate via the practico-inert, that is through the use of the body, objects, materials and language; for instance, when Brian draws his skeleton and accompanies this with mimetic actions directed at the camera he sends a message to the adults who have been constructing the outer frame.

What the assessment text shows is that there is some bartering around the use of the art materials in this assessment, and although the therapist may present the child with a task, this task is changed or adapted to form a more personal brief. This bargaining has the character of the 'troc' or barter that develops between the artist and his patron or audience (Baxandall, 1985). Before the start of the assessment Brian negotiated to be allowed to play his 'football' game with the paper aeroplanes whilst the therapist asked for a demonstration around making in return. In the squiggle game, for example, Brian is coerced to take turns and use the visual cues that the therapist provides, and he is encouraged to produce drawings using pencils. Brian then has to decide how he will use the squiggle and what drawings he will produce.

As we have seen, Brian is suspicious in relation to the situation; he does not trust the adults and he interrogates the therapist in relation to the camera. He wants to know what his parents and the professionals are doing. The therapist avoids a discussion of the camera and its implications. However, through his gestures Brian does comment on the surveillance that the camera represents. He communicates his objections to this aspect of the situation. The skeleton, especially, is a dramatic expression of disapproval and a warning to the adults. The skeleton can also be read as a portrayal of Brian's subjective feeling in the assessment situation.

The assessment text also shows that, in the art therapy assessment, the individual (the subject child) presents an image of himself or herself. She or he performs a self, in the spirit of a proposal, a proposed or provisional self, which seeks endorsement from the adult audience. These performances of self, achieved through the production of messages, involve play and the creation of an imaginary situation (Vygotsky, 1966). This allows for a presentation of self that has an 'as if' quality, that enables the exploration of identifications or identities in a playful mode, within the reverie of play. For example, Brian comes dressed in a football strip and he performs victory dances. As well as presenting himself as victorious, he presents himself as mocking and threatening towards the parental and adult figures.

In his drawing he presents combative figures, with which he identifies, as facing the other in a competitive and confrontational stance. Tasks are 'E::::asy' and he can recognise and contemplate the 'scary' and he also shows himself as one who knows – about football at least.

The other, the therapist, is interested in maintaining his definition of the situation in the face of potential disruptions (Goffman, 1971: 231–232). And he also presents or performs a self, a self which he wishes to promote, an image for which he seeks credit. He presents himself as one conducting an inquiry and an endorsement of his performance is sought from the team at Chestnut House and from parents and other professionals seeking help for the problem child. However, the therapist does also present himself as playful, even mischievous at times (the devil or cat) and perhaps thereby better able to engage with children. Goffman (1971) argues that interaction is a gamble, and certainly interactions with problem children have risks for the adult, especially where the adult proposes to present himself, through this interaction, as having the expertise to unravel difficulties, to assess the child's competencies and failures.

In presenting selves as subjects, the therapist and child propose a role for themselves in the assessment ceremony. Affirmation and compliance are often sought from the other and power is contested during the assessment. Loss of face is resisted and there is an avoidance of vulnerability. However, temporary agreements do make their appearance in the drama that constitutes the assessment, and such agreements lead to reciprocal exchanges, to an experience of mutuality and solidarity, for example, when Brian and the therapist enjoy the 'football' game. Asymmetrical power relations are the norm, but symmetrical power relations can appear briefly.

Summary and implications

Often in clinical settings, where mental health is in question, an identification of elements within art works as signs of pathology is undertaken, reminiscent of the manner in which the medical profession treats the body as a text (see Sebeok, 1991). Di Leo (1973) exemplifies this way of interpreting drawing. He presents a figure and adds the legend: 'Scatter of body parts. Emotionally disturbed child of 5 years' (p. 69). The written text proposes a particular reading of the drawing; 'the scatter of body parts', an interpretative description, invites the viewer to read the drawing as confirmation for the expression of and presence of emotional disturbance.

Di Leo's account of the child's figure drawing shows how professional practices limit the development of hermeneutic processes. Whilst there is amongst many professionals an appreciation that symbolic content or referential elements within the art work should be approached through an understanding of context, in clinical settings where the emphasis is placed on the pathology of the patient, clinicians are inclined to treat art as an unmediated projective process where internal, or intrapsychic and pathological phenomena are consciously, or inadvertently, signified, in marks, iconology or formal properties. A larger understanding of context is rarely sought and the sense of self as a social construct, and art as socially produced, is absent in the interpretative procedures just discussed.

Self as a construct formed, and reformed, in relation to others, has not been developed in the art therapy literature that explores work with children and with autistic subjects, although dynamic models have been favoured. Evans (1997) for example, used Stern's model of developmental stages in self construction (Stern, 1985), and Case (2005) Fordham's account of Jung's primary integrated self (Fordham, 1976). Whilst I would accept that there is a 'core self' which is body based, a 'system for recognising the difference between self and not-self' (Muller, 1996, p. 37), to understand how art products emerge in this setting and are related to the participants, therapist and client, we should give attention to this shifting dynamic of the cultural or social self.

We have seen that in the adult's production of documents a particular view of reality finds expression; together they identify difference and produce a subject who is related to an image of 'normal' development. And, as might be anticipated, I do describe Brian in the art therapy assessment report as controlling in his interaction, and as displaying some obsessive interests and repetitiveness in his play. But through giving close attention to discourses Brian's positive capacities were also identified and represented to others for use in determining need, for example, his ability to communicate effectively and express his feelings about a situation clearly, his willingness to share in his play and his enjoyment of social exchanges.

Exchange and social interaction have been given emphasis in this research because it relates directly to autism where social interaction is regarded as impaired, although, as I hope the case material shows, the nature of this impairment is not uncontested and not always obviously present and open to view. However, I would not want to argue that the research which I have presented here should be used to support art therapists who wish to avoid any involvement with diagnosis (see BAAT, 2007). At a practical level this might not be possible, and politically it may not be desirable. There are difficulties, tensions between the requirements of the group and the languages that the individual art therapist feels comfortable in adopting. But I would argue that we need to be willing to meet the challenge of dominant institutional paradigms, for example, in cognitive psychology where psychological functions are intended to explain all social phenomena. We need to cultivate our ability to give emphasis to the visual, and our understanding of its relation to the larger semiotic environment. In this area I believe the profession has something special to offer, something of importance to assessment with children and adults, particularly in situations where social interaction is in question. There is now a possibility of producing an assessment report that emphasises social semiosis, through an understanding of the way in which power relations constrain exchanges in the assessment setting. This should enable a more sympathetic account of subjects to emerge, an account that is more productive of solidarity, and helpful to the child, or adult, in attaining agency. A change in this direction entails the recognition that an assessment which is able to promote solidarity with clients has more value in promoting understanding of the phenomena of art production and in influencing treatment decisions.

Box 6.1   Key to transcript

/	End of utterance. A pause is usually present.
[ ]	Simultaneous utterance, brackets begin and end when simultaneous words appear, for example:

Therapist: What is it?/
Child: [its a] man/

.	A period indicates a falling tone, not necessarily the end of a sentence.
?	A rising inflection, not necessarily a question.
–	Underlining, indicates emphasis.
*	Indicates quieter passage.
:	Colon indicates extension of the sound, for example:

so:::: sorry re:::ally

((cry))	
((grunt))	
((laugh))	Sounds.
((singing))	
((sung))	The words in the utterance sung.

References

Althusser, L. (2001) *Lenin and Philosophy and Other Essays*, trans. B. Brewster. New York: Monthly Review Press.

Atkinson, P. and Coffey, A. (1997) 'Analysing documentary realities', in D. Silverman (ed.) *Qualitative Research Theory, Method and Practice*. London: Sage.

Austin, J. L. (1962) *How to Do Things with Words*. Oxford: Oxford University Press.

Baxandall, M. (1985) *Patterns of Intention: On the Historical Explanation of Pictures*. New Haven, CT: Yale Unversity Press.

Baxandall, M. (1991) 'The language of art criticism', in S. Kemal and I. Gaskell (eds) *The Language of Art History*. Cambridge: Cambridge University Press.

Brisset, D. and Edgley, C. (eds) 1990 *Life as Theatre*, 2nd edn. New York: Aldine de Gruyter.

British Association of Art Therapists (BAAT, 2007) *BAAT's Statement on Art Therapy and Diagnosis*. London: BAAT.

Burkitt, I. (2008) 'Subjectivity, self and everyday life in contemporary capitalism', *Subjectivity*, 23: 236–245.

Butler, J. (1997) *The Psychic Life of Power: Theories of Subjection*. Stanford, CA: Stanford University Press.

Cannon, B. (2005) 'Group therapy as revolutionary praxis: a Sartrean view,' in A. van den Hoven and A. Leak (eds) *Sartre Today: A Centenary Celebration*. New York and Oxford: Berghahn Books.

Case, C. (2005) *Imagining Animals: Art, Psychotherapy and Primitive States of Mind.* London and New York: Routledge.

Cobley, P. (ed.) (2001) *The Routledge Companion to Semiotics and Linguistics.* London and New York: Routledge.

Di Leo, J. (1973) *Children's Drawings as Diagnostic Aids.* New York: Brunner/Mazel.

Evans, K. (1997) 'Art therapy and the development of communicative abilities in children with autism'. Unpublished PhD thesis. Faculty of Art and Design, University of Hertfordshire.

Fordham, M. (1976) *The Self and Autism.* London: Academic Press.

Foucault, M. (1977) *Discipline and Punish: The Birth of the Prison,* trans. A. M. Sheridan. Harmondsworth: Penguin.

Foucault, M. (2002) *Power – Essential Works of Foucault 1954–1984,* Vol. 3, J. D. Faubion (ed.), trans. R. Hurley and others. London: Penguin.

Goffman, E. (1971) *The Presentation of Self in Everyday Life.* Harmondsworth: Penguin.

Hodge, R. and Kress, G. (1988) *Social Semiotics.* Cambridge: Polity Press.

Jaworski, A. and Coupland, N. (eds) (1999) *The Discourse Reader.* London and New York: Routledge.

Meltzer, D., Bremner, J., Hoxter, S., Weddell, D. and Wittenberg, I. (1975) *Explorations in Autism – A Psychoanalytical Study.* Strathtay: Clunie Press.

Muller, J. P. (1996) *Beyond the Psychoanalytic Dyad: Developmental Semiotics in Freud, Peirce and Lacan.* London and New York: Routledge.

Peirce, C. (1985) 'Logic as semiotic: the theory of signs', in R. E. Innis (ed.) *Semiotics: An Introductory Anthology.* Bloomington, IN: Indiana University Press.

Sartre, J.-P. (1960) *The Critique of Dialectical Reason,* J. Ree (ed.), trans. A. Sheridan-Smith. London: Verso/New Left Books.

Sebeok, T. (1991) *Semiotics in the United States.* Bloomington, IN: Indiana University Press.

Stern, D. N. (1985) *The Interpersonal World of the Infant.* New York: Basic Books.

Tipple, R. A. (1993) 'Challenging assumptions: the importance of transference processes in work with people with learning difficulties', *Inscape,* Summer: 2–9.

Tipple, R. A. (1994) 'Communication and interpretation in art therapy with people who have a learning disability,' *Inscape,* 2: 31–35.

Vygotsky, L. S. (1966) 'Play and its role in the mental development of the child', *Soviet Psychology,* 12 (6): 62–76.

Wetherell, M. (2008) 'Subjectivity or psycho-discursive practices? Investigating complex intersectional identities', *Subjectivity,* 22: 73–81.

Winnicott, D. W. (1996) *Therapeutic Consultations in Child Psychiatry.* London: Karnac Books.

Part II

Snapshots from the field

Plate 1 Disclosure

Plate 2 Guarded house

Plate 3 Abstract

Plate 4 Bird's nest

Plate 5 Grandpa

Plate 6 A person picking an apple from a tree (1)

Plate 7 A person picking an apple from a tree (2)

Plate 8 A person picking an apple from a tree (3)

Plate 9 A person picking an apple from a tree (4)

Assessing a young autistic boy in art therapy private practice

Arnell Etherington

Here's where I work

The art therapy I am engaged with is in private practice. My room has a sandplay set, a dollhouse, and shelves with art materials. There is a low table on which to make art with optional seating.

Referrals originate from social/employee services or private individuals. I see children, adolescents, families, and individual adults. The referral source expects an assessment as to whether the patient is adaptable to art therapy and is using it wisely. Written evaluations of this early vital entrance into therapy are not usual. As therapy progresses, whether the patient is making progress with symptom reduction, is more adaptable, flexible, content, more able to handle their life – this is of interest to the referral source. Each patient will have their own goals that make sense to themselves, to the therapist, and to their situation.

Here's what I assess

I assess the overall functionality of the patient through the initial contact via phone, in person, with information on the family and from information obtained through a written set of questions. This includes psychological, physical, social, cognitive, and spiritual aspects of the patient which leads to a better understanding of them and their presenting issues. Assessing culture, ethnicity, and financial status comes into an initial understanding of context. Most importantly one must meet the patient and begin an assessment based on one's experience of the person in the room, accessing one's own emotional response and factoring in one's educational experiences of relationships, psychotherapy and psychopathology.

Once in the session I continue to assess particularly for information that is about the individual's 'unconflicted space'. This is an aspect of their psyche which primarily has not been tarnished with anxiety or depression. I am looking for those moments when there is a sense of openness without fear toward themselves and/or the world. I want to focus on those moments, to extend them and in some way assist the patient, if that seems useful, in becoming more aware of that part of themselves. I observe facial expressions, any expression of feelings, changes in breathing that may indicate the unconflicted space, for it is here that the client is able to find creatively a sense of 'home', of well-being, answers to questions and particularly insight that is unfettered.

The unconflicted space is directly related to Kalff's (1980) 'safe and protected space' which she describes as occurring within the sandplay process, providing a deep unconscious movement within the psyche. In sandplay, the tray provides a literal boundary within which the patient is able to work on psychological material. Within the unconflicted space is a psychological 'space' in which the client comes into contact and is able to access their most valuable tool: the full self. One place the unconflicted space appears to be found is when art-making. As with the sand-play tray, the art itself may enable its appearance. It becomes a context that may help open that place inside.

Here's what I do

The first session begins with deciding whether the client might be more content to be given a particular directive in drawing or do a free drawing. I make this decision by initially asking if they like to do art. The child just diving into the material indicates a positive response. I then know that the child has some inner resources to help them with acting alone with the art. If the child is interested in drawing or painting but uncertain what to do, I suggest ideas such as their favorite animal, something they like to do, or to answer the question: 'What is it like to be your age?' If the child is not interested in art I try to engage them by asking if they know anything about how to handle the materials. I bring out the Cray-Pas™, for example, and demonstrate how the material works. I suggest they play with the materials. I assess their willingness to engage. Again, does fear or anxiety interfere with this exploration? In each case I watch how they approach the matter of art: apprehensively, with vigor, excitedly, shyly, secretively, etc. I note whether they verbalize what they are doing while they work as well as the feeling content. I am curious about their coming to understand something concerning what they have just created.

I note their intellectual acumen, emotional intelligence, and artistic facility. I ask them to tell me about their piece. Do they know anything about it? Is it just for pleasure? Does it surprise them? Is it about a particular psychological matter? I make little or no interpretation verbally and assess the art piece for content, affect, color, shape, and possible meaning.

The initial assessment phase of therapy covers the length it takes to gain rapport. One remains curious as to what nuances encourage rapport. Prior to gaining rapport, has one not understood some aspect of the patient? Thus the discovery period of who this patient is, will they be able to use art therapy, will they make progress in therapy, takes some time.

Here's an example

I have an autistic/Asperger spectrum male patient age six who initially did not make eye contact, spoke in rather odd syntax (English with French/Slavic phrasing) and had problems pushing peers and poor language at school and home. The parents, who wanted these behaviors to be reduced or eliminated, referred the patient.

Initially the patient wanders around the room anxious, looking at the materials available. He spies the Cray-Pas™, crayons and paper and sits at the table immediately and begins to calm down as he tries marking a few colors. He says he has these at home. He diligently begins to make block-like shapes of strong color. He intuitively knows how to put color next to color to make it more and more beautiful. In 15 minutes he has created an abstract that most artists would die to have. He becomes happier and happier in the doing of the piece. He is satisfied with his work. For these moments his breathing slows, he focuses on the art, he talks but not directly to me, he makes a few gestures with his body and head and for a few seconds his eyes glance to include me. I know now something about his unconflicted space. The art will be a medium for him to work in therapy. Afterward he must leave the room and show his parent who makes a fuss about the art but rolls their eyes at me as if it is nothing, this art. So now I additionally have some information about the parental interaction.

> It is in playing and only in playing that the individual child . . . is able to be creative and to use the whole personality, and it is only in being creative that the individual discovers the self.
>
> (Winnicott, 1971: 54)

His beginning art (see Plate 3, situated between pp. 100 and 101) is an abstract. It has the natural elements of understanding color and more importantly it satisfies him. As he works I comment regularly on how wonderful this work is, how skillful he is and how he understands color. He always agrees with me but in these moments he seems to simply repeat back my words. I am hoping they will be introjected and available to bolster his self-understanding at another time. He seems a bit unable to take in the support I offer in regards to his work. The work, though obviously a reflection of an organized individual with abilities in art beyond his age, is nevertheless void of any interaction with the outside world and especially other people. If I see someone doing better work, artistic, stylized work but it has no human interaction or no interaction with the environment, then I wonder if they may be lonely or unable to socialize.

He continues with abstract pieces. He repeats format and design with just a variety of color, despite my suggestions to do other work or engage in art therapy assessment drawings. I make suggestions to see if this unconflicted space, which he finds in these schemas, can be translated into different images and ideas. However, he knows what he wants. There is an appreciation that he moves into the unconflicted space but so far he is unable to either share that with anyone else or move it into other types of art. He remains isolated within these drawings. I continue to sit quietly with him and give him reliable and predictable support around the products in a gentle way.

During the next phase of assessment and therapy several events occur. The client begins to share with me his problems with verbalizing per se, especially his feelings and thoughts. He lightly hits his head when he is not able to say or get across his thoughts. I stop everything and say: 'I want to know your thoughts.' I am happy to wait. I look at him directly and calmly. He looks at me and keeps trying, then clearly articulates his thoughts. This happens numerous times. It becomes an interesting break in the play or art activities where he really attempts to communicate with a willing and waiting audience. He becomes agitated during these periods, upset with himself. There, in the here and now, is something that he cannot do. We confront this together. We are both waiting then. After he speaks and sees that I understand, he is satisfied and turns to calm himself afterward with art. I continue to assess this new ability to include others in his language problems as a very positive gesture.

In time he spontaneously draws a person. The person has no hands to reach out with nor feet to stand on. His long neck may be an attempt to connect his mind and body or depict his 'sticking his neck out' in his attempts to make contact with the outside world. The figure is undeveloped, awkward yet smiling. There are no ears to hear the world, nor to be heard perhaps. His mouth is prominent and red which may indicate his language difficulties. However, this spontaneous act of art has again contented him. He appears to find the unconflicted space in this drawing as well. Now he may have opened the door to access this part of himself within other contexts.

I begin periodically to draw him. He reviews these with interest. I show him through the drawings that I see and appreciate him. Here there is interaction with the art being the medium. His ability to form an interest in my drawings is another positive step towards opening to the outside world.

A further event occurs when the client decides he will respond to my suggestion for a specific drawing. His parents live separately and I wonder how this plays into his situation. Though the formal assessment may give some indication on how he sees his home, I am also interested to see if he can enjoy the process of painting a bird's nest with the same joy he makes his abstracts and person drawing. Can he enjoy a drawing that has been suggested to him as much as he does his spontaneous art? Does this painting and his ability to touch the unconflicted space stretch parameters? He assuages me by painting the assessment: the bird's nest (see Plate 4, situated between pp. 100 and 101).

Though the watercolor has run, the aspects of Kaiser's (1996) assessment are clear. Here is a large bird relative to a small nest. The bird has no space to nest, there is no food, nor mommy or daddy bird and there is neither tree to hold the nest nor any environment. The nest is isolated or in an undeveloped situation. This is, however, a very colorful bird. Perhaps this is the potential in this client.

The darkness of the bird has run into the nest. I wonder how much he feels responsible for his parents' separation and whether the tiny nest represents the dissolution of the family nest.

This level of assessment in the early stage of the patient's work speaks well to his ability to learn social skills, change behaviors, and develop his language. He has gained rapport with me and the assessment reflects beginning shifts in his inner world. Art therapy can be used to encourage his continued use of art to express his thoughts and feelings, finding the unconflicted space for solace.

References

Kaiser, D. (1996) 'Indications of attachment security in a drawing task', *Arts in Psychotherapy*, 23 (4): 333–340.

Kalff, D. (1980) *Sandplay: A Psychotherapeutic Approach to the Psyche*. Boston, MA: Sigo Press.

Winnicott, D. (1971) *Playing & Reality*. New York: Tavistock Publications.

An art-based assessment of a young, psychotic male

Rebecca Arnold

Here's where I work

The site is a 20-bed inpatient mental health unit that treats adults aged 18 to 54. Most individuals who are admitted have been previously diagnosed with mood disorders, anxiety disorders, personality disorders, and/or psychosis. All of the individuals admitted are in acute crisis and present with behaviors or verbalizations that indicate perceived or actual harm to self and/or others. The locked unit offers a medical model to treatment and patients often report the reason for admission as 'My meds aren't working right'.

I am part of the treatment team, which consists of psychiatry, nursing, art therapy, and social work. The team conforms to the structure of the *DSM-IV-TR* for charting and interdisciplinary communications (American Psychiatric Association, 2000). I am able to add a significant piece of the patient puzzle, which comes directly from the non-verbal interactions I collect from each individual. Moon (1994) discusses the concept of the art therapist within the treatment team as offering a non-verbal identity for the patient. He includes the concepts of respecting other professionals within the team as well as building and maintaining an art therapist identity amongst more verbal and analytical viewpoints. Because I have something very special to add to the evaluation and treatment of the individuals on the unit, I have become a respected member of the team and my review of the patient is often sought after outside of the clinical meetings held.

Here's what I assess

Each patient is identified by a wristband and all required paperwork is kept in a clinical chart which is held on the unit until time of discharge. The chart includes admission criteria, patient mental health and physical histories, daily progress notes, and any legal documentation. In addition, the members of the treatment team must provide completed evaluation forms within 72 hours of admission of any patient. Each team member has a distinct form that requires patient information related to the team member's expertise.

The art therapy evaluation form includes identifying information on the patient and offers a space where the patient is encouraged to create an image. The back of the form provides an art-based evaluation and space for clinical summation. This art-based practice of evaluation offers the patient a more open-ended approach which supports personal reasons for admission, current needs, and perceived barriers to treatment while on the unit. I often ask patients what they feel is important to work on during their stay. The greatest need expressed is that of wanting to understand: 'Why am I this way?'

The art-based assessment offers patients an introduction to an effective tool for coping with this existential question and provides the beginnings of a creative therapeutic relationship within an art context. Most important to the evaluation process are the individual's potential for acting out, reality orientation, and height of crisis. This collection of valuable information through initial examination and continued monitoring of the patient offers safe treatment practices that can be maintained with the setting (Feder and Feder, 1998).

Here's what I do

Art therapy is supported within the studio, but assessments are typically completed within community spaces. The studio can be overwhelming or intimidating to a new patient. Therefore, meeting an individual outside of the studio often helps alleviate hospital-related anxieties and facilitates a more balanced start to the therapeutic relationship. Patients' shortened length of stay and space limitations also play an active role in where assessments are completed.

The art-based assessment allows the patient to draw 'anything you'd like to share about yourself'. A more directive approach is offered if there is resistance or confusion. A supply of markers, colored pencils, and graphite pencil with eraser are laid out. These specific media choices provide: a 'clean' image for the chart, familiar tools that are easily retained on the unit and a certain level of safety and monitoring. Supplementary media is on hand if there is technical interest from the patient and then the image is copied for chart inclusion.

Most individuals report 'I'm no artist' and simply choose the drawing tool closest to their hand on the table. Some choose to draw in complete privacy and return the image to me at a later time, while others wish to entertain discussion during the drawing process. I honor the needs of the individual at this time. My review of the work includes asking about the story presented whether by poem, song lyrics, storytelling, or by title alone. This allows the patient an alternative way to share feelings associated with the art and provides me with a creative portrayal of the reasons for admission.

In instances when acute psychosis or active crisis is observed, not only the assessment process but also the individual's inclusion in the art therapy group may be impractical; stabilization becomes the primary treatment goal (Drapeau and Kronish, 2007). However, I have met some individuals who, although extremely unsafe in most situations on the unit, are able to respond positively to the inclusion of art therapy in their treatment. I find that most individuals who feel trusting of the newly formed therapeutic relationship with me and who have had their resistance softened by the process of creating art upon admission will more easily engage in self actualization and personal storytelling during treatment.

Here's an example

I approached the nurse's station with an art evaluation form and several drawing tools, including large markers, in my hands. My intention was to introduce myself to the young 19-year-old male, John, who had been admitted the day before due to confusion and paranoia. He had been complaining of racing thoughts for the past week and was brought to the hospital emergency unit by his mother who committed him involuntarily and reported he was 'doing strange things'. He had no previous history of any psychiatric admissions and his family reported he had been 'stable', maintaining a part-time job and helping to care for his younger sibling. I overheard him denying any need for treatment and as he became more agitated he began yelling to the nurses, 'The meds kill my thoughts!' and aggressively asking for them to let him go home. I stopped a few feet away from him to monitor his level of safety and to examine his ability to engage effectively in the evaluation process. This tentative approach to John was met with further confrontation as he refused to answer any questions I had for him.

As I noticed his eyes quickly travel to the package of markers I was holding, I asked, 'How do you feel about art?' John's yelling stopped and with more interest than he had previously displayed he asked what I wanted him to draw. My response was simply: 'Draw something you find interesting; something you feel comfortable putting on paper.' Were I to ask him to follow me to the studio and engage in art-making while being observed I may have invited more confrontation and resistance. Although he disliked being on the unit, he was comfortable where he stood. My approach had helped diffuse the situation and had offered the level ground on which the therapeutic relationship could begin since I did not appear to be telling him what to do.

John took the assessment form with the pack of large markers back to his room with no further interactions. He returned to the art studio 15 minutes later, image in hand and tears in his eyes. 'Can I talk to you?' he asked, handing me the markers but holding on to his work. John shared feelings of excessive worry about disclosure to the staff and denied feeling safe within the hospital setting. I immediately felt invited into the role of 'gentle persuader' in my budding relationship with John related directly to his interest in the arts (Moon, 1994: 179). He proceeded to tell me about his feelings of being 'a slave' and stated, 'I'm being dumbed down.' He reported he had been increasingly agitated with his parents and stated that his mother was using a type of Morse code 'finger tapping just to irritate me'. John viewed his father with complete disgust and became increasingly restless and irritable as he continued to speak about both parents and their decision to bring him in for treatment. The image John created 'enabled [him] to disclose very intimate and worrisome issues' (Drapeau and Kronish, 2007: 78) that may have remained hidden behind his verbal aggressions had he not been offered the non-verbal outlet.

Encouraging him to share his perspectives and listening to his personal commentary helped my assessment of John. As he became more trusting of me and was able to relay his hospital experiences in a creative manner, John's mood shifted and he handed me his assessment drawing (see Figure R2.1). I was immediately struck by the blues, oranges and yellows, which were highlighted against a teal background. A gray mass of contrasting line composed the bottom of the page and the work left me feeling as if being swallowed by an ocean, having no control and being at the mercy of external forces. An overwhelming need for safety and nurturance welled inside me. John said nothing about the image. Instead, we engaged in a discussion of our favorite artists and I learned he had created numerous computer art images, this being his favored art medium. His assessment image carried remnants of computer-generated line and mirrored the vibrant colors often found in computer art programs.

John continued our discussion by sharing with me an array of perceptual disturbances which included people 'changing their voices' in an attempt to confuse

Figure R2.1 Chart drawing.

him and 'using eye blinking' movements to control his thoughts. Had I offered 'no attention to the sensibility of the artist' (McNiff, 2004: 77) in the beginning of the meeting our relationship may have remained superficial. Trust was forming as John was able to share his anxieties and his own reasons why admission on to the unit might be helpful to him. He felt he was being heard as a person, respected as an artist and, consequently, he felt safer and displayed less resistance to treatment.

I shared the assessment drawing with the treatment team, along with my inter-actions and observations of John, including John's personal stories. The team concluded he was experiencing bizarre thought processes including delusions which caused social impairment. In addition, he was most likely experiencing a manic episode causing him to display poor coping with daily life stressors and an inability to remain safe outside of an inpatient facility. John's treatment plan comprised: anti-psychotic medications; nursing and social work groups for verbal sharing, socialization, and relaxation; individual, group and family art therapy sessions to foster reality orientation and encourage effective coping skills through creative expression.

During the eight years I've worked in mental health, I've come to rely heavily on the process of art-making and the benefits creativity offers those with whom I work. I provide a non-threatening approach to my assessments so that individuals can begin a level of care that supports their humanity instead of their diagnosis. This non-threatening approach, as identified by Hyland-Moon (2002), offers enhanced benefit during treatment challenges and allows the client a better under-standing that the work will be honored without being subject to interpretation by the art therapist.

References

American Psychiatric Association (2000) *Diagnostic and Statistical Manual of Mental Disorders: DSM-IV-TR*. Washington, DC: American Psychiatric Association.

Drapeau, M. and Kronish, N. (2007) 'Creative art therapy groups: a treatment modality for psychiatric outpatients', *Art Therapy: Journal of the American Art Therapy Association*, 24 (2): 76–81.

Feder, B. and Feder, E. (1998) *The Art and Science of Evaluation in the Arts Therapies: How Do You Know What's Working?* Springfield, IL: Charles C. Thomas.

Hyland-Moon, C. (2002) *Studio Art Therapy: Cultivating the Artist Identity in the Art Therapist*. Philadelphia, PA: Jessica Kingsley Publishers.

McNiff, S. (2004) *Art Heals: How Creativity Cures the Soul*. Boston, MA: Shambhala.

Moon, B. (1994) *Introduction to Art Therapy: Faith in the Product*. Springfield, IL: Charles C. Thomas.

Assessment of adults with intellectual disabilities and complex health needs

John McCulloch

Here's where I work

The setting is a National Health Service (NHS) inpatient admission and assessment unit for adults with intellectual disabilities. A medical model treatment approach is the predominant discourse used in this setting. At its core the unit comprises nursing, psychiatry, clinical psychology, dietetics, pharmacy and occupational therapy. Patients admitted to the unit can have a range of psychiatric diagnoses in addition to the primary diagnosis of learning disability, and many have long-term incapacitating symptoms. Many are known to the service prior to admission, with a number of individuals being admitted to the unit on more than one occasion.

Art therapy can provide assessment as and when required by the core assessment team. A request for assessment would be considered upon receipt of a written referral to the community-based art therapist. The art therapy service has devised criteria for specialist assessment to assist referrers in making an appropriate referral by prioritising those in most need: for example, people whose behaviour has recently changed, deteriorated or seems to be in response to other changes taking place.

The room in which art therapy assessment takes place is located immediately outside the assessment unit. It is a spacious art room with a number of large tables, chairs, and sink and is normally used by Occupational Therapy (OT) for recreational art groups.

Here's what I assess

Mental illness can be difficult to diagnose in this patient group due to atypical presentation, communication difficulties and, often, the absence of subjective complaint. An assessment can be requested by the core assessment team following a patient's admission to the unit and can typically be sought in response to a perceived deterioration in mental health. The purpose of such an enquiry might vary, but can be in response to helping the team gain an understanding of a patient's presentation since emotional distress or mental illness with this population can be disguised or expressed through disturbed behaviours. An assessment might therefore be requested in order for the team to build up a clearer picture of emotions underlying behaviour.

Working in this setting involves working with patients in acute states where illness can intensify feelings of loss, separation and confusion. Assessment helps me to form an opinion as to whether a patient is emotionally able to manage boundaries, tolerate difficult feelings, and whether someone is ready to engage in a therapeutic process, and able to consent to being involved in therapeutic endeavour. Assessment helps me to know whether the locus of attention in a treatment approach is on the art-making activity or on interpersonal aspects of the therapeutic encounter. I monitor response to art experiences; whether there is a sense of exploration and playfulness in working with art materials; the manner in which the patient interacts using the image, e.g. whether it is shared, devalued or discarded; and whether or not personal themes/ideas develop as a result of involvement in image making.

Here's what I do

I arrange to meet the patient and the referring agent (normally the patient's nurse key worker) and in this meeting I introduce myself and I explain that an assessment is a way to find out whether art therapy can be helpful, and the patient can have a say in what happens in the assessment. However, choice and consent, generally viewed as integral to the assessment process, can be problematic for people with intellectual disabilities, where making decisions about treatment is very often not in their control (Rees, 1998).

Assessment can be a protracted process when working with the degree of complexity presented by patients admitted to the assessment unit. Assessment can take longer than one session and can often last for several months. Assessment usually involves two people in gradually constructing an understanding of each other. However, when working with people with an intellectual disability, this can involve dialogue with others. Furthermore, in the acute setting other people's concern frequently seeps into the therapeutic space which can become crowded and consequently the therapist is never truly alone by himself with the patient (Corbett, 2009).

Here's an example

There is limited documented information regarding Mr D's early history, although it is known there had been a chequered history of hospitalisation and residential care within nursing homes. He has a history of schizophrenia and has received treatment with medication for this illness for a number of years. Mr D was a resident of the unit as a result of deteriorating physical health, which had been subject to extensive medical and neurological examination. At the time, the indications were that Mr D was likely to have a progressive degenerative illness of an as yet unspecified type. At the time of the referral being made, his medication was being gradually reduced with the aim of having a medication-free assessment period. Referral to art therapy was part of a wider psychological assessment to help understand the complex behaviours he displayed since his admission to the unit, manifesting in him refusing food, lying on the floor and falling to the floor. It was wondered whether there was an emotional component underlying these behaviours. During the period of medical and neurological investigations, psychological input halted while the biological bases contributing to his presentation were better understood. At the point of the referral being made Mr D was experiencing a period of respite where his physical skill level in terms of personal care and daily living tasks had increased. However, his motivation to perform these tasks independently fluctuated.

The pre-assessment process of information gathering did not prepare me for the moment when I finally met Mr D for an initial meeting. His nurse key worker was unexpectedly unable to attend this meeting and I was accompanied instead by two ward nurses for the visit. Mr D was lying slumped on the floor in a curled up position when I arrived. Background music was playing from his radio. He was raised from the floor by the nurses and positioned on a chair by his bedside. There was a flicker of recognition and a faint smile appeared as I introduced myself and enquired how he was. I wondered if he had remembered about my visit and if so what his understanding about the purpose of my visit was. I asked the nurses whether it would be possible for Mr D and me to be alone together for a while. Once alone in the room he gestured with his eyes towards the radio. I enquired whether he wished for the radio to be left on or turned off. Mr D did not reply, and I was left wondering if he had understood my question. His facial expression by this point seemed absent and gave no clues in getting an answer to my question. There was a short period of quietness during which time he begun to slowly slump sideways towards the floor. I tried to assist him but it appeared that his body was unable to support itself in an upright sitting position. I ended this encounter shortly after, and was left harbouring doubts whether Mr D was physically well enough at this stage to engage in a psychological assessment process. I was certainly left without a clear sense of whether he was consenting to being assessed.

Mr D was asleep when I arrived to meet him after a two-week interval. He was in his wheelchair which by this time had been adapted to hold his body from falling over. He recognised me and smiled. I enquired whether he needed help in transporting to the art room since I had earlier informed him that we would meet there to consider a period of assessment. I became aware of my voice becoming quieter and noticeably slowing down whilst speaking. I also became aware of his attention to my spoken words. When I stopped speaking his attention seemed to drift to other parts of the room, his facial expression becoming harder to read. This made me wonder whether my voice, its attention to intonation, adaptation of pitch and sentence length was helping Mr D to hold on to something supportive and alive. There was hesitation when I invited him to choose between the art materials laid out on the table. There were no words spoken but already a rudimentary form of communicating was beginning to emerge which involved him making fleeting eye contact with things in response to my questions, but this made it difficult for me to be entirely sure whether I was correctly understanding what was being communicated. He gestured towards the paint. He was able to hold a paintbrush in his hand but unable to lift it to the paper. There was a tremor in his hand which I noted but did not comment upon. I sensed there was an active attempt by Mr D to move the brush but it was as if an electrical connection between hand and brain had been switched off, preventing movement from happening. In response I moved the paper closer to him but his interest in painting seemed to evaporate at this point. I reflected on his inability to use the paintbrush and the frustration and disappointment that he may be feeling. Mr D watched intently as I spoke. After a short interval he gestured to be taken back to the ward. I suggested we met for a short assessment period. However, I was left unsure whether there was understanding or consent given.

I was greeted by a smile upon my arrival at the ward the following week. To my great surprise Mr D rises from his wheelchair and in a burst of energy runs down the ward corridor to show me his new bedroom. This unexpected transformation is made all the more surprising by the clarity in which words and language are used. There was a sense of urgency, and impatience to begin. I was stunned. Could this be the same person that was mute and immobilised in his chair the previous week?

Mr D requested paints. He wished to paint a 'rainbow'. There was a notable liveliness and rhythm attached to his movement that was distinctly absent in his previous encounter with the paintbrush. However, this did not last and a noticeable deceleration in his body's capacity to respond had begun to occur. It was as if being witness to the initial clamour and excitement of a mechanical wind-up toy as it performs its action before beginning to wind-down to an inevitable halt. After a while Mr D asks in a low and I thought rather defeated sounding voice whether I thought he was getting better. He asks me to be 'honest' with him. I was struck by this and wondered if in this invitation for honesty Mr D was also asking whether he felt he could confide in me at times like these when confronted with powerlessness and diminishing control over his environment.

My developing hypothesis was of a man struggling with awareness of loss and impingement to his sense of autonomy. The beginnings of a relationship had begun to develop with me during assessment at a time when attachment with others in the ward was proving extremely difficult. Being involved in painting appeared to enliven connections, allowing him opportunity to have some degree of control over his environment. The outcome of the assessment was his being offered therapy whilst resident at the unit. I have continued to provide therapy post discharge; the work transferred and was delivered closer to Mr D's home.

References

Corbett, A. (2009) 'Words as a second language: the psychotherapeutic challenge of severe intellectual disability', in T. Cottis (ed.) *Intellectual Disability, Trauma and Psychotherapy*. London and New York: Routledge.

Rees, M. (1998) 'Frames of reference,' in M. Rees (ed.) *Drawing on Difference*. London and New York: Routledge.

Art therapy assessment of adults in an inpatient forensic setting

Philippa Cronin

Here's where I work

The setting is an adult forensic psychiatric unit to which patients are admitted on a section of the Mental Health Act following an alleged offence or conviction. Their mental illness (primarily schizophrenia and schizoaffective disorder) results in hospital treatment rather than a prison sentence, the duration of treatment depending on the perception of risk either to others or the patient. Art therapy is part of multidisciplinary approach to treatment. The designated art therapy room within the secure unit offers an environment that is quite distinct from other clinical spaces, being furnished with plants, books and art materials and visible signs of the art-making activity that goes on, with patient's art work displayed on the walls and shelving.

Here's what I assess

Assessment in art therapy offers the team a different perspective from that of other interactions. It can contribute to an understanding of the patient's view of themselves and others, identifying factors which may have contributed to committing the offence. It also enables a formulation to be made about the patient's readiness to make use of psychological treatment, and informs about suitability for engagement with insight-oriented or art-making approaches through group or individual modalities. The clinical example given below will focus on the interpersonal aspects of art therapy assessment that inform me and the team about the patient's internal world and how this may help us to understand issues of risk.

The interpersonal relationships of patients are likely to be severely impaired and histories frequently include unstable family relationships in which violence and abuse have taken place. There may be little experience of another who can take in and make sense of disturbing and potentially dangerous and frightening feelings for the patient.

In many cases the index offence, or offence relating to the current conviction, has involved a violent attack on another person; an actual intrusion on their person or their physical space. This act may be understood as an attempt to force into the body and mind of another a psychic experience which has to be fended off because it is felt to pose a catastrophic threat to the self. Action or enactment takes the place of thought. Treating patients in this setting might be about facilitating the development of thought. With reference to Bion, one aim might be to help patients develop 'an apparatus (or function) that transforms raw sense impressions into experiences which can be known and felt' (Bell, 1995: 78). It is helpful to think of this function being concretely held in the first instance by the institution and staff, who hopefully can be receptive to the raw experiences, which the patient does not yet have the means of knowing as thoughts. The experiences of each team member are crucial in this endeavour and can either inform us or create divisions in our ability to work together (Gordon and Kirtchuk, 2008). The setting of art therapy in which I include the room, materials and the images, together with the receptivity of the therapist, can function as part of this 'container' for the patient's thoughts and feelings.

Here's what I do

In reality an assessment may start with information gathered from various team members before meeting the patient. Strong impressions may be formed from hearing about a patient's history and accounts of others' experience of them. It is likely to consist of two meetings a week or so apart giving an opportunity for a response to the first meeting to emerge. I explain to the patient that the purpose of the assessment is to give both of us the opportunity to consider whether art therapy may be helpful and that the time may be spent both using the art materials and talking. My approach is largely non-directive and I invite the patient to find out what there is to use. How do they respond to this, and the information I give them? Are they curious or reticent? Do I feel I am instructing or inviting them? Is there something in the patient that can tolerate unfamiliarity, or does this provoke anxiety and a closing down? Do I act to pre-empt anxiety, or perhaps the patient does this by moving quickly into art-making? In considering all these possibilities careful attention is given to what it feels like being with the patient. It is likely to be the case that patients will not say much about their experience and will use the therapist instead as a recipient of feelings which they cannot think about.

I ask myself how the patient responds to the art medium and if they relate to the image, verbally or otherwise, as having meaning. What do I feel about the image and what role do I feel invited to take on as observer of the image-making? Sitting with a patient, observing but not engaging myself in art work, can be an uncomfortable, even persecutory experience.

Here's an example

Mr S was in his forties when convicted of an unprovoked assault on a ticket inspector on a train. He had knocked this man unconscious. He grew up in a large, somewhat deprived and chaotic family who had come to the UK from a region in Europe known for violent action in the cause of political independence. In a team meeting I was given a description of a rather competent sounding man with no overt symptoms who appeared not quite to belong in this sort of service and would soon be discharged. As he had told his consultant he liked art, it was suggested I meet with him. During a preliminary discussion to ascertain whether he might wish to consider an art therapy assessment I was curious to notice that I was behaving with an almost apologetic urgency to offer him art therapy. Significantly, I realised this was driven by concern he might be bored, rather than the task of offering an assessment. I also felt at odds with the view expressed by other members of the team that he would soon be out of hospital.

By the time I met with Mr S for our first meeting he had moved from the admissions ward to a rehabilitation unit, reflecting a reduction in perceived risk. I was curious about this happening without us knowing much about him, feeling that his personable and gently humorous manner contributed to a picture that nothing much was the matter. At the time arranged he was asleep but hurriedly got ready, to arrive looking startled and caught off balance. I felt sympathetic towards his unprepared state but my acknowledgement of this was met with a defiant stare and a softly spoken, 'oh no, it's just fine.' Now I felt off balance.

He started measuring and dividing a large piece of paper with diagonal pencil lines; the impression was of a flag in the making. Quite suddenly, as he painted part of the image green he caught my eye and with a look of excitement said the colour reminded him of the political gatherings in his home region, known to be flashpoints of confrontation with security forces. Caught up with this vivid association I ventured to suggest these events were known to him. 'Oh no, I'm from the North of England,' he challenged with an intense and defiant stare. I felt a palpable warning to stay away. Having been drawn into taking up his association with these violent scenes, I was left feeling they were my thoughts alone. He noted the unevenness of the painting and set about correcting this with long fluid brush strokes of colour. My thoughts were of the preceding turbulence between us being smoothed over; I felt quite sleepy.

Mr S arrived for our second meeting with an overfamiliar 'Hi' as he strode into the room and searched for his painting. As he added new colours to the image, identifying it as a flag, I found myself again drawn into the observations he made, but each time my curiosity was pushed away. As we looked at his now complete image, I observed the function of flags to identify territory. Smiling ambiguously he said, 'Now I can put up my flag and mark out my territory. I don't want to lead you up the wrong road but if a man's got a green sash and he meets someone from the other side there'll be trouble.' As well as firmly warning me off, was he also alerting me to these territorial divisions as a way of keeping something hostile in himself in check?

I asked Mr S about his experience of being on the ward. He spoke of the difficulty of being with others who are not so well and having to ignore patients who look at you in a threatening way. I felt he was describing the very real difficulty he experienced in managing the close proximity of our meeting, that he had to shut down his feelings. My own sense was of being left in a bewildered and unsettled state related to his charged and excited associations.

What does this material tell me? At the start I felt invited to think of Mr S as not really a patient in difficulty. At the same time I found myself taking up a quite different position in the team, questioning whether something was in danger of being overlooked, based on my countertransference in the assessment. On the one hand I was being invited to join with a non-thinking part of him that overlooked his problems, but then I felt I was taking up an uncomfortable and oppositional view by identifying his ongoing potential for violence.

He was responsive to the art-making and his image conveyed powerful associations to some sort of conflict that was located in a bloody struggle between government and rebel forces. When I demonstrated that I had my own thoughts about his image, namely that it might represent a struggle within himself related to a perspective different to his own, his reaction left me feeling that, at that moment, he experienced us as indeed in mid-conflict. My aim as part of the assessment was to see if there was potential for mutual exploration of his image. The indication was that a different view was highly provocative, indicating perhaps why it had felt so uncomfortable to have an opinion about him that did not fit with the team's view. I reflected on feeling as if I'd been physically struck by the intensity of his verbal responses at the moment of trying to make contact with him. I felt I had become the oppressor. Although there was no indication why he had attacked his victim, Mr S may have identified the ticket inspector as someone full of the hostility and curiosity that Mr S was unable to know about in himself. His history indicated that offending was usually the precursor of an admission to hospital, in other words a man who could not easily turn to others for help. In the clinical setting it seemed there was the potential for a re-enactment of the attack on the guard, in the form of an attack on the team's ability to come together to fully know about this patient.

Mr S's image and interactions with me communicated something very disturbed and volatile about his internal world. Something very excited was stirred up which invited me to respond, but this was clearly provocative and potentially dangerous. My thoughts were that work would need to proceed at a very gentle pace allowing Mr S to use the art work to express and hold these highly volatile feelings, whilst keeping the therapist responses on quite a concrete level.

The outcome of the assessment was his being offered a place in a group This was facilitated by two therapists allowing him to operate a defensive split; he could locate his persecutory feelings in one or other of the therapists whilst retaining a good enough relationship with the other to sustain treatment.

References

Bell, D. (1995) 'Knowledge and its pretenders: Bion's contribution to knowledge and thought', in J. Ellwood (ed.) *Psychosis: Understanding and Treatment*. London: Jessica Kingsley Publishers.

Gordon, J. and Kirtchuk, G. (2008) *Psychic Assaults and Frightened Clinicians: Countertransference in Forensic Settings*. London: Karnac Books.

Art therapy assessment in an adolescent day service

Jane Saotome

Here's where I work

I am employed in a therapeutic day service for adolescents (11 years to 18 years) with serious mental, emotional and behavioural difficulties. The young people come from a wide range of backgrounds including the statutory care system. Jointly funded and staffed by the National Health Service (NHS), social services and education, it is an innovative service in line with government initiatives regarding integrated multi-agency working. The service provides an alternative to inpatient or residential care. Referrals into the service come through two routes: child and adolescent mental health services (CAMHS) and social services. Once a young person is accepted into the day service programme, referral for any therapy generally comes via a young person's care co-ordinator and discussion with therapists at a weekly meeting. Some young people self refer for individual art therapy which may have come from their engagement in the weekly open art therapy group. These referrals would be similarly discussed and assessed.

The day service programme consists of a mixture of group and individual therapy, education and activities. Up to ten young people can attend all day, up to five days a week, from six months to a year, but some stay much longer. The service is highly staffed. The whole day and whatever happens in it is considered to be the therapeutic milieu. There is a blurring and merging of therapeutic boundaries with therapists contributing to twice-daily community groups and eating lunch with the young people.

Here's what I assess

Young people arrive in the service with myriad background reports, assessments and diagnosis from involved agencies. After referral to the service a further assessment is made by a care co-ordinator. This comprises a detailed family and personal history and risk assessment, and includes the young person's views about their current situation. At the point of referral to art therapy I already have access to considerable information about a young person and they may be known to me in the broader context of the day service.

My assessment role is to consider a young person's current state of mind and situation and how and if they might benefit from individual art therapy. In a service with a wide diversity of serious presenting problems, nature and depth of engagement and what will be the approach are major considerations. For some disaffected young people, assessment can be less about suitability and more about whether there is a willingness to engage on any level. This is in line with the ethos and remit of the service to include difficult to engage young people. As a supportive factor the physical and emotional containment of the service as a whole allows a flexibility and broad inclusiveness in therapy, which might not otherwise be possible.

Here's what I do

After referral for individual art therapy, I offer an initial meeting to discuss the possibility of art therapy. Most adolescents have a heightened sensitivity to an assessment environment and I avoid the word 'assessment' with its connotations of judgement. This meeting takes place in the art therapy room, which is a dedicated space with abundant and varied materials. There are some young people's images, graffiti tags, writing, poems and handprints on the walls and a general atmosphere of informality. An initial meeting is usually for an hour but is adjusted to accommodate those who are hyperactive or have difficulties in concentration. The approach is also adjusted to their age and developmental stage. I give a brief explanation about art therapy and the parameters of confidentiality of sessions in relation to the team as a whole, introduce the materials and explain the storage of their work in their own folders. The use of art materials is offered in the assessment and this may or may not be taken up.

The assessment for art therapy presents particular difficulties relating to the nature of the adolescent client group. Approaches and considerations that I have in mind and which inform an assessment include: the unreliability of self-presentation of adolescents; their mistrust of the therapist and fear of intrusion; the denial of difficulties; identifying the therapist with authority figures; and the internalising or externalising of difficulties.

The mercurial moods of adolescents, their uncertain, fragile, adopted and changeable personas make assessments notoriously unreliable if not anathema. The presentation of self can rapidly change even within an initial assessment. There can be moves from grandiosity to self-doubt and from regressed behaviour to mature and startling insights. Presentations that mimic psychiatric symptoms and expressions of extreme thoughts are common and can be worrying. There is a danger (and temptation perhaps) of pathologising adolescent turmoil into psychiatric diagnosis. As Winnicott aptly noted: 'That which shows in the normal adolescent is related to that which shows in various kinds of ill persons' (Winnicott, 2004: 153). For some young people the idea of 'madness' powerfully resonates and offers an explanation for their own confusion and internal conflict. This is sometimes supported by an identification with areas of youth music and culture where there is a preoccupation with violence, suicide and self-harm. Both mental state and actual risk can, at times, be difficult to assess and may require some disentangling. However, such young people tend to be significantly interested in their internal worlds and can engage rapidly in an initial assessment.

Many adolescents are sensitive to the stigma attached to mental health issues and are resistant to any notion of therapy or therapists. Whether a young person will be able to tolerate an emphasis on the therapeutic relationship is a factor that would inform the nature of engagement rather than suitability for therapy. Some have a background of trauma, abuse and neglect. I therefore give careful acknowledgment to expressions of mistrust and fears of intrusion. There is often anxiety that I will 'see things' in their art work and know that which is private or secret. Other young people are deeply attracted to this possibility. Some adolescents maintain a denial that anything is wrong, despite all external and alarming evidence. In an initial assessment this is a defence that needs respecting.

Identifying the therapist as authority figures with whom young people may have been or are in conflict may arise in assessment and can be a serious disincentive to engagement. This is particularly evident in young people with behaviour problems and who are excluded from school or in trouble with the police. Frankel suggests that adolescents may immediately identify the therapist with the 'negative prohibitory force' and that the therapist must differentiate themselves 'from the adolescent's projection of collective morality' (Frankel, 1999: 201). The therapist's artist identity, the informality and atmosphere of the art therapy room are helpful here.

Whether young people internalise or externalise their feelings and distress in terms of their behaviour is an important practical factor in assessment for art therapy. This perceived, but not always clear, division of behaviour was starkly described by one young person in the service as 'nutters and delinquents'. Outwardly directed disturbance often takes the form of verbal abuse of staff and attacks on the containing environment, represented by the contents and fabric of the building. For such young people assessment for art therapy must include the potential danger of the uncontained, destructive use of art materials. Consideration of the contained and expressive use of fluid, flexible and highly physical art materials within the art room is part of the initial assessment and of the work itself with these young people.

Here's an example

William was a 14 year old from a mixed ethnic background. He was seriously neglected as an infant and taken into care. He had very little early experience of a 'secure base' and had been sexually abused. William had lived in multiple foster placements, children's homes and on occasion has slept rough. At the point of referral to the day service William's foster placement was relatively stable but quickly broke down leaving him in a state of perceived homelessness as he was moved between temporary foster placements. His behaviour was frenetic and he had been permanently excluded from school for more than two years. He coped at times by using alcohol and marijuana. Art therapy was suggested by his care co-ordinator because he was unable to process his distress verbally and William himself had expressed an interest in art therapy. From information I already held, I felt that this interest was more to do with issues of attachment and historical experiences of rejection than curiosity about art therapy. I thought he was attracted to the possibility of closeness within a safe relationship, but would probably provoke a rejecting response in me in order to confirm his own perception of himself as 'not wanted'; a pattern repeated in his history of many self-sabotaged foster placements.

On entering the art room for the assessment there was no opportunity for discussion about the process or purpose of art therapy, issues of confidentiality or the assurance that his work would be kept safely. William was restless. I felt anxiety as he moved furiously around touching and testing materials. With his back to me he surreptitiously squirted and emptied a full 568 ml bottle of yellow paint into a corner of the art room. Pointing it out to me, he cheerfully denied having done it, though the paint was notable on his jeans and trainers. I was struck by his contemptuous, challenging and symbolic use of paint (pissing in a corner) and the projection of his own feelings of having been 'pissed on' in his life. Things escalated and began to feel out of control, damage to the room seemed likely. I wondered aloud would art therapy be possible? I asked William to find me the following day and tell me if he seriously wanted to do art therapy, and if yes could he manage not to damage the room and things in it. At this point William left the room, leaving me to clean up.

In this assessment there was a confusion of a regressed infantile attack and an adolescent challenge to a perceived authority figure. There seemed to be a projection on to me as being a 'negative prohibitory force'. William's toddler-like presentation belied his age. In asking William to find me the next day I addressed his adolescent potential for maturity and underlined his ability to choose. William sought me out early the next morning and in marked contrast to his self-presentation of the day before, requested to do art therapy.

William explored and tested out the boundaries of the assessment, the containment of the room and of my resilience and tolerance. My response was not one of rejection but of stating a basic boundary of containment and hopefully suggested the possibility of containment of his own regressed infant self. His exploration and attack on the fabric of the art therapy room is typical of the outwardly focused expression of disturbance of many young people whose earliest experiences are characterised by neglect. William's behaviour in this assessment could be thought of as containment seeking and perhaps an indicator of the focus of art therapy via the physical properties of the art materials.

William engaged in art therapy and in the early sessions used art materials in a physical and regressed way. There was an outpouring of affect, with William at times being very distressed. Although he frequently took mess to its limits, it never spilt out of the room. He was just containable in the therapeutic relationship, in the art room and by the art materials. Reflection on a symbolic level was difficult. As a strange echo of the assessment, William occasionally secretly squirted paint into hidden places of the art room, which I only found by chance at later dates some time after he had left.

References

Frankel, R. (1999) *The Adolescent Psyche*. London and New York: Routledge.
Winnicott, D. W. (2004) *Deprivation and Delinquency*. London: Brunner/Routledge.

Report 6

Assessing the suitability of adult clients in community mental health

Marian Liebmann

Here's where I work

I work in an inner city community mental health team in Bristol which has several teams within it: support and recovery (long term), assessment and intervention (short term), early intervention (schizophrenia), outreach, deaf people, asylum seekers and refugees, community resources, and approved social workers. I take referrals from all these teams, based in a multicultural area of Bristol. The staff teams include professionals from many different disciplines and ethnic backgrounds. There is a high turnover of staff for a number of reasons, such as secondments, temporary jobs, promotions elsewhere, and so on; and there are always several trainee professionals of all disciplines. I run regular sessions entitled 'What Is Art Therapy?' to introduce what I do and improve the quality of referrals.

Here's what I assess

For individuals, I mainly assess suitability for art therapy. First, I check motivation – is the client keen, or is it someone else's idea? In our team worn-out staff sometimes refer someone to art therapy as the one thing not yet tried. A recent client referred for work on anger, when asked about the problem responded, 'I don't have a problem with anger, it's just that the mental health service keeps winding me up!'

Next I check: why art therapy? Sometimes a non-verbal therapy is needed because issues are difficult to express in words. I have also co-worked with a psychologist using verbal therapy (e.g. Cognitive Behavioural Therapy, CBT), while art therapy provided a more fluid way of expressing and dealing with feelings.

For clients referred for 'something to occupy themselves', I have gathered information on informal art classes and groups, and also helped to start a local branch of Studio Upstairs (a community art studio for adults with mental and emotional distress). I update this 'creative art opportunities' list annually, and give it to clients and referrers, marking the most relevant ones for them.

One vital question is: can they turn up for appointments? In the inner city many service users' lives are chaotic and unpredictable. They are usually visited at home by a community psychiatric nurse or social worker when they are likely to be in, for example, late morning, as they are just getting up. Although I am happy to make a home visit to meet someone for the first time, all the art materials are at the service base. I discuss with service users how they will remember appointments, from bits of paper to wall calendars; I am overjoyed if someone pulls out a diary and writes in their appointments.

I explore whether clients are prepared to take an active role in their treatment, and are willing to contemplate change. Some longstanding clients, accustomed to taking tablets, assume that painting one picture will result in them magically feeling better. When clients ask 'Will it work?', I say that in my experience it works if clients are prepared to put the work in. I also ask whether they can cope with some upset as they work through difficult things, so that they do not have unrealistic ideas about getting better overnight.

As I work part-time for two days per week, I cannot take on people who are going to need art therapy for ever. So I look for an 'art therapy task' we can work on. This may be short-term work in association with the assessment team (two to six months), or longer work, in association with the support and recovery team. I promise such clients up to a year, which can be extended a bit to finish a task.

I have mixed feelings about including art therapy work in an assessment. On one occasion, when I suggested that a client used paints, the client became overwhelmed, only coming back when reassured that she could use more controllable art materials like a black felt-tip pen. This helped me realise how scared many clients are about using art materials. On the other hand, some clients find words and interviews so difficult that using art materials is a relief. So I usually start with words, and discuss with the client how they would like to use the art materials, so that they feel safe doing this. If talking proves difficult, I offer art materials as a way forward, which clients then use to explain their difficulties.

Meanwhile, of course, the client is assessing me at the same time, thinking, 'Do I really want this? Will it work or be a waste of time? Is this person someone I can work with?' Sometimes they decide art therapy is not for them, or they don't find me congenial to work with. With black clients, I sometimes ask if they have any issues about working with a white therapist.

Here's what I do

Referrals come to me in different ways. Often other staff stop me in a corridor and say, 'Oh, I've been meaning to talk to you about someone I'm thinking of referring.' We might sit down and discuss the referral. Or they might send me a letter or email, or fill in my referral form – then I talk to the referrer, and also check on some basic details. For example, are they in our area? Are they being referred to other things at the same time, for example, psychotherapy? In which case I would ask for some discussion, or suggest just referring to one therapy at a time.

Then I send a letter with an appointment and a leaflet describing art therapy. At this first assessment session I listen to the client's story and then discuss whether art therapy is the best way forward – if not, I try to signpost them to something more appropriate, for example, an art class or verbal counselling. If art therapy seems suitable, we discuss how to work together, for example, length of time, frequency, special needs, risks, etc. Sometimes fortnightly sessions suit clients better than weekly ones, which they find too intense. Some have special needs/risks, such as epilepsy, and I ask how to deal with these. If people are worried about getting too deeply into things, we arrange a 'winding down' time before the session ends. The main thing is tailoring art therapy around the client's needs.

In a second assessment session we identify the problems more closely. Some people like to write these down themselves, but many prefer talking, with me as their 'secretary'. We use a five-point scale to gauge severity. This gives me a good idea of clients' problems and priorities. Clients too find it useful to see their problems listed. We go back to this list after a few months to see if anything has changed. I also ask a future-focused question, i.e. how will you know you are better? I include a space for people to list their strengths, which are often overlooked by mental health professionals and by clients themselves.

I discuss with clients how they want to use the art materials. Some clients are familiar with these and quickly choose ones they like. Others have not done any art since early schooldays, and I offer some sessions to try out art materials, without any expectation of working on their issues. So they might try pastels and pencils the first session, paint next, then clay, then maybe collage. By then they usually know what they like – and what they don't like. And they are also more comfortable with me and more ready to work on their issues.

I have arrived at this way of working partly through experience and partly through my personal philosophy, believing there is no 'right' or 'wrong' way to engage clients provided I respect them and their culture and put them at the centre. I believe the art therapy process has a momentum of its own, so I do everything possible to help someone get started.

Here's an example

Sophia was an African-Caribbean service user, aged 40, suffering from depression linked to childhood sexual abuse from her father. In our first assessment session she talked about flashbacks she experienced during child abuse training while working for the Connexions (youth employment advice) service. She left the job and was claiming benefits. She had been in psychiatric hospital four years previously, and had used the crisis service two years later. She had seen a psychiatrist several times (and took medication) and had had 16 sessions with a psychologist, talking about the sexual abuse. While she was grateful for this help, the problems still persisted, as the surfacing of the abuse had split the family. She was also in the process of separating from her husband.

Sophia had a degree in French and Spanish. She had also studied German, Italian, Japanese and Portuguese. She had enjoyed art at school and hoped art therapy might help more than verbal therapy, especially for her anger problems. These seemed good reasons, and she was well motivated, so I offered her individual art therapy for up to a year. We used the second assessment session to identify her problems more closely. She preferred writing them down herself:

1   Dealing with the aftermath of sexual abuse – feelings of anger and guilt at the disintegration of the family.
2   Sadness and bouts of depression that my marriage is over and I cannot fulfill my dream of having my own family.
3   Feelings of isolation and loneliness – no longer used to long periods on my own, especially evenings at home.
4   Lack of confidence and uncertainty about what to do for a job.
5   Worrying about my financial situation and feeling a burden on my family, especially my younger sister and brother, who help me out but also have their own problems and families to support (guilt).
6   Dealing with the new family set-up.
7   Fear of entering into a new relationship – do I disclose my past?

From this list, she identified anger and guilt as difficulties that were 'top of the scale'.

In answer to the question 'How will you know when you are better?', she wrote:

1   I will be happier, not so depressed and tearful and stressed.
2   I will be able to cope with problems better and be more independent, e.g. when things go wrong with the house and dealing with the council, I will be able to get them sorted without calling on my 'ex' to help me out.
3   I will feel more 'in charge'/ fit for work.
4   I will be signed off from my psychiatrist.
5   Feelings of guilt and anger will not be so strong or may even disappear.

For her strengths, Sophia wrote:

•   Physical – like to exercise and dance, which relieves stress.
•   Now able to open up to close friends so I don't bottle everything up.
•   Now able to ask for some help/support sometimes, although I do find it difficult.

We discussed how we would work together. Sophia was happy talking to me but still a bit hesitant about art therapy. Together we started making a plan, which we completed the following session:

1   Trial period of two months, to see if art therapy can help.
2   Start fortnightly, to avoid getting 'buried' in negative stuff.
3   Bring something positive out of each session at the end.
4   Explore different aspects of anger management.
5   Look at guilt issues, especially re current family situation.
6   Try to leave everything here at the end of the session.

We did not discuss art materials as Sophia felt confident about choosing these.

In this third session we completed the plan and there was time for art work. Sophia chose paints and portrayed a large tree with branches, leaves and flowers. She enjoyed using paints and continued with them during subsequent sessions. In the fourth session we started on the anger issues at the top of Sophia's list. We discussed some aspects of anger, and she painted a picture about its good and bad aspects and what might lie underneath. By this time, we were well on the way.

The challenge of art therapy assessment in bereavement work with children and teens

Laura V. Loumeau-May

Here's where I work

As an art therapist in The Journeys Program of Valley Home Care, located in New Jersey, I provide individual and group bereavement support for children and teens. Originally established as an outpatient resource for children and grandchildren of hospice patients, Journeys has expanded over 20 years to provide a service to the larger community and youth who have lost loved ones under sudden and identifiably traumatic circumstances such as automobile accidents, drowning, suicide, heart attacks, and the 2001 terrorist attacks in New York City. There are now three art therapists on staff.

Referrals come from Valley Home Care itself, schools, pediatricians, hospitals, other hospices, and by 'word of mouth' from former clients who are familiar with the program. The hospice treatment team consists of nurses, social workers, a chaplain, and a psychiatrist. Most families seen in Journeys have been discharged from hospice following the death of their loved one, or have not been on the hospice program. Journeys and the hospice team support each other as consultants on an 'as needed' basis.

Journeys has its own suite in an administrative building, which includes a waiting area, an office for meetings with parents, and a large art therapy room. The art room is furnished with tables, an easel, a sandtable and figurines, a puppet theater, a sink, a toy medical 'crash cart' with intravenous pole and x-ray machine, dollhouses, a case with books and games, cabinets and shelves for storage of art materials and art projects, and bulletin boards which display client artwork.

Initial assessment consists of information gathering with bereaved adult caregivers. This takes place in the smaller, less stimulating, more 'professional' office. Parents receive information on normal reactions to grief and therapist's approach to treatment, which is intended to be reassuring. Further assessment with the children themselves is ongoing and contiguous with treatment, in the art room setting, through the observation of their art work, play and behavior.

Here's what I assess

Youth referred to Journeys have suffered a loss. The focus for treatment is bereavement; occasionally post traumatic stress disorder (PTSD) must be ruled out. At the start of treatment I conduct an interview with the primary caregiver which serves as an initial assessment and enables the formulation of art therapy goals. Information is obtained about the nature of the loss, the quality of the relationship with the deceased, family history of trauma and loss, academic performance, behavioral and emotional responses, cultural and spiritual attitudes toward illness, healing and death, resilience factors such as ego strengths and support, and what the parent is seeking in bereavement support for their child. Throughout treatment, art materials and processes are used directly with the child to determine stage of grief, area of greatest distress and changing focus. Parent conferences are scheduled regularly to evaluate ongoing progress.

Because the experience of loss, and therefore effective grief work, is determined by many factors, assessment and treatment approaches vary from individual to individual. The age of the child plays a major role in how death is understood, their ability to regulate feelings, and the developmental capacity for art-making. Early art assessment with a young child may include encouraging the child to depict their concept of what death is, or what they think happens to a person after they die (Doka, 1995). If the death was unanticipated and violent, trauma may be present. This must be evaluated and addressed in order to establish safety and provide proper support before expressive grief work is encouraged (Cohen *et al.*, 2006). The relationship of the deceased to the child is also a significant factor. The loss of a non-primary caregiver such as a grandparent will be grieved differently than the loss of someone on whom the child depends. Personal death awareness and survivor guilt are more likely to be activated following a sibling's death (Worden, 1996). The quality of the relationship with the person who died will influence the grief process as well as ongoing relationships with remaining family members. Cultural, spiritual, and social influences affect the rituals and support available, as well as the context in which death has been explained to the child. The intake interview with the parent prepares an initial frame through which the child is seen. Subsequent evaluation through the art work monitors emotional expression, portrayal of the deceased, level of engagement in art-making, self-image, acceptance of loss, and future outlook. Continuous processing of spontaneous material as well as the use of formal, art-based assessments informs the direction and duration of treatment.

Here's what I do

In bereavement work, it is important to recognize and respect defenses so as not to move too quickly with material or retraumatize. At the same time, observation and nurturance of symbols and metaphors that arise from the unconscious helps guide the journey of grief, provides meaning to loss and a new sense of wholeness or healing. At the beginning of treatment, I follow the lead of the child or teen, confident that they will introduce material they feel capable of addressing. My initial goal is to establish a trusting working relationship. Allowing the initial picture in therapy to be a free drawing provides children with an opportunity to tell about themselves at their own comfort level. Subject matter as well as materials selected will reveal defenses, strengths, and whether they are ready to delve into the subject of loss right away. As treatment continues with a child or teen reluctant to address their loss directly, I may suggest specific subject matter or perform a formal, art-based assessment which can identify issues that need addressing and stimulate deeper exploration.

For example, the Kinetic Family Drawing (K-F-D) is useful in the early stages of grief work because of its focus on relationship (Burns and Kaufman, 1970). Closeness, distance, identification, role in family, conflict, and quality of interactions are revealed through this assessment tool. Rawley Silver's Draw-A-Story assessment (1983) reveals resilience factors such as problem solving, optimism, creativity, and humor. The Formal Elements Art Therapy Scale (FEATS) is easy to do and a good screening for depression, anxiety, problem solving and perceived ability to meet nurturance needs (Gantt and Tabone, 1998). Several metaphoric directives can be useful at various points in bereavement work. Among these are bridge drawings (Hays and Lyons, 1981). These drawings depict past, present, and future as well as direction, significant events and surrounding environment. This can provide information about expectations, perception of safety and support.

No assessment tool by itself is a measure of grief. Rather each can be chosen at specific points during treatment to evaluate an area of concern. Much information is obtained through interpretation of spontaneous imagery or observation of the quality of engagement in the creative process.

Here's an example

Robert, a seven year old whose maternal grandfather had died, was brought to the Journeys Program for art therapy treatment by his mother. She noticed that Robert had become withdrawn, occasionally tearful, and was having bad dreams which he would not talk about. She felt a non-verbal approach would help him express his feelings about his grandfather's illness and death. His mother was also concerned that her frequent crying might be having a negative impact on Robert.

Robert loved animals and drew them often in his first sessions. They later served as a metaphor for his grief process. However, he was initially avoidant of the subject of his grandfather. I advocated the topic by asking Robert to draw himself doing something with his grandfather (see Plate 5, situated between pp. 100 and 101).

Robert created an image of playing catch with Grandpa – an activity they had done frequently prior to his cancer diagnosis. Robert drew himself large with outstretched arms and huge open hands, leaning back as the ball almost flies past him. However, his grandfather is diminutive with a stunted body and frail, ribbon-like fingers. Robert realized he was making his grandfather smaller than himself and gave Grandpa a large head with lots of hair 'because he was taller than me'. This drawing stimulated talk about what his grandfather was like before and during his illness and led to more meaningful exploration of his fears concerning death and grief in subsequent sessions, including occasional dreams in which pursuing animals figured prominently.

After five months of treatment his mother reported that the nightmares had ceased and Robert was again cheerful at home. She asked if he was ready to stop attending Journeys. I selected the Silver Draw-A-Story assessment to evaluate Robert for termination of treatment. This tool was chosen because of its potential to reveal optimistic versus pessimistic themes and strengths. It was also chosen because it offers animal and human stimulus images, increasing the likelihood of a story depicting a relationship theme. Robert selected the cat and the mouse and created a stereotypical chase scene. Robert's drawing was purely linear, void of the many details he typically embellishes with. This possibly indicated depression, but his behavior contradicted that. He was quite pleased with the picture and energized after drawing it. I considered that this assessment calls for use of pencil only and is drawn on 8½ by 11 inch paper, whereas Robert typically selected a variety of coloring media and large paper which allowed him to be more expansive. I recommended to his mother that we observe him for two more sessions; that his drawing did not reveal enough to fully assess his state of mind.

Although Robert's response to the stimulus drawings was non-remarkable, they continued to command his imagination. At his next session, Robert announced he wanted to draw the cat and mouse again. This time both animals were drawn in full color with dramatic details, which he delighted in (Figure R7.1). The cat in

Figure R7.1 Draw a story (1).

this picture is quite large and looks as if it is about to overtake the mouse, who seems to be sitting calmly with its back to the cat. When asked to identify with one of the animals, Robert said he was the mouse, adding that he was not frightened of the cat. He pointed out that the mouse was on skis, not just sitting still.

In his final session Robert drew scenes in which the clever mouse lured the cat into pursuing it to an underwater locale and then back to dry land, where the mouse was finally seen escaping in a Richard-Scarry-like 'pumpkin car' as the exhausted cat shook off the water in defeat and exasperation (Scarry, 1998) (see Figure R7.2). Similarly to his story, Robert had dealt with a 'cat and mouse' game of trying to evade feelings of fear and confusion which threatened to overwhelm him, bravely navigating the deep waters of his and his mother's tears, and had finally emerged triumphant – 'in the driver's seat' feeling proud and empowered by his success.

In conclusion, appropriate assessment for art therapy grief work, especially with children and teens, is as complex as the grief process itself. To evaluate effectively, one must be knowledgeable and aware of the many factors that influence grief. No one assessment tool or approach can measure every aspect of bereavement; the same image responses may have either positive or negative implications depending on the stage of grief as well as individual experience of it. My approach therefore is directed by caution, attentiveness, and respect for each child's unique ability to navigate this journey.

Figure R7.2 Draw a story (2).

References

Burns, R. and Kaufman, S. H. (1970) *Kinetic Family Drawings (K-F-D)*. New York: Brunner/Mazel.

Cohen, J., Mannarino, A. and Deblinger, E. (2006) *Treating Trauma and Traumatic Grief in Children and Adolescents*. New York: Guilford Press.

Doka, K. (1995) *Children Mourning, Mourning Children*. Washington, DC: Hospice Foundation of America.

Gantt, L. and Tabone, C. (1998) *The Formal Elements Art Therapy Scale*. Morgantown, WV: Gargoyle Press.

Hays, R. and Lyons, S. (1981) 'The bridge drawing: a projective technique for assessment in art therapy', *Arts in Psychotherapy*, 8 (4): 207–219.

Scarry, R. (1998) *Cars, and Trucks, and Things that Go*. New York: Random House.

Silver, R. (1983) *Silver Drawing Test of Cognitive and Creative Skills*. Seattle, WA: Special Child Publications.

Worden, J. W. (1996) *Children and Grief*. New York: Guilford Press.

Part III

A more distant calculation

Chapter 7

Nightsea Crossing
Assessment for art psychotherapy
Andrew Marshall-Tierney

Nightsea Crossing

Nightsea Crossing is the collective name for a series of performances by Marina Abramović and Frank Uwe Laysiepen in which they sat motionless and in silence at a table. The environment (different rooms in different countries) and number of days over which the performance would be carried out varied, but the same mahogany table and the same two chairs were always used. Sometimes they placed an object on the table, mostly the table was bare. The artists sat at either end of the table, facing each other so that the audience was looking at their profiles: silently observing each other whilst being observed.

Being at sea and being in the dark

Observing myself sitting at a table with my patients, the motif of two artists sitting quietly doing nothing was one I returned to consistently to critique my work. There were times during ongoing work when enduring proximity in silence for extended periods was a core aspect of my role. *Nightsea Crossing* seemed so like and yet so unlike my practice, bringing into focus the performed aspects of art psychotherapy, which are often missing from the literature (see Rogers, 2002 and also, Skaife, 2008). The artists, furniture and the gaze of the audience can be thought of as being art 'materials' and also as psychoanalytic 'objects'. By way of comparison I can describe the two practices as follows.

Nightsea Crossing:

- Two people sit at a table for an agreed length of time.
- The table is always the same table.
- Sometimes there is an object on the table.
- This object is never used other than as an object of their gaze.
- The encounter takes place in silence.
- It is witnessed by an audience.
- The encounter is documented in a variety of ways.
- There seems to be a balance of power between the two people.
- This sitting together is framed within the discourse of visual culture.

Art psychotherapy:

- Two people sit at a table for an agreed length of time.
- The table is always the same table.
- Materials and objects are frequently brought to the table.
- These materials and objects are used in a variety of ways, being touched, joined together and looked at.
- Sometimes the encounter takes place in silence, but optimally there is conversation.
- No one witnesses events other than the two people themselves and their own internal audiences.
- It is documented in a variety of ways.
- There is an imbalance of power between the two people.
- This sitting together is framed with the discourse of art therapy.

The question I put to myself at the time was: if the artist's body and the audience's gaze are the art work, then what is the status of the 'art materials' in my art psychotherapy assessment practice? I now think that the anxious question behind this was: supposing the patient just sits quietly doing nothing during assessment?

Art psychotherapists just can't say no!

With a few exceptions, art psychotherapists in the UK seem to have avoided detailed discussion of assessment. Many of the profession's core beliefs about people, relationships and art make decision making in this area particularly complex. We tend to privilege therapist passivity, uncertainty and not knowing; we believe that meaning is provisional and negotiated interpersonally; we value the purposelessness of play. However, we are coming under external pressure: employers, regulators and the public all expect expertise in assessment.

Assessment asks us to think critically about our core beliefs. As an art psychotherapist you either believe that everyone in a given client group can benefit from art therapy, in which case assessment is unnecessary, or you believe that some people might benefit more than others (and that some will not benefit at all), in which case you need clear criteria to aid your decision making. This is crucial because the emotional climate of assessment is anxiety: the anxiety of meeting a stranger; the anxiety of making art; and the anxiety, as described by Gilroy (2006), of practice in a potentially hostile research environment. We could sit quietly and we could let the patient do nothing. I think there are compelling reasons not to do so.

'Talking quite a lot'

Whilst I was developing my assessment practice several texts from the psychoanalytic literature, particularly Coltart (1993) and Mace (1995), influenced my thinking. I took three key ideas from Coltart. First, that the assessment must not be 'traumatic' for the client and that it is the therapist's task to ensure this by adopting a 'friendly and sympathetic attitude'. Coltart (1987: 134) insists that it is 'narcissistic and uncreative' for a therapist to 'sit and do nothing' in assessment. The dynamics of *Nightsea Crossing*, watching in silence, would surely constitute trauma here. Second, Coltart says that it is important to be clear about what qualities a client needs in order to benefit from a particular therapy; in her case this is psychological mindedness. Tantam (1995) has contested the concept of psychological mindedness (asking, for instance whether it is a personality characteristic or a set of values) but the idea of using assessment to identify desirable qualities became central to my assessment practice. Third, and I think most importantly, is Coltart's statement that: 'One is in no position to make a judgment about psychological mindedness unless the patient has talked quite a lot, and therefore, as skillfully and unobtrusively as possible one wants to enable him to do so' (Coltart, 1993: 78).

The question that I asked myself from this was: if a client needs to 'talk quite a lot' in an assessment for a talking therapy, do they equally need to use art materials quite a lot in assessment for art psychotherapy?

The mind's eye and the real world

My model of assessment evolved from reflective practice. However, three papers (Case, 1998; Tipple, 2003; Dudley, 2004) were contemporary with my emerging practice and these authoritatively set out the territory to be explored. The other aspect of the profession's discourse to note is the British Association of Art Therapists assessment training workshop (convenors De Heger and Woddis) which I attended in 2006.

The consensus in the UK is that art psychotherapy assessment aims to discover whether the client can use the therapist and/or the materials safely. Most texts (except Tipple's) are unclear about how to help the client make use of the art materials; this seems congruent with the privileging of non-directive practice. De Heger and Woddis's training echoes Coltart in saying that it is traumatic to organize assessment like an ordinary session (De Heger and Woddis, personal communication, 2006); they add that it is essential to adapt practice to each unique assessment context.

Case (1998) makes two points: that assessment must not blur into ongoing therapy; and that the decision about whether or not to work with a client is informed by images in her 'mind's eye' built up from the transference and the art work. Dudley (2004) writes about work with adults with mental health problems. Whilst privileging the cultural, Dudley also says that much of the decision is made using 'unconscious knowledge and intuition' (2004: 20). Dudley does not clarify how the therapist is to help the client establish a relationship with art materials whilst also addressing the socio-political context. Tipple (2003) is the only person to describe a structure of assessment and is clear that it is the therapist's task to ensure art materials are used. He is fundamentally concerned with the dilemma of inter-preting a 'patient' to a 'team'. Although Tipple does not explicitly contest Case, he argues clearly that art psychotherapy discourse contains assumptions about art-making that marginalize the social context. More than this, he says that counter-transference feelings can too easily be used to shape the description of context.

Being indoors with the door shut

My model of assessment for art psychotherapy was developed in National Health Service (NHS) community mental health teams (CMHTs) from 2001 to 2007. The CMHT art therapy rooms were neither studios nor clinics. They were imbued with the aesthetics and idiosyncrasies of the NHS, which I experienced as a form of holding. They gave me all that was required: a space in which I could meet a client without interruption and an environment in which clients could use art materials. The room was the passive, least complex aspect of the assessment environment, representing neutrality and abstinence and tending to elicit little curiosity from this client group.

I represented the interpersonal and most complex aspect of the assessment. Aspiring to benign neutrality but eliciting curiosity in the transference, I was an object that could not be touched. The art materials, conversely, were there to be touched; the client's curiosity was given free rein so that the materials could be treated in ways that I (and most other people in most other situations) could not.

I provided a range of art materials for two-dimensional and three-dimensional work that were typical of those in art therapy rooms throughout the UK. Some of these were good quality, some poor quality; this seemed like a useful aspect of reality for a patient to engage with. I relied on well-stocked scrap boxes for my assessment practice. The rule of abstinence particularly applies to scrap materials but the CMHT provided a surprising variety of packaging materials to add to found offcuts of wood, wire, fabrics and plastics.

Narrow gates

The CMHT had a gate-keeping system that used *DSM-IV* criteria (American Psychiatric Association, 2000), but I did not assess by diagnosis. My concern was to discover whether one-to-one art therapy of between 6 and 18 months duration might meet an individual's needs. There were no groups, art psychotherapy or otherwise, in the service as CMHT premises could not accommodate rooms that were large enough.

Being referred, a client is bound to have an unconscious component and being dependent on a team for referrals (which at root is being dependent on the team for professional survival) is undoubtedly loaded with meaning. A psychodynamic point of view would expect this giving and receiving to be characterized by ambivalence. This only lent weight to the need for transparent and objective referral criteria.

Looked at from an economic perspective, the key areas were resources, risk, and capacity to benefit. In other words, can this particular person be helped, can they be helped now, and can they best be helped by art psychotherapy? The central dilemma is to identify both those clients most likely to benefit and those clients most in need of services. Since these two groups might well be mutually exclusive, the idea of indentifying those clients at an optimal point of need of services who also had the capacity to benefit from art psychotherapy became central to my assessment work. In this context I judged that the client should use the art materials, with myself observing, for the majority of the time we were together. I would then further assess if they were also open to the idea that there might be connections between their art work and their presenting problem.

'Use art materials whilst telling me about yourself'

Each client's assessment began with a referral form giving a succinct description of the current problem, previous interventions (successful and unsuccessful), desired outcomes, risk and personal history (milestones, losses, etc.). Receiving the form always went hand in hand with a brief discussion with the referrer; this was usually when an impression first formed in the countertransference.

I aimed to send a standard appointment letter within 10 working days of referral. On the day of the assessment I would often find myself experiencing mixtures of curiosity and apprehension, checking my appearance in the mirror and re-reading the referral form as I waited for the reception staff to announce the client's arrival. Having a clear model of assessment in mind meant that my anxieties were contained within a feeling of competence.

During assessment, the patient and I sat on identical chairs (almost at touching distance) with the patient at the longer side of the table and most of the art materials on nearby surfaces. I began by saying that our meeting would last one hour, that we might need to meet for a further assessment appointment, that the purpose was to see if art therapy could be of help to them and that the best way to find out was for them to use art materials whilst telling me about themselves. I added that any future art therapy would be non-directive, meaning that I would be a quieter presence and ask fewer questions. This was often enough for the patient to get started; I was always struck by patients' ability to do so.

If a patient was unable to choose art materials then I would ask them to go to the scrap box, choose several things that caught their eye, bring these back to table and do something with them. The scrap box provided material that already had substance, that could be touched, joined together and rearranged; something tangible rather than the experience of nothingness that blank paper can sometimes suggest. Again, this proved helpful in the majority of cases.

If the client still struggled to find materials or do anything with them I would (rather than move on to a discussion of the presenting problem) try to have a conversation about the difficulty of using materials with the hope that we could revisit the actions above. As a last resort I would, if the client's anxieties were too high, use the art materials myself. However, I only needed to do this once in about 50 assessments during this period. If a client attended two sessions and did not use art materials then it seemed to me that art therapy was contra-indicated.

I encouraged clients to spend as much time as possible art-making, usually inviting them to aim to do so for 'most' of the session. Longer periods of time making art forge a stronger attachment to an image whilst giving more opportunity for the client to adapt to the constraints of the materials or learn to tolerate chance events. This seems close to Dissanayake's concept of 'making special' (see Learmonth, 2009).

Asking clients to use art materials whilst telling me about themselves was key to my assessment practice. I did so for two reasons: first, because hearing their story alongside the emergence of an image helped me to begin to make a formulation; second, because, with eyes both up and down, it minimized the potentially traumatic feeling of being under scrutiny. A conversation with the art materials whilst thinking out loud in the presence of another is art psychotherapy as a reflective loop, an iterative process. Isserow (2008) has recently introduced the model of joint attention skills which seems useful here. Conversation during assessment has several functions: building a relationship, modelling reflective practice, unobtrusively gathering history, making interpretations, and so on.

By the end of the first session I would know whether or not we needed to meet for a further hour before coming to a decision; this was because a clear 'yes' or a clear 'no' could usually be arrived at in just one session. I would sum up succinctly and clarify my impression (based on their use of art materials and of myself) about how I thought art psychotherapy might or might not benefit each patient, aiming for just a few jargon-free sentences.

Overall I saw my role during assessment as facilitating art-making, seeking information, making provisional links in my mind and cautiously voicing them. From the patient's point of view, using art materials in the presence of the art therapist, discussing this reflectively, sketching out their story, and seeing how the art psychotherapist responds puts them in a position to give informed consent. However, unlike the greater mutuality of ongoing work, the responsibility for the decision to offer art psychotherapy sits with the therapist.

Once the client had left the building, the art work was left behind on the table (I am contrasting this with *Nightsea Crossing*). Photographing it, handling it for the first time, storing it and uploading the photograph all contributed to holding the image in mind, of curating it psychologically. I then returned to the team office to make my notes on a computer, joining my experience of the client to the Trust's recording systems; secure, but accessible by colleagues from within the service.

Shades of grey

If the function of assessment is to arrive at a decision, then both positive and negative outcomes must be possible. Decision making provokes least anxiety when based on observable phenomena: yes, the client did use art materials; or no, the client did not give any history. Underlying this was a maxim much used in the CMHT that the best predictor of future behaviour is past behaviour. A client who struggles with art materials in assessment is likely to struggle with them long term.

It is not my intention to explore assessments where decisions are arrived at easily. It is those assessments that throw up complex and contradictory material that require discussion. I used the idea that there was a range of outcomes possible: yes, probably, probably not, and no. 'Yes', if a client used art materials under observation with some degree of spontaneity, talked reflectively and made or accepted links with their presenting problem. 'Probably', if a client used art materials and talked fairly openly without necessarily making links. 'Probably not', if a client struggled with art materials and was unable to discuss this reflectively. 'No', if a client did not use art materials and responded to me in an anxious, persecutory and non-reflective way.

The complex decisions ('probably, probably not') require something more than observable phenomena. It is these grey areas that require skilful readings of subtle, elusive information. 'Probably not' is harder than 'probably' because of our difficulty in saying 'no'. My practice was to offer clients a second session if the outcome was unclear at the end of the first, the second session being the crucial one for decision making. Active reflection between sessions was essential to clarify themes. It was rare for me to use supervision to make the decision: my experience was more like an internal supervisor (see Casement, 1985) viewing the tableaux vivants of assessment. It was at this point that building a formulation from key images and key narratives proved helpful. The key text here is Hinshelwood (1995) who says that early relationships set the pattern for later relationships and that the transference recapitulates the problematic relationships in the patient's life.

I played with the emerging stories and images in my mind, viewing each (the art work, the client's current situation, past relationships and transference) through the lens of the other until they gravitated towards a working formulation. Making a formulation using images and stories from the transference gave shape to things that were slippery, elusive and yet strangely palpable.

A fragile meadow, an unreliable lampshade and a spirit long house

I will illustrate my assessment practice with three case vignettes that I have named from their key images. These three clients were from broadly similar white, working-class backgrounds, struggling with depression coupled with other psychological problems and, of course, all unique complex people. During their first sessions they all made use of art materials and they all made use of me, but because they did so ambivalently I offered them second sessions. The second session gave the client (who arrived knowing what to expect) a second chance to use the materials and a second chance to use me. Consequently I had more time and more material with which to make a decision.

A fragile meadow (first session)

The referral came from a close colleague who seemed uncharacteristically weary with this client, a woman who, suffering from Parkinson's disease which led to frequent falls at home, retired early after being bullied in her workplace. There was a lift to the art therapy room but despite her difficulty walking she was determined to use the stairs and, although collaborative throughout, remained quietly spoken and apologetic, reluctant to discuss either her own history or the presenting problem.

From my invitation to go to the art materials, her eye was caught by shredded green cellophane which she tentatively spread on faded green sugar paper. Then, using sharp scissors, she weakly snipped yellow felt into small irregular pieces which she sprinkled on top. Nothing was glued in place. She worked slowly throughout the session and was cautiously pleased with the effect of flowers in deep grass, calling her picture 'Summer Meadow' and saying that it would be a better place to be than where she is now.

She had had several admissions for depression, and told me that she had felt tired, unhappy and unfulfilled throughout her adult life. The client told me she had felt looked after as a child, had friends and went out, but no longer really enjoys family and friends. She talked with her brother on the phone every evening but complained of 'pain and hurt' because all her siblings were involved in their own families. My impression was of her physical frailty and her own ambivalence around this. I found myself thinking that I could have made her art work in minutes and realized how easily she could be bullied.

On her way back down the stairs she started leaning forward alarmingly, stumbled and, grabbing the banister, only just stopped falling badly. I felt shaken, both for her and for nearly failing in my duty of care. Once she had gone I discovered that her art work was so fragile that it could barely be moved without the pieces blowing away. Before the next session I experienced flashes of anger about her inability to look after herself and found myself wondering why compassion was so elusive. I thought about her determination going up the stairs and recklessness going down, her complaints about her family not looking after her, about fragile objects treated carelessly.

A fragile meadow (second session)

Quietly but firmly I asked her to use the lift up to her second session. Once in the room she showed no interest in either art materials or conversation, saying only that she was tired and preferred just to sit quietly. Her art work remained on the table, ignored. We sat in silence doing nothing. Her eyes grew heavy and after a while she fell asleep. I did not know what to do, unsure about what sort of position I had been placed in. To begin with it felt too intrusive even to look in her direction. As time passed my gaze was increasingly able to rest on her; it felt as if I were now watching over her. She looked vulnerable and I began, at last, to feel concern for her.

A working formulation began to take shape in my mind: she lived alone, feeling hurt by friends and family; there was bullying on the periphery of the transference and a lack of empathy. Her art work was a good object for her but for me something fragile and hard to care for. She had been able to use me (a range of countertransference experience), able to use art materials (some tenderness, a hint of ruthlessness), but despite this the image was of her weariness and of a fragile, neglected good object and split off aggression. As my concern grew, a picture formed in my mind of something too fragile to be worked with and when she woke I said, gently, to her expressed relief, that art psychotherapy did not seem to be what she needed.

An unreliable lampshade (first session)

This client, experiencing long-standing depression with obsessive traits, had never really engaged with the CMHT. He was referred from a team meeting to clarify his need of the service. Although he arrived a little late for his first appointment, my impression was of geniality and nothing particularly problematic being played out with me.

This client needed little prompting to choose net-like packaging material and wire. He readily engaged in conversation, bending and twisting the wire into a shape like a large lampshade. He described his problems as being to do with motivation. He was, for example, overweight and wanted to get fit: to get fit he would need to repair his bike, to repair his bike he would need to tidy the shed, and to tidy the shed . . . and so on. The typical pattern was that he would start something, take a break, extend the break over several days, lose interest and then feel hopeless. He said that he had been a creative child but became 'devious' in adolescence to avoid his stepfather's temper, daydreaming about motor bikes and bands. In adulthood he worked as a stage technician, struggled with alcohol and lost contact with his wife and son after his marriage failed. Although maintaining a good relationship with his daughter, he described continued fallings out with friends.

After shaping the wire he wrapped the packaging material around it, taping it quickly to the wire and describing the piece as a lampshade. Although he disliked its 'rough and ready' manufacture, he really liked its 'ethnic' style. It seemed to be as much a piece of imaginary home furnishing as an art object, something with a symbolic and a quasi-functional value. It seemed to me neither obsessive nor depressed, nor like daydreaming: an object with a carefree, artless quality that I found pleasing. He summed it up saying that the light leaked through the lampshade just as his own motivation to do things always seeped away. As he said this I realized how large the holes in the lampshade's 'netting' actually were. He agreed to meet a second time to explore issues of motivation and ambivalence.

Between sessions I found myself cautiously looking forward to meeting him again and thinking about the permeable function of lampshades, how their purpose is to keep some light in whilst not letting too much light out. I thought that for him daydreaming had become a form of avoidance, a state of mind, which both staved off and led to depression.

An unreliable lampshade (second session)

The client did not attend his second appointment and made no contact either by phone or letter. I found myself sitting quietly doing nothing. In his absence I thought about the lampshade being a fallible object; it seemed somehow redundant waiting on the table. I thought about how a lampshade needs a lamp and how a therapist needs a client. I liked him, I liked his art work, but it was becoming clear that the team did not think his case was a high priority and he had now (as with so many other people in his life) set up a problematic relationship with me by not attending. I thought about how the creative child became an avoiding, daydreaming teenager and how avoidance both staved off and led to depression. The image was of an unreliable object, full of good intentions, with hope and creativity leaking away. I found myself wanting to know more about his relationship with his stepfather and realized I was reluctant to hold the space for him. Keeping in mind the matrix of working with those most in need and most able to benefit, a picture formed in my mind of the usefulness of art therapy leaking away. This crystallized into a sense that this client would be unlikely to attend regularly enough for therapy to be viable. I wrote to him saying that art therapy did not seem likely to meet his needs and my feedback to the team led to his discharge from the CMHT.

Spirit long house (first session)

This man was referred by a colleague who I did not know well but liked and respected and whom in turn liked her client. He had recently not attended appointments with the team's cognitive behavioural therapist to address his long history of anxiety and depression following major heart surgery. Before his contact with mental health services he had a significant forensic history and was a recovering alcoholic, now dependent on his wife whom he had previously mistreated.

I experienced some anxiety before meeting him but when I first saw him huddled against his wife in the waiting room he struck me as being frail and defeated by life. However slowly I walked to the art psychotherapy room, he lagged behind me. He gave such a vague history and was so hard to reach in conversation that I could not form a picture of him in my mind other than a countertransference fantasy that he was presenting with early onset dementia.

He rummaged through the scrap box and chose thin card, orange paper and a thick cardboard tube. He folded the card to make a short triangular tube covered with orange paper and sawed the tube roughly into three equal pieces that he used for legs. To my surprise he described this as a 'spirit house on stilts for a tribe of honey eaters' and put a small piece of golden foil inside to represent honey. He did not know what to use for a ladder and after a cursory search took a new pencil and placed it like a slide. He said that he believes he is watched over by spirits but was at pains (understandably, given the context) to explain this was not a psychotic thought. I offered him a second session with little hope, given his history of non-attendance, that I would see him again or if he would be able to demonstrate any reflective thinking.

Between sessions I thought about his art work, a small unlikely object that set up a compelling image in my mind: honey eating spirits living communally in swampland. This seemed tentatively linked with his physical frailty and my fantasy of his mental frailty but it was hard to link to stories of his past violence.

Spirit long house (second session)

He still managed not to walk by my side on his way to the second session but readily told me that he had struggled to find a focus in the first session having taken valium to cope with the anxiety of attending. He drew an elderly depressed woman he had seen in the waiting room, using the pencil with flair and confidence and letting the character emerge from the lines. As the session progressed, the character changed into an angry prisoner, a heartless, middle-class man convicted of corruption. He added a CCTV camera in the corner. He said that his father died when he was a boy and that he had never played as a child because he had been sent out on to the streets to earn a living dealing in scrap metal. He linked this to his ability 'to make something from nothing' in the first session, adding that he had discovered drawing in Borstal aged 14. His lifelong career in scrap metal had been regularly punctuated by lost weekends and custodial sentences. He had experienced his heart surgery as traumatic and now avoided going outside.

The impression I gained was of a boy who never had a chance to play and of a man who fought his way through life on the streets but was now defeated and frightened. The image successfully brought together ageing, depression and anger, with the CCTV perhaps representing the scrutiny of assessment. Clearly he was able to use both art materials and me, and so met my criteria for ongoing work. He made good use of subsequent sessions and it emerged that in prison he had learnt always to walk behind the officers.

Discussion: a table with something on it

Returning to my comparison between *Nightsea Crossing* and art psychotherapy, I can now describe my model of assessment in similar terms:

- Two strangers meet and sit at a table for a prearranged length of time.
- One person knows the table well; for the other the whole environment is strange.
- One person's task is to ensure that the other brings materials to the table and uses them creatively.

- There will be occasional silence but it is one person's task to initiate conversation.
- There is an explicit imbalance of power between the two people.
- This sitting together is framed with the discourse of art psychotherapy.
- A decision is made about whether or not to meet again.
- The meeting is documented within the discourse of mental health.

I began this chapter thinking about the anxiety underlying the question: supposing the client sits quietly doing nothing? I have argued that in assessment a more active therapist is required, that art-making needs to be central, that conversation is beneficial and that information from the transference is crucial when there is uncertainty.

In assessment I privilege the use of art materials over use of the therapist because materials can be treated permissively and because doing so moves the gaze of the other away from the patient. Art-making gives patient and art therapist something else to look at, think and talk about. Although doing nothing can at times be a powerful communication, it does not take the assessment forward; an empty table is not a positive indicator.

If the therapist's first task is to unobtrusively facilitate art-making, the second is to simultaneously engage in conversation. Assessment calls for empathy and distance in the therapist and for what could be described as optimal levels of anxiety in the patient. There might be tension between privileging art-making and engaging a client in conversation, but it is a strategy that diminishes scrutiny whilst eliciting a verbal narrative. There are, of course, risks that result from more assertive therapist behaviour: the risk of compliance in the client and the risk that the therapist will be experienced as an intrusive object. These can be explored, whether conceptualized as part of the transference or not. As Skaife (2008) says, we need to tease out how each particular client experiences the difference between talking and art-making, because it is the intersubjective aspects of assessment that are central to the exploration and negotiation of meaning.

Silence and conversation are both objects that can have malign and benign aspects. Whilst conversation can provide maternal functions of holding and attunement, it also has a political function to do with whose narrative is privileged. If silence can be a transference communication, it can also be a political statement but, like the empty table, it is not a positive indicator.

A central point of my argument is that the difficult decisions in assessment call for information from a variety of sources, including the use of the transference. I want to revisit Tipple's (2003) concerns about the use of the transference at the expense of the socio-economic. Clearly one must not marginalize the other. Assessment is a site that requires us to be especially attuned to difference. Hogan (2003) has argued that art psychotherapy is uniquely placed to challenge and critique restrictive social norms from a cultural and interpersonal viewpoint. Art psychotherapists have an expertise in exploring the uncertainties of images within interpersonal relationships; connecting these with the client's own narrative reveals the socially constructed uniqueness of their situation. Formulations can end up erasing paradox and contradiction; attention to the socio-economic can be the anchor that ensures complexity is not avoided.

Despite my feeling of being at home in the CMHT it is important to be mindful of the way in which the discourse of mental health also functions as a system of control. Conversations about difference are highly charged, particularly so at a first meeting. It would not be surprising if mental health problems undermined a client's ability to speak directly about discrimination. If difference is played out interpersonally the transference will be similarly imbued with experiences of grievance and injustice. Up until now I have been writing as if transference and difference are in a dialectical relationship, but it increasingly seems clear to me that what we call transference is an expression of power relationships from infancy to adulthood (Heron, 1997).

To return to the third vignette, my client's second drawing began as an elderly, depressed woman and ended as a heartless, middle-class 'villain'. How better could he have brought difference (ageing, physical and mental disabilities, sexuality and class politics) to the table?

Conclusion: benefits and recommendations

To return to one of my opening thoughts about assessment: supposing the patient just sits quietly and does nothing? It now seems clear to me that although there will be times during ongoing work when it is essential for the patient to sit quietly and do nothing, and although sitting quietly whilst being observed made *Nightsea Crossing* a seminal piece of performance art, it is not helpful for a patient to sit quietly and do nothing in assessment for art psychotherapy. Assessment requires us to behave differently, to have confidence in our ability to make a decision about whether or not we can help each particular individual. When it comes to assessment, employers, regulators and the public all require a more active art psychotherapist. In a CMHT context the art psychotherapist's role in assessment is to help the client make art whilst also telling their story.

References

American Psychiatric Association (2000) *Diagnostic and Statistical Manual of Mental Disorders: DSM-IV-TR*. Washington, DC: American Psychiatric Association.

Case, C. (1998) 'Brief encounters: thinking about images in assessment', *Inscape*, 3 (1): 26–33.

Casement, P. (1985) *On Learning from the Patient*. London: Tavistock/Routledge.

Coltart, N. (1987) 'Diagnosis and assessment for suitability for psycho-analytical psychotherapy', *British Journal of Psychotherapy*, 4 (2): 127–134.

Coltart, N. (1993) *How to Survive as a Psychotherapist*. London: Sheldon Press.

De Heger, J. and Woddis, J. '*Assessment skills for art therapists*'. British Association of Art Therapists continuing professional development workshop, attended 16 September 2006.

Dudley, J. (2004) 'Art psychotherapy and the use of psychiatric diagnosis', *Inscape*, 9 (1): 14–25.

Gilroy, A. (2006) *Art Therapy, Research and Evidence-Based Practice*. London: Sage.

Heron, J. (1997) 'The politics of transference', in R. House and N. Totton (eds) *Implausible Professions: Arguments for Pluralism and Autonomy in Psychotherapy and Counselling*. Ross-on-Wye: PCCS Books.

Hinshelwood, R. (1995) 'Psychodynamic formulation in assessment for psychoanalytic psychotherapy', in C. Mace (ed.) *The Art and Science of Assessment in Psychotherapy*. London and New York: Routledge.

Hogan, S. (ed.) (2003) *Gender Issues in Art Therapy*. London: Jessica Kingsley Publishers.

Isserow, J. (2008) 'Looking together: joint attention in art therapy', *Inscape*, 13 (1): 34–42.

Learmonth, M. (2009) 'The evolution of theory, the theory of evolution: towards new rationales for art therapy', *Inscape*, 14 (1): 2–10.

Mace, C. (ed.) (1995) *The Art and Science of Assessment in Psychotherapy*. London and New York: Routledge.

Rogers, M. (2002) 'Absent figures: a personal reflection on the value of art therapists' own image-making', *Inscape*, 7 (2): 59–71.

Skaife, S. (2008) 'Off-shore: a deconstruction of David Maclagan's and David Mann's *Inscape* papers', *Inscape*, 13 (2): 44–52.

Tantam, D. (1995) 'Why assess?', in C. Mace (ed.) *The Art and Science of Assessment in Psychotherapy*. London and New York: Routledge.

Tipple, R. (2003) 'The interpretation of children's artwork in a paediatric disability setting', *Inscape*, 8 (2): 48–59.

Chapter 8

Three Starting Points (3SP)

An art-based assessment method

Kim Thomas and Martin Cody

Introduction

This chapter describes the development and use of an art-based assessment method used in our clinical work with adults who have severe, enduring and complex mental health needs. It is a method of assessment that includes a standard set of art-based tasks to introduce using art materials and making images in an art therapy context. The Three Starting Points (3SP) requires the client to respond in an active way and at a later stage introduces them to the idea of reflecting on their use of art and the art object in the presence of the therapist. For the therapist, this method allows her to witness and gather information about the client's responses to using art materials and making their art. By doing so it becomes possible to make an assessment regarding what form of art therapy might best suit the client. Furthermore, these observations provide information from which an initial art therapy formulation about the client's difficulties can be made while, for the client, these experiences can inform their decision to consent to the therapy.

First we give a general outline of common factors affecting development of our assessment model, describing how it grew from experiential workshops with student and staff groups, and how it became part of our routine clinical assessment. We then look at British art therapy assessment literature to contextualise our approach, with a brief reference to pertinent American literature. Following this the general features of our assessment method are described, introducing the 3SP. In the discussion we draw together ideas and observations about what the use of 3SP achieves and show how we use the approach through an illustrated case vignette.

Developing an art-based assessment method 1990–2000

> Through trying out different ways of working with clients and experimenting with different media and methods, the art therapist may begin to formulate ideas about creating his or her own unique tool that is tailored to fit with a particular client population.
>
> (Betts, 2005: 80)

Our assessment method arose from a combination of experiment and familiarity gained through experiential education sessions for trainees and staff drawn mainly from nursing, occupational therapy, social work and psychology. We introduced basic ideas about art therapy by encouraging the participants to use art materials which in turn revealed the strong impact image-making has expressively and emotionally. The practical part of the session paved the way for a bit of theory and this combination seemed to work well most of the time. These sessions were attended by a variety of participants of whom we had no prior knowledge and who in the main had no understanding of what happens in a therapeutic relationship within a psychodynamic frame. We were often amused at the way students responded to the encouragement to use the art materials. Many of them appeared to expect more 'chalk and talk' teaching from us and the encouragement to make a drawing or painting was received either with alarm or pleasure. This taught us to refine the form of art-making to suit the level and depth to which participants were taken so that our interventions provided optimum containment and safe exploration.

After a while we realised that these educational sessions closely reflected aspects of our clinical work, suggesting to us that the 3SP method could be useful with clients, particularly at the assessment stage of their contact with our service. An art-based method promised to be a way of working with our clients' usually limited experience of using art materials, art-making and therapy. By creating an art object and receiving a tangible experience of the therapeutic situation we estimated this would help them, as vulnerable people, to reach the serious decision to take up therapy in a more informed way. The original educational sessions guided us to structure the clinical sessions in the interests of communicating aspects of art therapy we thought clients needed to experience whilst helping them maintain a degree of comfort and control. Later, we came to think about the method as a way of communicating the *difference* of art therapy quite quickly to people who usually had several years experience of being *managed* in one way or another by members of the care system around them. Not least, the method was a way in which the therapist could get to know something about the client, his difficulties and his resources; this was an essential matter after often receiving limited or incomplete referral information. Our method also recognised the importance of hearing the client's story first hand.

The art therapy service in context

The authors provide an art therapy service located in non-residential adult psychiatry settings. Initially each of the two full-time posts were part of separate community mental health teams. We developed similar but slightly different approaches that reflected the needs and circumstances of the teams and client groups we worked with. The main part of our art therapy work was providing weekly open groups, offering long-term contact as an option within day services or as an outpatient provision. Individual sessions were also available to outpatients and initially, early on, involved a longer assessment period that sometimes blurred into therapy.

As the organisation changed it became possible to form a discrete art therapy service which enabled us to build up a more balanced caseload by increasing individual therapy. We felt this would help promote the distinctiveness of our profession within an organisation that often misunderstood art therapy, not recognising the depth and range of processes involved. We believed that working with individuals demonstrated the high level of accountability inherent in the art therapeutic relationship. This required us to develop and communicate the formal processes, structures and boundaries we saw as central to our clinical work and through which we could relate to other mental health professionals. It was the turning point that prompted us to use the 3SP as a clinical assessment method. In this incarnation, we accepted referrals from eight multidisciplinary community mental health teams spread across a large area of inner city and suburban communities, seeing clients in up to three venues. Before describing the 3SP approach we take a brief look at the current available literature for art therapy assessment.

Literature

We have found some discussion of assessment in the British art therapy literature (Wood, 1990; Case and Dalley, 1992; Hacking, 1999; Dudley, 2004) and also indirect references within case studies to the use of art materials in first sessions (Dalley et al., 1993: 34; Waldman, 1999: 12). Wood (1990) explicitly addresses the use and place of art at the beginning of therapy with adult clients, writing of her 'unspoken assumptions' (p. 7) when examining what happens on first meeting a client and identifying elements that form the basis of assessment. She reflects upon the importance of keeping in mind how a client uses the whole environment (the room, therapist, art materials and art objects), acknowledging that art therapy may be a 'strange, even alien' experience (p. 8). She registers the powerful influence these first encounters can have on future therapy through the ways in which art and the client are introduced to each other, making the point that some degree of structure or direction is inevitable when bringing the client and art together. Alternatively, Case and Dalley (1992) describe the process of 'initial interview' in purely verbal terms which seemingly does not involve the active use of art materials, this being reserved for sessions following agreement to therapy (p. 179).

Clearly there is a need to impart a lot of information during the initial stages of contact but our view is that it is essential for the client to experience using art materials and for the therapist to observe their responses before consenting to therapy. Otherwise how can an informed consent to art therapy be made? Dudley (2004) merits a mention here for two reasons: first, because she identifies that assessment is about the 'unfolding' relationship between therapist, client and the art that is made; second, because she touches on the importance of thinking about the language that art therapists employ. Ours is a similar view: that art-making and the resulting images should lead the way art therapists verbally describe the art works and respond to the client rather than the other way round.

Hacking (1999) piloted the Descriptive Assessment of Psychiatric Artwork (DAPA; Hacking and Foreman, 1994) and examined a method of rating art work. This was used originally as a psychiatric assessment tool that aimed to 'objectively define and describe psychopathological criteria of paintings' (Hacking, 1999: 327). This is closer to material on assessment tools found in American literature, most of which are intended to function diagnostically.

American art therapists have produced more literature over a longer period of time (e.g. Gantt, 1986; Williams *et al.*, 1996; Feder and Feder, 1998; Thayer-Cox *et al.*, 2000; Wadeson, 2002; Kaplan, 2003; Betts, 2005). We discern two distinct schools of thought regarding art-based assessment. Wadeson (2002), for example, takes a position closest to British art therapists, holding the view that 'assessment is a minute by minute operation that pervades therapy' (2002: 169). She believes that we continuously evaluate client progress and emphasises the need to create our own models and language to describe what we do. Her view regarding the preference for formal assessment models (a subject taught as part of American art therapy training) is that they can give false certainty if used unquestioningly or routinely without consideration of their limitations or appropriateness to the client group, the environment and the type of information being sought.

Kaplan (2003) suggests there is some value in formal art-based assessments which consider the 'global features' of client art work, citing Smith and Dumont's (1995) definition that such measures 'consider the drawing as a whole or a set of specific features in the drawing' (Kaplans, 2003: 27). This also concentrates on measuring form rather than content in the artwork, an approach apparent in other models of assessment developed by art therapists (Cohen *et al.*, 1988, 1994; Hacking, 1999; Gantt, 2004). Kaplan stresses that formal assessment tools contribute to a comprehensive art-based assessment alongside therapists' observations of how clients engage in art-making as well as discussion between therapist and client about the art work. Betts (2005) similarly reflects the value of both sides of the debate. Her analysis of art therapy assessment and rating tools highlights how far the profession still needs to go to develop robust methods, strongly advocating that therapists should be aware and informed of the range of approaches and research methods while also concluding that they need to 'identify their own personal philosophy . . . embracing both sides of this issue' (p. 77).

Gantt has contributed widely to the debate (1986, 1998, 2004; Gantt and Tabone, 2003), arguing cogently for the development of standardised assessment tools that offer us our own methods and provide ways of evaluating the effectiveness of assessment interventions. Gantt condemns what she sees as the 'rather casual approach to the process of assessment of most art therapists' (Gantt, 2004: 18), taking issue with their lack of rigour. She is particularly concerned that informal approaches have no real means of offering comparison; that the information gathered cannot be generalised and that the terms and definitions used are unclear. Gantt is supported in these views by several other art therapists, some of whom have similarly developed art-based assessment tools (Cohen *et al.*, 1988; Thayer-Cox *et al.*, 2000).

It is clear from the literature that art therapists hold a range of views regarding the form an assessment might take. The fundamental difference between them is not that they question the process of assessment per se, rather that they explore how to go about it while remaining open and receptive to the unique qualities of each individual person and their art work. There is general agreement that assessment must involve some form of comparison for it to offer meaningful material to be interpreted. Bruscia (1988) stresses the importance of being clear about the purpose of an assessment and suggests it can have one of four objectives: to be diagnostic, interpretive, descriptive or prescriptive (1988: 5). Further agreement is evident regarding the need to develop our own language which describes the image on its own terms (Dudley, 2004). Despite differences in how this might be achieved, there appears to be consensus that evaluating the form rather than the content of art produces more reliable information, although Hacking observed that her findings gave significant support to the usefulness of 'subjective criteria' (1999: 330).

We suggest that the 3SP method falls within the range of interpretive or descriptive assessment, described in the literature as semi-structured or informal in approach. It is not at this stage a standardised or otherwise validated measure. By developing our own art-based assessment method we sought to give ourselves a structure that would enable comparison to be made, give us a language to describe what the art work contains and achieve our main purpose of obtaining and providing enough information to enable informed consent to be given to proceed with art therapy. In the next section we go on to describe the 3SP approach in detail.

Introducing the 3SP

Usually an assessment will take up to three introductory meetings with the client in order for the client and the therapist to reach an informed decision to proceed to therapy and to identify what form the therapy should take. In the event of it being difficult to reach a decision, despite a clear sense that art therapy may be useful, we have the option of extending the assessment period for up to six sessions. Meetings take place in the art therapy room where a small range of good quality art materials are available. As well as observing and thinking about the client's use of the art, we encourage them to tell us in their own words what they would like help with. In addition, and with most but not all clients, we ask that they complete a Clinical Outcomes Routine Evaluation (CORE; Barkham *et al.*, 1998) as a way of registering their experiences in four areas of difficulty: their subjective sense of well-being; general functioning in life and relationships; risk of harm to self and others; and difficulties caused by specific symptoms and problems. Completion of this questionnaire is optional but, as a validated measure, it is useful to have alongside other sets of observations.

We find the first meeting is usually given to verbal exchanges of information although the art materials are on a table next to the client and the use of art materials and the 3SP are mentioned by the therapist. During the course of the meeting we give information about the service and about how art therapy 'works'.

The client may say a little or a lot about their difficulties and personal resources. Usually an opportunity arises where we ask about the client's previous involvement with art, their own 'art history'. The invitation to begin the 3SP may happen in this first meeting, especially where a client is anxious or prefers to communicate non-verbally. More typically, clients begin the 3SP at the second meeting, continuing and completing it during the third. If we find that barriers are thrown up to the use of the art materials in the second or the third session, this is considered as a significant factor in the assessment process.

The 3SP method

When it is timely to use the 3SP, the first starting point is introduced in the following way:

> 'When you're ready, choose a piece of paper and something to draw with and make a mark of some kind, somewhere on the paper. Use this mark as a starting point for a wave of colour, a splash of colour. Draw quickly and freely without thinking too much about it. Take about five minutes and I'll keep the time.'

Just before the end of the five-minute time period we say:

> 'There is a minute or so left, so bring this drawing to an end in some way even though you may feel you haven't completed it.'

When the client stops drawing, we add:

> 'Take a few moments to look at the drawing you've made and just notice what it has been like to make this drawing. Notice what thoughts or feelings went through your mind as you were making the drawing and just register those for yourself. You don't have to talk to me about your drawing now, just notice for yourself.'

This quick plunge into the use of art materials is intended to concretely introduce and encourage in the client's mind the notion that art therapy consists of action and reflection on that action in the presence of a therapist who observes silently, who also thinks and speaks and who takes some responsibility for boundaries (time keeping, reflection, etc.). This sequence is repeated and affirmed in starting points two and three that follow.

The second starting point is intended to take the client a step further in their image-making, getting them to look, notice and decide things about the first image as well as producing something new. We say:

> 'Now look for a small area of your first drawing that catches your eye in some way. It could be a colour, a line, a shape, just a small area and use this as a

starting point for a second drawing. Again work quickly and freely without thinking too much about it for five minutes and I'll keep the time.'

Near the end of the five minutes the statement to the client about noticing and registering their experience is repeated.

The client is now normally over the hurdles of touching the art materials, using them and staying with their image and it is possible to guide him towards creating a more personal image and to foster a sense of personal connection with it. Extended time is offered so that he can slow the pace down and perhaps become more absorbed in the image-making. We now say:

> 'Use any of the art materials you see on the table and make an image that is about someone, somewhere or something that matters to you. There is more time to do this image, about fifteen minutes, so you can work a bit more slowly and put as much as you can into the image.'

After the client has stopped using the art materials, we again invite him to reflect on the experience of the image-making process. In addition we state that there is now time to talk and to look together at this image and /or the previous two.

By now we have accumulated a number of observations about the client's use of the art materials, the resulting images and our internal responses. This information may suggest remarks to make to the client that, in the therapist's view, are helpful to the assessment at this point, although the therapist also has the option of holding their comments in mind for the present. In any case this third starting point should provide some indication of the client's response to specific ideas that have emerged or to the issues affecting them.

How the 3SP helps us reach a formulation

The 3SP provides an art-based structure in the context of a generic art therapy assessment through which:

1   The client has a real, practical, qualitative and informative experience of art therapy.
2   The therapist can gather information to match the client with the most helpful form of art therapy. This information encompasses the formal or global qualities of the art work; the subjective content of the image revealed by the client's verbal and non-verbal responses and also registered by the therapist's sensations and reflections in relation to the client's image;
3   As a consequence the therapist can begin to make a formulation of the client's difficulties and resources from an art therapy perspective using a method of comparison based on three broad criteria that address the client's primary needs (see Table 8.1). Each image is considered against these criteria using the therapist's *reasonable expectation of client response*

Table 8.1 3SP matching chart

A	B	C
3SP response **By and large responds as instructed** e.g. Task 1: use of colour and space available Task 2: choice of detail and clear elaboration on separate paper Task 3: image holds personal connection.	**3SP response** **Responds in expected way up to a point** e.g. Task 1: uses colour but drawing restricted Task 2: separate image using same sheet of paper Task 3: detailed image, flattened, thin quality.	**3SP response** **Wide variation from expected response** e.g. Task 1: monochrome image Task 2: minimal difference from first image Task 3: struggle to make image that has personal connection, avoids, hides, neutralises meaning.
Presentation	**Presentation**	**Presentation**
This client presents difficulties coping with the demands of their present relationships and/or work situation. The client's thinking, feeling and behaviour appear to be dominated by emotions and ideas that are active but outside his or her immediate awareness.	This client appears to connect with the task up to a point but is unable to sustain that connection.	This client presents having an extensive sense of constriction or restriction in their personal connection with their image-making.
Priority	**Priority**	**Priority**
A priority for this client is to develop a connection with and understanding of unconscious influences in their relationship to others.	A priority for this client is to experience a sense of containment and creative control. This is done through repeated interactions with their art-making and the therapist.	A priority for this client is to experience their therapy as a safe place in which to develop their capacity to think and feel.

Function of art

In the process of using art materials, marks, shapes and images are created which give a concrete and symbolic form to unconscious ideas and associated feelings.

Goals of art therapy

A goal for art therapy in this case is to give meaning to the client's unconscious thoughts and feelings as represented through their art work. This knowledge can then be integrated into the client's everyday relationships.

Function of art

Making artwork provides the client with a repeated experience of having contact with and separation from representations of their internal world.

Goals of art therapy

A goal for art therapy in this case is to provide an experience of contact and separation from the art work which becomes explicit and available for reflection and thought.

Function of art

Making a piece of artwork introduces the client to a potentially safer, less traumatic means of relating to others. It provides a means through which art materials can be creatively controlled and experimented with, enabling the client to develop a more flexible or spontaneous response towards something outside him or herself.

Goals of art therapy

A goal for art therapy in this case is the strengthening of the client's ability to feel in control of their thoughts and feelings. They can learn that relationships with others can be a reasonably good experience that need not be intrusive or overwhelming.

and of *variance* from that expectation. This is key to the way our assessment model works

4   The therapist also holds in mind the wealth of assessment art work gathered over time which serves to guide her thinking, offering a further means of comparison.

Our norms for comparison originated in the student workshops. Although not set up for this purpose, they offered us a broad enough range of what an 'expected' response to the 3SP tasks were likely to be that could be used to establish a norm. This notion of 'reasonable response' and 'client variance' is a recognisable part of standard research methodology, which we think helps strengthen the 3SP as a valid model.

The information or data created by the client in response to the 3SP can be matched and considered against the chart, enabling the therapist to make broad comparisons. This offers a means of capturing the therapist's appraisal and judgement of the degree to which the client varies from the 'expected responses' to the 3SP tasks. It takes the therapist through a series of 'thought steps' which assist in the formulation and identification of goals for art therapy that can be discussed and agreed with the client. Evidence indicates that if agreement occurs about treatment goals, a better outcome for therapy is indicated (Norcross, 2002).

Our experience of using the 3SP indicates that it has two distinct functions: first, it gives the client a qualitative and informative experience of art therapy; second, it provides the therapist with a means of gathering information – about the individual and for the purposes of comparison. It allows observation of a client's responses when using art materials and making art which can be thought about in relation to their emotional and psychological needs and their abilities (for example, decision making, imaginative play, etc.). These needs and abilities can be considered through the formal qualities of the art work while the subjective content is responded to mainly through discussion with the client, the therapist's reflections on their countertransference and their aesthetic responses to the art work. These functions are achieved because the graded, 'therapy-like' experience of the 3SP provides the client with an introduction to using art in the presence of another, attentive person which is likely, as mentioned earlier, to be their first experience of the *difference* of art therapy. We take the view that the therapist's task from the beginning is to create an opportunity for the client to experience a sense of emotional safety while registering the risk and play involved in using art materials to make images in a therapeutic framework. The three activities communicate the basic approach and values of art therapy; that of activity, reflection and personal agency, introducing the notion that the client is going to be active on their own behalf.

The 3SP also gives clients permission to play and to be spontaneous, the response to which is usually of great assessment interest. We try not to underestimate the complexity of this. While it may be very freeing, as intended, equally it may be unexpected or challenging. This permission is given in the context of 'warm-up' through the first and second 3SP tasks when the therapist emphasises working quickly and freely without thinking too much. The client's responses may include comments about 'being at school', 'doing art with my kids', expressing concern about doing what has been asked or possibly requesting further instruction. It is not uncommon for clients to ask if they should use a new piece of paper for each task; this is reflected back by the therapist to the client as their choice. Some will then decide to find a space on the first image and create their elaboration there. We also think about atypical and exceptional responses such as using charcoal or clay after receiving the suggestion to make 'a splash of colour'. In each case the therapist must register how an unexpected response like this one *feels* to her.

The second starting point, the invitation to elaborate part of the first image, also implies taking things 'a bit further', to think more deeply and make some conscious decisions about what to choose, invent and imagine. Again the client's responses, compared with expected responses, are instructive. For instance, a second drawing that appears indistinguishable from the first is a noticeably different result to what the therapist might reasonably expect; this is of interest in its own right.

While the first and second task may result in a wide range of visual responses, abstract to figurative, the third generally always brings out figurative, descriptive imagery that is expected to have more personal content. This is intentional and meant to provide clients with a direct experience of using image-making to specifically represent something that holds personal meaning. For the therapist it helps her to assess whether the client has a capacity to symbolise their subjectivity. Through this task the client's significant material can become visible and available to both client and therapist. The therapist observes and assesses the impact of this.

A further important element of the 3SP is to give the client and the therapist an experience that is manageable. Both parties cannot know how the power of image-making will play out with *this* client, *today* working with these materials and *this* therapist. The starting points are intended to give a client just enough of a dip into art-making and reflection, and to being held in mind by the therapist, in order to see if the client can cope. The different viewpoint that the therapist provides can, as we know, open things up. This can be experienced as intrusive or create a satisfying feeling of being understood at a deep emotional level, or it can be completely ignored. This connects with why we have more than one assessment meeting. The gaps between sessions provide valuable time for both client and therapist to think further about what they made of the experience. The therapist is also able to observe and assess what the client appears to have done with his experience of the previous session (here we concur with Wood, 1990).

The therapist can also expect communications from the client at the counter-transference level. Information about the client's difficulties and resources is gathered through the therapist's active and detailed empathic observation of external and internal events. By internal events we mean the therapist's observation of her own subjectivity, her own thoughts, feelings and bodily sensations in relation to the client's activity and communications. Some key communications that we watch out for are as follows:

- the extent to which the client appears to communicate through symbolisation or through projection
- the degree to which the client appears to understand and respond to the 3SP directions and the tasks of activity and reflection
- the degree to which the client appears to accept at some level, the therapeutic relationship
- to try out and test what a client does when the therapist shares some of her thinking, e.g. a trial interpretation.

Case vignette

The following case vignette provides an example of the way in which we use 3SP. It portrays Amy, a woman in her early forties, and describes in detail the second session when Amy felt ready to use the art materials.

The first meeting was entirely verbal. Amy gave a history of her life and current concerns and Kim answered questions Amy had regarding how art therapy might help. Boundaries such as confidentiality were discussed and they agreed to meet for a second time to use art materials.

Amy arrived early for the second meeting and was clearly in a very fragile state because, she said, things were so awful at home. She spoke of sleeping much of the time in order to avoid and forget her difficulties, then added that she wanted to disappear and not exist. Amy told Kim that her nurse was currently managing the quantity of medication available to her due to a fear that she might seriously harm herself.

Kim asked Amy what she wanted to do, describing how they could continue either by talking or using the art. Amy was keen to use the art hoping it might help her forget. Kim suggested it could offer ways of thinking about what was happening. Amy was still willing to continue so Kim suggested the first starting point, to make a mark and so on, as described earlier. Amy selected red paper and felt pens, sitting at the table by the window. Taking a moment before starting, she proceeded to work steadily for several minutes before sitting back and looking towards Kim who asked her to reflect on her drawing and then to use a detail as a starting point for a second image (Figure 8.1). Using the same paper Amy drew more quickly this time and when stopping seemed to struggle to breathe as if anxious.

Kim invited Amy to bring the drawings to another part of the room so they could look at them together. Amy said she had felt an initial desire to cover the paper with black lines but feared Kim would think her crazy. Next came lines that were breaking up, like her. Most important was Amy's struggle to make connections between the lines and how it seemed impossible because there wasn't enough room. She said she felt frustrated by this and, in order to end the first drawing, had decided to add more lines and red eyes.

It was the eyes that became the starting point for Amy's second image, culminating in them 'bleeding' and the last one becoming her eye. Amy's response to this was to use the words 'nothing', 'empty', 'not connected with anything'.

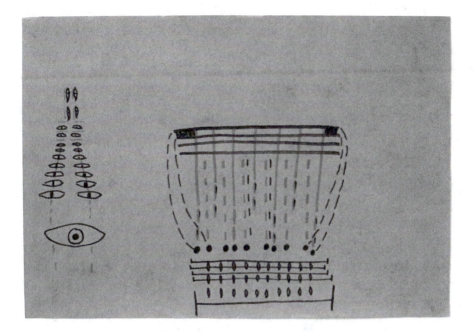

Figure 8.1 Starting point two.

She described seeing herself as 'nothing', 'not existing'. At this point Amy struggled to remember an alternative idea from the first meeting about how she could build up her confidence in the fact she does exist and that it is okay. Amy could not tolerate further thinking about this. What she could do was be concrete about needing others to help her through this difficult time, including coming to the second assessment meeting so as not to let Kim down.

Introducing the third task, Kim asked Amy to create an image about something important. At first she struggled to depict a cat but then found a means to continue and create her two cats in a cage with no door or key (Figure 8.2). From what Amy said about the drawing, Kim's view was that the cage itself was her, while at the same time she was inside it. Amy said this was a prison and somewhere safe because she was in a place of no responsibility. Amy and Kim had reached the end of the session and agreed to a third meeting in a week's time when they would decide whether art therapy could be helpful and what form it might take. Kim noticed that Amy seemed brighter as she left the session.

For the third meeting Amy and Kim discussed what she made of her experiences from the previous sessions and from this they reached an agreement to proceed into individual therapy.

Reflecting on Amy's responses to the 3SP tasks, Kim concluded that she was 'someone who responds in an expected way up to a point' (see Table 8.1,

Figure 8.2 Starting point three.

column B, p. 160). While her capacity to take in and respond to the tasks and to her artwork fluctuated, there was evidence that she could connect with art-making, creating images that held personal meaning and could hold something of this experience in her mind between sessions. It was also clear that Amy would struggle to maintain these connections so a main task of art therapy was likely to involve repeated contact and separation through her relationship with her art work and the therapist.

Conclusion

After using the 3SP method with a number of clients over several years we are reasonably confident that the qualitative and informative experience it offers to the client results in the intended outcomes. For the client these are that it communicates that art therapy primarily happens through activity (the use of art materials) and reflection by client and therapist on that activity. It demonstrates the difference of art therapy to other forms of psychological and psychiatric intervention, fostering informed consent. For the art therapist the method produces enough visual material from which observations and responses can be gathered to construct an initial formulation. The goals and purpose of art therapy for the client in assessment, arrived at through the 3SP method and described in the matching chart (see Table 8.1), does not in itself indicate directly whether individual or group sessions should be offered. However, we think that there are valid inferences to be made drawn from the priorities for therapy that appear, particularly in pathways B and C in Table 8.1, where questions of 'a safe place' and 'a sense of containment and creative control' may influence the discussion with the client about the choice of individual or group sessions.

References

Barkham, M., Evans, C., Margison, M., McGrath, G., Mellor-Clark, J., Milne, D., and Connell, J. (1998) 'Clinical Outcome Routine Evaluation (CORE). Outcome measure. (F)', in CORE System Group *CORE System (Information Management) Handbook.* Leeds: CORE System Group.

Betts, D. (2005) 'A systematic analysis of art therapy assessment and rating instrument literature'. Dissertation. Florida State University School of Visual Arts and Dance. Available at http://www.art-therapy.us/images/Donna_Betts.pdf

Bruscia, K. (1988) 'Standards for clinical assessment in the arts therapies', *Arts in Psychotherapy*, 15: 5–10.

Case, C. and Dalley, T. (1992) 'Art therapy with individual clients', in C. Case and T. Dalley *The Handbook of Art Therapy*. London and New York: Routledge.

Cohen, B., Hammer, J. and Singer, S. (1988) 'The diagnostic drawing series: a systematic approach to art therapy evaluation and research', *Arts in Psychotherapy*, 15: 11–21.

Cohen, B., Mills, A. and Kwapien-Kijak, A. (1994) 'An introduction to the diagnostic drawing series: a standardized tool for diagnostic and clinical use', *Art Therapy: Journal of the American Art Therapy Association*, 11 (2): 105–110.

Dalley, T., Rifkind, G. and Terry, K. (1993) *Three Voices in Art Therapy*. London and New York: Routledge.

Dudley, J. (2004) 'Art psychotherapy and the use of psychiatric diagnosis. Assessment for art psychotherapy', *Inscape*, 9 (1): 14–24.

Feder, B. and Feder, E. (1998) *The Art and Science of Evaluation in the Arts Therapies. How Do You Know What's Working?* Springfield, IL: Charles C. Thomas.

Gantt, L. (1986) 'Systematic investigation of art works: some research methods drawn from neighbouring fields', *American Journal of Art Therapy*, 24: 111–118.

Gantt, L. (1998) 'A discussion of art therapy as a science', *Art Therapy: Journal of the American Art Therapy Association*, 15: 3–12.

Gantt, L. (2004) 'The case for formal art therapy assessments', *Art Therapy: Journal of the American Art Therapy Association*, 21 (1): 18–29.

Gantt, L. and Tabone, C. (2003) 'The Formal Elements Art Therapy Scale and "draw a person picking an apple from a tree"', in C. Malchoidi (ed.) *Handbook of Art Therapy*, New York: Guilford Press.

Hacking, S. (1999) 'The psychopathology of everyday art: a qualitative study'. Unpublished MPhil thesis, University of Keele. Available at: http://www.wfmt.info/musictherapy world/modules/archive/stuff/papers/Hacking.pdf

Hacking, S. and Foreman, D. (1994) 'DAPA. Descriptive Assessment of Psychiatric Artwork. Pilot study', in D. Betts (2005) 'A systematic analysis of art therapy assessment and rating instrument literature'. Dissertation. Florida State University School of Visual Arts and Dance. Available at: http://www.art-therapy.us/images/Donna_Betts.pdf

Kaplan, F. (2003) 'Art based assessments', in C. Malchoidi (ed.) *Handbook of Art Therapy*. New York: Guilford Press.

Norcross, J. C. (ed.) (2002) *Psychotherapy Relationships that Work: Therapist Contributions and Responsiveness to Patients*. New York: Oxford University Press.

Smith, D. and Dumont, F. (1995). 'A cautionary study: unwarranted interpretations of the Draw-A-Person Test', *Professional Psychology: Research and Practice*, 26 (3): 298–303.

Thayer-Cox, C., Agell, G., Cohen, B. and Gantt, L. (2000) 'Are you assessing what I am assessing? Let's take a look!', *American Journal of Art Therapy*, 39: 48–67.

Wadeson, H. (2002) 'The anti-assessment devil's advocate', *Art Therapy: Journal of the American Art Therapy Association*, 19 (4): 168–170.

Waldman, J. (1999) 'Breaking the mould. A woman's psychosocial and artistic journey with clay', *Inscape*, 4 (1): 10–19.

Williams, K. J., Agell, G., Gantt, L. and Goodman, R. F. (1996) 'Art-based diagnosis: fact or fantasy?', *American Journal of Art Therapy*, 35: 9–31.

Wood, C. (1990) 'The triangular relationship. The beginnings and endings of art therapy relationships', *Inscape*, Winter: 7–13.

Chapter 9

The Levick Emotional and Cognitive Art Therapy Assessment (LECATA)

Myra F. Levick

Why assessment?

In 1980 I had the opportunity to spend five weeks as the 'art lady' at the Hampstead Child Therapy Clinic in London. I participated in team meetings conducted by Anna Freud and would like to quote her description of the 'Diagnostic Profile' completed for each child in that setting:

> The Diagnostic Profile . . . is intended to draw the diagnostician's concentration away from the child's pathology and to return it instead to an assessment of his developmental status and the picture of his total personality. . . . diagnostic assessment is more than a mere intellectual exercise for the clinician. It is, in fact, the only true guide to the choice of therapeutic method.
>
> (A. Freud, in R. S. Eissler *et al.*, 1971: 184)

That experience and the need to learn more culminated in my years of teaching graduate art therapy students. It also served as a model and basis for my original work (Levick, 1983), and the development of the Levick Emotional and Cognitive Art Therapy Assessment (LECATA) in 1986.

In the beginning

Only after the American Art Therapy Association (AATA) was established in 1969, of which I was a Founder and first President, were education standards adopted and new graduate programs in this field evolved. The scope of this chapter cannot begin to document the growth of art therapy as a new discipline in the USA (see Junge, 2010). Nevertheless, from my perspective as an officer of AATA and an educator in the field, I know that the 19+ graduate programs that developed early on, as well as those that followed, did not embrace a unified core curriculum. They were diverse in focus – some psychodynamically oriented embracing art in therapy, while others embraced art as therapy. A few continue to design their program based on an educational model as opposed to a clinical one.

Trained as an art therapist in a psychoanalytic milieu, I developed the first year art therapy curriculum at the (then) Hahnemann Medical College and Hospital based primarily on the writings of Margaret Naumburg but including those of other published practicing art therapists at that time. As a result of my graduate work in which I was introduced to other psychological theories including behavioral, reality oriented, self-actualization and family therapy, the second year curriculum incorporated these approaches as well.

This diversity impacted the development and use of assessments. The psychodynamic, developmentally oriented programs were concerned with and sought out assessments that would support diagnosis in order to direct and define treatment goals. Those schools that adhered strictly to art as therapy were not committed to the concept of assessment and diagnosis. For many this implied labeling and this was not acceptable. The problem for educators like me, who truly believed in evaluating patients and making diagnosis to develop treatment plans, was the parity of available assessments, other than psychological tests. The best known and most frequently utilized were the Draw A Person (DAP) test (Machover, 1949), Human Figure Drawing (HFD) test (Koppitz, 1968) and the House-Tree-Person (H-T-P) test (Buck, 1948).

While committed to learning and teaching diagnosis and educating our students to appreciate the importance of such a procedure in the process of treating mentally ill patients, we did not introduce or utilize known psychological tests. The graduate program at Hahnemann was anchored strongly in the belief that art productions were a graphic representation of both symbolic and realistic, conscious and unconscious thoughts and feelings. We believed that graphic images were the road to the unconscious and that the role of the art therapist was to facilitate the artist's/patient's understanding and interpretation of their image. Therefore, in those early years, our core art therapy course work, co-taught by me and a staff psychiatrist, was to review patient art work and their associations. As we explored and learned about the relationship between the manifest and latent content of the imagery we began to understand the interface of this relationship with symptom formation, levels of development, examples of coping skills and diagnosis. My forte as an instructor emerged in the area of ego mechanisms of defense and their manifestations in patient art work. With the growth of programs and art therapy as a profession, we exchanged ideas and new knowledge with our fellow educators to create art-based assessments.

The early art therapy assessments

To place my assessment within the context of the history and development of art therapy, I will only (briefly) discuss those art-based assessments created by practicing art therapists in the United States. Projective techniques incorporating art productions were described as early as 1958 by Emanuel Hammer. His work, which follows the development of the use of projective drawings, has been revised and reprinted as recently as 1997. Hammer's focus was and is on drawings produced in psychological tests. However, in his very first edition Margaret Naumburg states:

> The fundamental difference between projective drawings obtained in psychological tests and those produced in art therapy is that test designs are necessarily prompted and those in art therapy are entirely spontaneous.
>
> (in Hammer, 1958: 513)

It soon became apparent that if we art therapists were to develop our own assessments it would be essential for us to adopt procedures that encompassed prompting images as well as facilitating spontaneous creations.

One of the earliest and best known assessments is the family art therapy system designed and published by Kwiatkowska (1978). Her evaluation consists of six drawings and reveals a wealth of information, but the scoring is complex and, while used by many art therapists, it was never standardized. Following Kwiatkowska's ground-breaking approach to the diagnosis of family systems and family dynamics, Wadeson (1980) and Landgarten (1987) designed assessments incorporating the concept of mutual drawings for couples and families in therapy. Wadeson's work revealed information on the relationship, while Landgarten's approach is described as 'clinical and intuitive' (Feder and Feder, 1998: 279). Landgarten pursued assessment further and developed a family art psychotherapy assessment consisting of three drawings. Although there is no normative data on these assessments they are considered valuable clinically by art therapists working with mentally ill individuals and dysfunctional families. It is interesting to note that these assessments were all designed by psychodynamically oriented art therapists. Wadeson and Landgarten also founded and directored graduate art therapy programs.

By the mid-1980s and 1990s there were more graduate art therapy programs, more practicing art therapists and a growing interest in developing art therapy assessments. But those providing standardized, normative data were still few and far between. Some demonstrated significant research. For example, Cohen and his colleagues (1986) created the Diagnostic Drawing Series (DDS) and have continued to accumulate thousands of series supporting the reliability and validity of this instrument (Cohen *et al.*, 1994). The Formal Elements Art Therapy Scale Scale (FEATS) was Linda Gantt's doctoral dissertation (1990). She created a test which consists of a single drawing and is designed specifically to address diagnostic categories. Her research has demonstrated reliability and validity when used for mentally ill populations. First published in 1983, the Silver Drawing Test (SDT) measured cognitive skills and adjustment, and was revised in 1990 to measure depression and emotional needs. Silver (2005) also developed the Draw A Story test that assesses aggression and depression through art; this assessment has considerable data to support its use in working with disturbed adolescents.

The primary direction of these assessments was to identify pathology in mental patients concomitant with diagnostic categories listed in the American Psychiatric Association's *Diagnostic Manual* available at that time. But at the same time there was also an effort to create a developmental art therapy evaluation. Williams and Wood (1977) created a rating scale to measure progress in art therapy made by children with physical, emotional and intellectual handicaps. Based on 'well documented literature', the conclusions for progress seen in the art work for this population must 'rest ultimately on assumption and inferences' (Feder and Feder, 1998: 288).

The LECATA

My initial training in a psychoanalytic milieu influenced my direction as an educator in art therapy and I gravitated toward a greater understanding of mechanisms of defense. I became a student and teacher of Sigmund and Anna Freud's work on this subject (S. Freud, 1959; A. Freud, 1966). Halsey (1977) discusses Sigmund Freud's views on art productions. He writes that Freud 'freely admitted that he had approached the psychological insights of artists with the primary intention of confirming the findings he had made in examining unpoetic, neurotic human beings' (p. 99). Halsey believed that Freud's 'greatest service to the understanding of art is his convincing reminder to us that works of art cannot be comprehended without an awareness of the dynamic role psychological factors play in both their creation and assimilation' (p. 101).

I began to question the efficacy of focusing only on dysfunctional behaviors that generally indicated pathology and that the absence of indicators of pathology indicated normality. In the 1970s a course on intellectual development, based on Piagetian theory, was added to our graduate training program. An affiliation between Hahnemann Hospital and Medical College and Anna Freud's Hampstead Child Therapy Clinic in London gave me an opportunity to seek permission to illustrate her book (A. Freud, 1966). Work in Anna Freud's clinic during my sabbatical provided the basis for my PhD dissertation, which later became a text for art therapy students and practicing art therapists around the country (Levick, 1983). Students and colleagues began to utilize the criteria I had designed for recognizing defenses in drawings in their clinical work with child and adult patients and the data were disseminated among us (Levick, 2009).

In 1986, Janet Bush, a graduate of the art therapy program at Hahnemann and then director of the Clinical Art Therapy Program at Miami-Dade County School District, spearheaded the development of the LECATA. Her objective was to develop a single art therapy assessment that would bridge the communication gap between the art therapists, school counselors and psychologists. Her motivation was based on the fact that within the 11 art therapists in her employ there were at least five different assessments being used to determine diagnoses, treatment plans and progress for the special needs population she was responsible for. With permission from the administration, she invited me to meet with her staff and develop an assessment based on my book that would meet her requirements. What was planned as a one-year project extended over a three-year period (Levick, 1989, 2009).

It is the relationship between normal emotional and cognitive development that shaped the basis for the creation of the LECATA. This assessment was designed to be given at the first meeting with a student/patient and provide information on strengths and weaknesses, pathology versus normality, in order to develop a treatment plan. It was copyrighted by me in 1989 and soon became an integral part of the Miami-Dade school program for children with special needs. Over the years, Janet Bush and I, and later Craig Siegel, an art therapist in the Miami-Dade School District and current Director of that program, continued to conduct training seminars and supervision for those professionals interested in utilizing this instrument for adults and children identified as having a broad range of cognitive and/ or emotional problems.

After many years of reviewing positive feedback and data from art therapists, working with children and adults from many different populations, I concluded it was time to develop a normative study. The assessment was based on my previous work (Levick, 1983), the literature reviewed and years of experience looking at drawings from an emotional and cognitive developmental perspective. Kellogg (1970), reported the influence of age and level of maturation on children's drawings. Hardiman and Zernick (1980) described a relationship between Piaget's cognitive theory and the artistic development of children's drawings. Lowenfeld (1969) looked at the nature of creativity on a developmental hierarchy. Koppitz (1968) based her Human Figure Drawing (HFD) test, a psychological evaluation of children's human figure drawings, on the earlier works of Goodenough (1926) and Machover (1949, 1953, 1960, 1978). She, more than other investigators, identified emotional indicators manifested in children's drawings in relation to symptoms and behavior. In addition to the pros and cons on the reliability and validity of projective techniques as a diagnostic instrument (Hammer, 1958), there was little in the literature supporting psychoanalytic theory and particularly defense mechanisms of the ego as the basis for a drawing assessment. This became my goal.

Defining test criteria

To record the presence of defenses in drawings required that I define criteria for identifying each defense. To simplify the process, I selected only the original 19 defenses outlined by Anna Freud (1966). Table 9.1 (Levick, 1983) provides the definition for the defense (Moore and Fine, 1968) unless otherwise noted, and the criteria I authored for identifying defenses in drawings.

The relationship between normal emotional and cognitive development as seen in the art work of children is developed in Table 9.2 (Levick, 1983). The cognitive criteria are based on Piaget's cognitive stages of development (Rosen, 1977); artistic lines are based primarily on the work of Kellogg and O'Dell (1967). Psychosexual sequences of development are based on Sigmund Freud's theories (1969) and the hierarchical scale of ego mechanisms of defenses are listed as defined by Anna Freud (1966).

According to the literature, children do not normally begin to scribble until at least 18 months of age and shapes making recognizable images do not normally appear until around two and a half to three years of age (Kellogg and O'Dell, 1967). While defenses are described from infancy up through the years, obviously they cannot be identified in graphic images until a child begins to draw.

Table 9.1 Definitions and criteria for identifying defenses manifested in graphic productions

Defense	Definition	Criteria
Incorporation	A type of introjection and an early mechanism in the process of identification. It connotes a change by imagined oral consumption of an object (person). This defense is usually employed by individuals with psychoses, impulsive disorders, oral character disorders and states of severe regression.	Symbols, forms, objects are encapsulated within other forms. Usually seen in graphic images which also indicate regression and are not generally differentiated from regression.
Projection	The source of a painful impulse or idea is perceived to exist in the external world.	Manifested in the earliest scribbles where some part of the self is represented in the lines and forms drawn on paper or some object symbolic or representative of the outside world. In more sophisticated drawings some characteristic, thought or feeling of the artist is attributed to some form or object other than self.
Regression	A defense employed by the individual when confronted with anxiety related to a specific aspect of maturation. A retreat to an earlier phase of psychosexual development and/or cognitive functioning that is manifested in behavior.	Graphic productions will reflect regression when age appropriate representations of psychosexual, cognitive and artistic development are drawn side by side with lower age representations.
Undoing	A defense employed by the ego when an unacceptable aggressive or sexual wish is expressed and symbolically reversed or undone.	Graphically represented when the artist has changed the representation of an object, form or idea so that it is reversed, drastically changed, or obliterated (undone).
Reversal	A defense employed by the ego when an unacceptable aggressive or sexual wish is expressed and symbolically reversed or undone.	Feelings, situations, facts related to objects, people in the environment, represented graphically, in a 'reversed' form.

Term	Description	Graphic manifestation
Denial	A primitive defense employed by the ego to keep from awareness some painful aspect of reality. Fantasy may also be utilized to erase from the mind that unwanted part of reality.	Absence of body part and/or some realistic aspects of persons or objects in the environment, where the artist is known to be capable of appropriate representation.
Avoidance	A primitive and natural defense seen in normal development and utilized to keep an unconscious wish of narcissistic mortification from conscious awareness. Sexual and aggressive impulses are usually related to object of function being avoided.	Graphically, represented by side (profile), and/or back views of objects and people in the environment.
Imitation	A less primitive defense than incorporation in the process of identification. This is a conscious process (A. Freud, 1965).	All representational images reflect imitation of objects and persons in the environment.
Symbolism	In the process of evolving symbols, the ego provides a way (language) to disguise the unacceptable.	Manifested in drawings through subjective graphic representations of specific objects and thoughts.
Isolation	A process in which ideas are split off from feelings which were originally associated. Used to avoid guilt, carry through a logical train of thought without contamination and distraction.	Manifested in the representation of objects drawn singly on a page; unconnected inappropriately to other forms on the page; ungrounded; separate in or from the environment.
Isolation of affect	Same process as above.	Concretely manifested in graphic images where color (an expression of feeling) is used or omitted inconsistently and erratically in depicting a specific form or object.
Identification	An unconscious process of the ego in which the individual takes on one or more characteristics of another person and becomes like that person; usually a loved or admired person.	Images that graphically represent figures that reflect some aspects of the artist and those of some other object (person) real or fantasy, in the environment.
Identification with the aggressor	The same process leading to identification, but coupled with fantasy. This allows for reversal of the role of the victim and identification with the real (or perceived) aggressor in the environment (A. Freud, 1966).	Represented in drawings of figures that reflect aspects of the artist and some aspects of an object or person in the environment who is perceived as the aggressor.

(Continued overleaf)

Table 9.1 Continued

Defense	Definition	Criteria
Repression	A process in which the ego keeps from conscious awareness an idea or feeling that may have been experienced consciously or curbed before it reached consciousness.	Inherent in images of figures produced after age 6–7 where some aspects of sexual characteristics are omitted. Observed in drawings where known unacceptable thoughts and feelings are transformed or omitted.
Displacement	A process in which repressed feelings for an object (person) are experienced in relation to another person who becomes a substitute for the original object.	Manifested in graphic productions in which the artist's known or perceived thoughts and feelings about one object are expressed graphically in relation to another object.
Reaction formation	This process follows repression of an unacceptable idea or feeling and replaces it in conscious awareness with one that is its opposite.	This is manifested in graphic images that reflect positive, acceptable ideas and feelings about a situation or object that is known to have been the source of (repressed) negative and/or painful ideas and feelings.
Rationalization	An unconscious process that allows an individual to justify in a tolerable fashion, by plausible means, intolerable feelings, behavior and motives (Kolb, 1969).	Seen graphically in images that reflect an early attempt at a logical resolution to an unacceptable idea or feeling related to a specific situation or person in the environment.
Introjection	Utilized in the process of identification in which the child carries out caretaker's (parent's) demands as if they were his own even when parents are absent.	Assumed to be present in graphic images reflecting identification and values of person(s) identified with.
Intellectualization	A process in which the ego binds instinctual drives through intellectual activity.	A more elaborate, sophisticated representation of a logical resolution to an unacceptable idea or feeling than the manifestation of rationalization.

Definitions: Moore and Fine (1968) *The Glossary of Psychoanalytic Terms and Concepts* (unless otherwise noted). *Criteria:* Levick (1983).

Table 9.2 Correlation of developmental lines of cognitive, artistic, psychosexual sequences, and defense mechanisms of the ego appropriate for those periods of development

Two and a half to five years of age

Cognitive	Artistic	Psychosexual	Defenses
Early preoperational	**Period of progression from random scribbles to shapes**	**Anal stage to Oedipal stage**	**Early anal (2½–3)**
Thinking is centered			Regression
Only one aspect of something is attended to at a time		Issues:	Incorporation
	Shapes become combined	Self-assertion	Reversal
Thought is representational		Control	Undoing
Symbolization present	Forms become balanced	Regulation of body functions	Denial
Differentiation between self and others present	Beginning of spatial organization		**Late anal (3–4½)**
			Avoidance
Animism, realism, artificialism in thought still present	Emergence of recognizable objects		Projection
			Symbolism
			Oedipal (3½–5)
			Imitation

Five to seven years of age

Cognitive	Artistic	Psychosexual	Defenses
Animism, realism, artificialism may appear in form of magical thinking	Period of greatest quantitative difference within sequences	**Post-Oedipal stage**	Identification
		Major task is process towards resolution of Oedipal conflict and identification	Reaction formation
Early development of logical consistency	Period of greatest qualitative differences between sequences		Isolation
			Isolation of affect
Early development of capacity to understand concepts of classification and conservation	Images reflect movement from a single aspect to an object or form to pictorial drawing		Displacement
		Positive identification with same sex parent	Simple rationalization
More than one aspect of something can be attended to at the same time	Several objects may be related in one drawing	Negative identification with parent of opposite sex	Earlier defenses are available and used appropriately
	Pictorial images begin to tell stories		**Note: defenses may develop in any sequence between 5–7 years of age.**

(Continued overleaf)

Table 9.2 Continued

Seven to 11+ years of age

Cognitive	Artistic	Psychosexual	Defenses
Concrete operational period	**Period of realistic representation of familiar objects**	**Latency period**	Repression
Thinking moves away from centration and irreversibility		Infantile past closed off	Reaction formation
	Relationships are drawn in more orderly fashion	Parental attitudes and values internalized	Simple rationalization
Cognitive reversibility emerges			Introjection
Advancement to a higher stage of equilibrium occurs	Elevated base lines and ground lines appear	Child's attention directed primarily toward learning and peer relationships	Denial
			Identification
Reasoning can move from the beginning to the end of a process	Horizon line		Identification with the aggressor*
	Human figures move from static to action		Intellectualization
	More frontal and profile views of people and objects appear	New role models perceived in teachers, movie and television stars, and sports heroes	**Notes: Earlier defenses are available and used appropriately. Defenses may develop in any sequence between 7–11+ years of age.**
	Houses and people take on a more proportional relationship		*This defense may appear at any age

Criteria: Levick (1983, 2009).

Therefore Table 9.2 begins with the early pre-operational stage, and parallels with the period of progression from random scribbles to shapes and the anal stage to the Oedipal stage. Investigators in these domains also agree that by around age 11 all normally functioning children have progressed through the concrete operational stage, are now able to realistically represent familiar objects and are moving from the post-Oedipal stage through latency into the pre-adolescent stage. By around 11 years of age all normal individuals have acquired the cognitive skills and ego mechanisms of defense to progress from adolescence to adulthood (Levick, 1983, 2009).

Designing the tasks

The process began by reviewing the tasks in the family art therapy evaluation by Kwiatkowska (1978). The first, the free drawing is intended to create a sense of freedom and was adopted as a logical beginning. The request for a story about the image was added. This task also serves as a baseline in identifying defenses most frequently used by the individual being tested. A picture of the self was selected for the next image and the direction is to draw a picture of your whole self at the age you are now.

Doing a scribble and making a picture from it was first described by Naumburg (1947) and viewed by many as efficacious. This initially became the third and fourth tasks but were later numbered the third task with two parts. Making something from the scribble was also seen as providing an estimation of the degree to which an individual was capable of cognitive abstraction. Piaget's theory maintains that abstraction is a higher level of cognitive functioning and generally appears in formal operations, around 11 years of age. The family drawing was essential and is the last task. The testee is asked to draw a picture of a family – if possible your family. The objective here is to make it as open a request for a family picture as possible.

The tasks selected seemed very satisfactory in providing the direction for imaging the developmental indicators being sought, with the exception of introjection. This defense is very important in the identification process as an individual begins to carry out the demands of the caretaker (parent) as if they were his or her own, even when parents are not present. The criteria I had developed assumed that the values of the person(s) the artist was in the process of identifying with were also in the process of being internalized by the artist. Therefore, the fourth task was a request to draw a place that is important, and to explain why that place was chosen. In preliminary testing, I found that children under the age of five years were not sure what the word important meant. It was agreed that for children between three and five years the task would be to 'draw a place you would like to be' and for children of six years and up the task would be to 'draw a place that is important'. For both conditions, the subject was asked to tell why that place was chosen.

A manual was designed and has been revised twice, most recently in 2001. It includes a specific, structured format to ensure consistency in administration, a scoring procedure, a script for presentation of each of the five tasks, a score sheet for each task and a scoring worksheet. In addition there is a sample report form, a sample case and blank score sheets that may be copied. This manual, previously available directly through this author, is now appended to the publication of the normative study and may be copied as needed (see Levick, 2009).

Summary of normative study of LECATA

Having designed the LECATA, it then had to be tested. Two hypotheses were formulated:

1   There will be no statistically significant difference between the chronological age and the age performance in the cognitive and emotional domains overall

and on each task. The two-tailed *t* tests, which assume the two samples have been drawn from the same population, tested this hypothesis.

2   There will be a statistically significant relationship between the chronological age and the age performance in the cognitive and emotional domains overall and on each task. The Pearson *r* (2-tailed) tested this hypothesis. Data were analyzed using the Statistical Package for Social Scientists (SPSS) program.

The LECATA was administered to 330 normal emotional and cognitive development children, kindergarten through sixth grade. All were enrolled in six different public schools in the Palm Beach School District, Florida, chosen because the population is diverse and included Caucasian, Afro-American, Hispanic, Haitian and Asian students. The proposal for this study was accepted by the director of research for this school district, permission from principals and school counselors was granted and consent forms from parents/guardians were obtained. All subjects were coded by grade and number with names known only to the school counselor. The subjects were all considered normal by school counselors and teachers, 'normal' being defined as functioning on an average level in the classroom, without any behavioral or emotional problems and not on any medication.

Results indicated that kindergarten, first and second grade children were performing age appropriate or better in both domains supporting both hypotheses. However, beginning with third grade through fourth and fifth grade, the data indicate performance one to three years lower than chronological age in both domains. The two hypotheses were proven statistically only sporadically in the first, second, third and fifth grade children, but more often than not throughout much of the data the mean scores for all tasks, with the exception of task three (the scribble drawing), fell within one year on the half-year parameters defined in the LECATA. It was expected that this study would provide further validity insofar as the population tested was defined as normal children, all performing on an age-appropriate level for each grade. Reliability, documented over the years, is also confirmed with consensus scoring of drawings by several art therapists.

Implications

The LECATA is therefore consistent with the literature identifying normal and cognitive development, but important questions were also raised. As the work was in process and data were being accumulated, I presented it to different groups of mental health professionals, including art therapists, psychologists and school counselors. Many concurred that a new norm was emerging, agreed by every group I met with to be emanating from what we have come to call the 'latchkey child'; this being one whose parents are either both working, separated or divorced and who comes home to an empty house after school. The more I thought about this obvious slowing down of development that had been identified, the more I realized the need to return to the literature which formed the basis for the assessment (Levick, 2009).

Piaget concurred with Sigmund Freud that there is neither a 'purely affective state' nor a 'purely cognitive state' and believed they are parallel (Rosen, 1977: 30). Piaget also regards 'affective operation' equal to cognitive operations in the concrete operational stage (p. 26). Defining developmental lines in the process of assessing normality versus pathology, Anna Freud (1965) emphasized throughout that in normality the cognitive and emotional domains will develop in a parallel process.

Many investigators of child development, peers and those that followed Piaget and the Freuds, concurred that their research more often than not was consistent with those of Piaget and Anna Freud. Those identifying ego development, defining a developmental relationship between the cognitive and emotional domains, also agree that a parallel process is necessary for adaptation. This prompted another question: is there a significant correlation between the average cognitive score and the average emotional score? I returned to my SPSS program and performed a Pearson *r* test on the average cognitive score and the average emotional score for each grade (see Table 9.3).

I found that kindergarten, first, second and third grades were significant at the highest level, indicating that in these grades the children tested were developing normally, i.e. according to the literature. Cognitive and emotional domains were progressing in a consistent, parallel process. In fourth, fifth and sixth grades, the student's cognitive and emotional scores were also progressing in a parallel process. While still statistically significant, these scores are a little less so. I believe that is consistent with the data that indicated they were moving slower than the younger children.

Conclusion

These data clearly indicated that we are indeed seeing a new norm, reflecting a decline in the norm postulated and accepted in the past. It must, however, also be

Table 9.3 Correlation of average cognitive and average emotional means for each grade – Pearson *r*

Grade/average M	Average cognitive	Average emotional	Pearson r
K/5.9	6.4941	5.8084	0.371**
1st grade/7.02	7.3234	6.1921	0.635**
2nd grade/7.8614	7.7641	6.6714	0.606**
3rd grade/9.1646	7.9118	6.9703	0.574**
4th grade/9.9641	8.5257	7.1396	0.654**
5th grade/10.7495	8.5638	7.3593	0.370*
6th grade/11.8932	8.7302	7.5129	0.573**

** Correlation is significant at the 0.01 level (2 tailed).
* Correlation is significant at the 0.05 level (2 tailed).

acknowledged that when past norms were defined there was no television or computers, more families were intact and fewer mothers were in the workforce. There is obviously a great need for more research to examine the relationship between these critical changes in our society and cognitive and emotional development in normal children.

No children included in the study gave any indication in their classroom performance that there were any learning problems or emotional problems. However, in the 330 children tested, the results of the LECATA, as predicted, indicated problems in four children. I will briefly describe two in order to demonstrate the efficiency of the LECATA in identifying children at risk. One child in kindergarten produced drawings that suggested there may be some minimal brain dysfunction. This child's teacher informed me that she was also beginning to suspect this. Armed with the results of the LECATA, she was more prepared to follow this child's progress. The drawings of a third grade child were age appropriate for all tasks. However, the figure drawings in task two and task five, while complete, were strange and suggested a medical problem. I shared these images and my views with his teacher. She informed me that the 'condition' I suspected was familial and she too was beginning to see signs of it in the classroom. It is not unusual to see manifestations of medical problems and/or physical impairment in drawings.

Finally, something must be said about the whole process of assessment. Not all art therapists are interested in traditional assessments of the mentally or cognitively impaired individuals they may be working with and some view assessments and diagnosis as labeling their patients and find this objectionable. However, from my years of experience as a clinician and educator I may state:

> It is inconceivable to me to consider art therapy tasks for someone, child or adult without assessing that individual's strengths, weaknesses, levels of functioning cognitively and emotionally. Also, completing this study, I am more convinced than ever of the efficiency and efficacy of art as an assessment not only in the area of establishing treatment goals, but in identifying children and adolescents at risk before symptoms erupt in the environment.
>
> (Levick, 2009: 131)

Example of an assessment

Because this assessment is based on normal development as described above, it is an efficient and useful evaluation of any individual presenting symptoms of pathology. It identifies levels of functioning in both domains and data for establishing treatment goals, and can be used across the age range with different patient populations. In order to demonstrate its utility I will now describe giving the LECATA to a 74-year-old man whom I will call Samuel Richards. While visiting the south of Florida, he was referred by a colleague. He and his wife were seeking further evaluation of his cognitive and coping skills in lieu of a diagnosis of Alzheimer's disease. This diagnosis was made approximately four years prior to this evaluation, and he was put on medication and involved in a writing program. He and his wife reported there had been no further regression. Prior to the diagnosis Samuel was a successful business man and at this time he was continuing to handle some personal financial matters.

Assessment results

The criteria for the LECATA are based on the correlation of developmental lines of cognitive, artistic, psychosexual sequences and defense mechanisms of the ego appropriate for these periods of development (Levick, 1983) and the criteria for identifying defenses manifested in graphic productions (Levick, 1983) The scores indicating developmental level of functioning are approximate and reflect performance at this time (see Table 9.4).

Summary

Based on graphic representations, Samuel Richards's average cognitive and emotional scores are both nine years and six months. It should be noted here that most investigators of cognitive and emotional development conclude that all individuals acquire the necessary skills in domains for adolescent and adult passage

Table 9.4 LECATA assessment results

Task/title	Cognitive levels	Emotional levels
1	8.5–9.5	8.5–9.5
A free drawing/story (Figure 9.1 A clown)	Beginning of elaboration proportions; gender identity; sequencing of story	Symbolism; isolation; identification
2	8.5–9.5	8.5–9.5
The self (Figure 9.2 Sam – the artist)	All parts in detail; beginning of elaboration	Identification
3	10.5–11+	10.5–11+
A scribble and image (Figure 9.3 Garbage)	Deliberate, inventive, creative	Intellectualization
4	9.5–10.5	9.5–10.5
A place that is important (Figure 9.4 My home)	Grounded; image shows complete pictorial sequencing	Introjection
5	7.5–8.5	7.5–8.5
A family (Figure 9.5 My family)	Beginning of sequencing; verbalizations cohesive	Regression; isolation; identification

to maturity between the ages of ten and a half and 11+ years (Levick, 1983). This patient therefore appears to be functioning at a level around one year below what would be normal for an average adult. However, the scores are not consistent and this is discussed below.

In the first task (Figure 9.1), Samuel was hesitant, declaring he could not draw and did not know what to draw. With encouragement and a reminder that this was not an art class, he produced a smiling male figure and elaborated with a hat, big ears and buttons. He then decided the figure was a clown, with big ears that he flaps, who wears funny clothes and does funny things. Compared to the following images, there is some regression and isolation. The image of self in task two (Figure 9.2) remains the same cognitively and emotionally. By task three (Figure 9.3), Samuel appeared to be more comfortable and demonstrated here his ability to think abstractly. Using the lines of the scribble as directed, he deliberately and creatively drew a cartoon face, a kite and a dog. The score for both domains here is very close to average for an adult individual.

Samuel then drew a grounded image of his home to represent a place of importance (Figure 9.4). In discussing this drawing, he described not only the house, but the property and the circumstances under which he purchased it many, many years ago. At this point he also described in detail how he became involved in his father's business and some of the successful changes he made. In this instance his memory appeared to be very intact. Emotionally the image still reflects isolation and limited affect.

In the final task, a drawing of the family (Figure 9.5), Samuel included himself, his wife, his two children and their children. In reviewing the drawings at a subsequent meeting, he had no idea why he omitted his children's spouses. While the gender differentiation is complete, the figures are again isolated and regressed when compared to figures in tasks one and two.

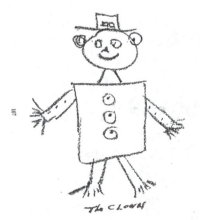

Figure 9.1 A clown.

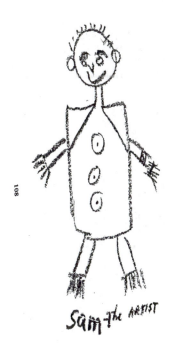

108

Figure 9.2 Sam – the artist.

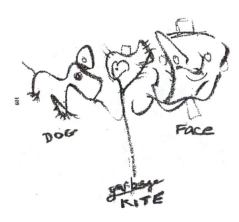

109

NAME: Samuel Richards
LECATA TASK #: 3
SCRIBBLE AND IMAGE
TITLE: Garbage
DATE: 3/19/01

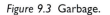

Figure 9.3 Garbage.

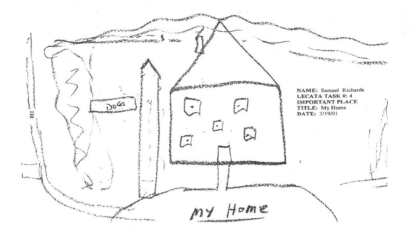

NAME: Samuel Richards
LECATA TASK #: 4
IMPORTANT PLACE
TITLE: My Home
DATE: 3/19/01

Figure 9.4 My home.

NAME: Samuel Richards
LECATA TASK #: 5
FAMILY
TITLE: My Family
DATE: 3/19/01

Figure 9.5 My family.

Conclusions and recommendations

Given the diagnosis of Alzheimer's disease, it is encouraging to note that there is no evidence here of any organicity. Mr Richards had no difficulty closing circles and meeting corners in his forms. None of the images was slanted and the lines are definitive. While it is known that Mr Richards functioned on a level well above average, was creative and successful in business, the performance here did not indicate a major loss of cognitive ability. Emotionally, his images suggest some depression, and when asked how he felt about his illness he reported that he feels very isolated. He acknowledged that he does not particularly like the writing program, but agreed it helps him focus. It is believed that art therapy sessions, structured to creating images rather than psychotherapy, would also aid in supporting his capacity to focus.

References

Buck, J. (1948) 'The H-T-P technique. A qualitative and quantitative scoring manual', *Journal of Clinical Psychology*, 4: 317–396.

Cohen, B. (1986/1994) *Diagnostic Drawing Series – Drawing Analysis Form*. Alexandria, VA: Author.

Cohen, B., Mills, A. and Kijak, A. (1994) 'An introduction to the Diagnostic Drawing Series: a standardized tool for diagnostic and clinical use', *American Journal of Art Therapy*, 34 (1): 19–23.

Eissler, R. S., Freud, A., Kris, M., Lustman, S. L., and Solnit, A. (eds) (1971) *The Psychoanalytic Study of the Child*, Vol. 26. Chicago: Quadrangle Books.

Feder, E. and Feder, B. (1998) *The Art and Science of Evaluation in the Arts Therapies*. Springfield, IL: Charles C. Thomas.

Freud, A. (1965) *Normality and Pathology in Childhood: Assessments of Development*. New York: International Universities Press.

Freud, A. (1966) *Ego and Mechanisms of Defense*. New York: International Universities Press.

Freud, S. (1959) 'Further remarks on the neuron-psychoses of defense', J. Strachey ed. and trans. *The Standard Edition of the Complete Works of Sigmund Freud. Volume 3*. London: Hogarth Press.

Freud, S. (1969) *An Outline of Psychoanalysis*, trans. J. Strachey. New York: Norton.

Gantt, L. (1990) 'A validity study of the Formal Elements Art Therapy Scale'. Unpublished doctoral dissertation. University of Pittsburgh, Pittsburgh, PA.

Goodenough, F. (1926) *Measurement of Intelligence by Drawings*. Yonkers-on-Hudson, NY: World Book Co.

Halsey, B. (1977) 'Freud on the nature of art', *American Journal of Art Therapy*, 16: 99–104.

Hammer, E. (1958) *The Clinical Application of Projective Drawing*. Springfield, IL: Charles C. Thomas.

Hammer, E. (1997) *Advances in Projective Drawing Interpretation*. Springfield, IL: Charles C. Thomas.

Hardiman, C. W. and Zernick, T. (1980) 'Some considerations of Piaget's cognitive structuralist theory and children's artistic development', *Studies in Art Education*, 23 (3): 12–19.

Junge, M. (2010) *The Modern History of Art Therapy in the United States*. Springfield, IL. Charles C. Thomas.

Kellogg, R. (1970). *Analyzing Children's Art*. Palo Alto, CA: Mayfield.

Kellogg, R. and O'Dell, S. (1967) *The Psychology of Children's Art*. New York: Random House.

Kolb, L. C. (1969) *A Psychiatric Glossary*. Washington, DC: American Psychiatric Association.

Koppitz, E. (1968) *Psychological Evaluation of Children's Human Figure Drawings*. New York: Grune and Stratton.

Kwiatkowska, H. (1978) *Family Therapy and Evaluation Through Art*. Springfield, IL: Charles C. Thomas.

Landgarten, H. (1981) *Clinical Art Therapy: A Comprehensive Guide*. New York: Brunner/Mazel.

Landgarten, H. (1987) *Family Art Psychotherapy*. New York: Brunner/Mazel.

Levick, M. (1983) *They Could Not Talk and So They Drew: Children's Styles of Coping and Thinking*. Springfield, IL: Charles C. Thomas.

Levick, M. (1989) 'Reflections: on the road to educating the creative arts therapist', *Arts in Psychotherapy*, 11: 57–60.

Levick, M. (1998/2003) *See What I'm Saying: What Children Tell Us Through Their Art*. Boca Raton, FL: Myra F. Levick Books.

Levick, M. (2009) *The Levick Emotional and Cognitive Art Therapy Assessment: A Normative Study*. Boca Raton, FL: Myra F. Levick Books.

Lowenfeld, V. (1969) 'The nature of creative activity', in R. Alschuler and L. Hattwick *Painting and Personality*. Chicago: University of Chicago Press.

Machover, K. (1949) *Personality Projection in the Drawing of the Human Figure*. Springfield, IL: Charles C. Thomas.

Machover, K. (1953) 'Human figure drawings of children', *Journal of Projective Techniques*, 17: 85–91.

Machover, K. (1960) 'Sex differences in the developmental pattern of children as seen in Human Figure Drawings', in A. Rabin and M. Haworth (eds) *Projective Techniques with Children*. New York: Grune and Stratton.

Machover, K. (1978) *Personality Projection in the Drawing of the Human Figure*. Springfield, IL: Charles. C. Thomas.

Moore, B. and Fine, B. (1968) *A Glossary of Psychoanalytic Terms and Concepts*. New York: American Psychoanalytic Association.

Naumburg, M. (1947) *Studies of Free Art Expression in Behavior of Children as a Means of Diagnosis and Therapy*. New York: Coolidge Foundation.

Rosen, H. (1977) *Pathway to Piaget*. Cherry Hill, NJ: Postgraduate International.

Silver, R. (1983) *Silver Drawing Test of Cognitive and Creative Skills*. Seattle: Special Child Publications. Revised 1990 and retitled *Silver Drawing Test of Cognitive Skills and Adjustment*. Mamaroneck, NY: Ablin Press.

Silver, R. (ed.) (2005) *Aggression and Depression Assessed Through Art*. New York and Hove: Brunner-Routledge.

Wadeson, H. (1980) *Art Psychotherapy*. New York: Wiley.

Williams, G. and Wood, M. (1977) *Developmental Art Therapy*. Baltimore, MD: University Park Press.

Chapter 10

Tending to the 'art' in art therapy assessment

Linda Gantt

> If art therapists have a system of thinking about art and what in that art gives us important clinical information, we'd better be the ones to direct the studies on it, because chances are no one else is thinking that way.
>
> (Gantt in Goodman *et al.*, 1998: 64).

Introduction

This chapter focuses on issues in art therapy assessment that are related to the formal variables of two-dimensional art exclusive of content. It views those issues from a historical perspective and discusses key concepts of a rating system for global characteristics in art. Whilst research on projective drawings in psychology has come to a dead end, art therapy research shows considerable promise. By stressing the components of art-making rather than content and symbolism, art therapists can develop assessments more consistent with their ways of understanding art.

The utility of this approach is that it focuses on form, not content. This makes it easier to compare one drawing to another. Such comparisons can be done between groups, across cultures or across time (for example, with an individual before, during, and after treatment). If we want to know whether there are differences in the ways various groups of people draw, the approach described below provides a practical method that can be subjected to statistical measures.

History of using art in assessment

Beginning in the mid-1800s, European investigators attempted to find diagnostic information in the art made by residents of psychiatric asylums (MacGregor, 1989). These attempts were rudimentary since the art was done voluntarily by a small percentage of residents. However, this small sample did suggest some potential for using art for assessment.

Cesare Lombroso (1888), an Italian psychiatrist, published examples of psychiatric art that greatly influenced other writers but no systematic studies based on a truly representative sample of patients have been done. This is a major difficulty in the art therapy literature. Although case studies can be compelling and the accompanying art work may be interesting, they are weak as scientific evidence. Truly scientific studies may be relatively rare in our field but they are possible (Gantt, 1998; Julliard, 1998; Kaplan, 2000).

As physicians developed medications for psychiatric conditions, art work became an important monitor of patients' responses. Lehmann and Risquez (1953) used finger painting to gauge the effectiveness of the first major tranquilizer on clinical state. Their requirements for an art-based assessment still apply – that it could be used with any patient, is repeatable, and can be reliably rated.

The influence of projective drawings

Psychologists developed projective drawings to assess intelligence, developmental level, family dynamics, and emotional issues (for example, Goodenough, 1926; Buck, 1947; Machover, 1949; Hammer, 1958a; Burns and Kaufman, 1970, 1972; Di Leo, 1970, 1973, 1977). This literature considerably influenced art therapy, especially in the United States. However, psychology and art therapy have different historical roots, and therefore different assumptions, theories, materials, methods of collecting, and units of analysis. Table 10.1 compares the two approaches as they originally developed over 50 years ago.

Unfortunately, in borrowing ideas from the psychologists, art therapists did not thoroughly examine the underlying premises. Now, psychologists are jettisoning not only projective drawings but other projective assessments shown not to be scientifically sound (Lilienfeld *et al.*, 2000). The American Psychological Association has recommended that graduate psychology programs cease teaching projective techniques (Grove, 2000). This makes it imperative that art therapists explain why we would espouse using art in assessment when others are abandoning it.

Why has the psychological approach found so little scientific support? There are several factors: the assumption that specific signs or details are correlated with certain personality traits has not been borne out; the scoring systems have not been reliable; and specific signs have not been found to be valid. (See Lilienfeld *et al.*, 2000 for a detailed critique of projective drawings, the Thematic Apperception Test, and the Rorschach test.)

From impressionistic judgments to systematic study

During the same time that the psychologists were investigating projective drawings, art therapists were developing their own approach. Influenced by Naumburg (1966) and Kramer (1979; Kramer and Schehr, 1983), most art therapists were interested in 'free' art, including paintings and sculpture.

Paula Howie and I began pairing characteristics of drawings done in separate mental health agencies with diagnostic criteria from the *Diagnostic and Statistical Manual: DSM-III* (American Psychiatric Association, 1980). We found drawings

Table 10.1 Comparing two systems for using drawings in clinical settings

	Psychology	Art therapy
Approach	Nomothetic (characteristics of groups).	Idiographic (characteristics of an individual).
Materials	Testing materials (writing paper and pencils).	Art materials (paint, pastels, clay, etc.).
Theory	Psychometric.	Psychodynamic.
Emphasis	Molecular (atomistic details).	Global (formal variables).
Form of reporting	Research report; formal report or evaluation.	Case studies.
Directions or instructions	Specified subject; timed administration.	'Free' choice of subject and materials (Rubin, 1984); specific series of drawings (Ulman, 1975; Silver, 1982, 1988; Cohen et al., 1988); or specific sequence of materials (Kramer and Schehr, 1983).
Fundamental assumptions	Art reflects enduring character traits.	Art reflects changing psychological state.
Purpose or goal	Assessment; evaluation.	Therapy.
Method of determining meaning	Closeness of fit with specific theory; meaning is independent of artist's associations.	Solely dependent on associations of the artist; symbolic speech (Naumburg, 1966).

Source: From L. Gantt (2004). Adapted with permission.

done by people with the same or similar diagnoses to be stylistically similar. Our professors at the George Washington University, Elinor Ulman, Hanna Yaxa Kwiatkowska and Bernard I. Levy, had been studying how art carried psychological information (Levy and Ulman, 1967; Ulman and Levy, 1968, 1973, 1974) but these studies were quite rudimentary. Kwiatkowska (1978) approached the problem the most systematically, having developed a system that applied a numerical rating to certain global variables.

Exactly how does art carry diagnostic information? Carmello Tabone and I began studying drawings of a Person Picking an Apple from a Tree (PPAT) gathered in a psychiatric hospital. We soon realized that keeping the content of the drawings the same and standardizing the instructions, and the materials (white paper sized 8½ by 11 inches and a set of 12 colors of 'Mr. Sketch'™ markers) made it easier to compare the pictures. This became an art-based rating system, the Formal Elements Art Therapy Scale (FEATS; Gantt and Tabone, 1998; Gantt, 2001).

Pattern matching as a crucial process

Sifting through the PPATs we began to see common features in the form of the drawings (for example, integration, use of space and color, and line quality). Although we did not realize it at first, we were doing pattern matching. This is the process we use when we see a painting for the first time but immediately recognize it as being by a certain artist with whose works we are familiar. It is the method used by art historians who classify works according to styles or schools. It is also the fundamental process used by medical specialists who compare visual characteristics of cells and gross tumors to make a diagnosis. When experienced art therapists see diagnostic clues in drawings, they are performing an instantaneous pattern-matching process (Gantt, 2000: 44). This visually oriented approach is considerably different than the sign-based one for projective drawings and is much more consistent with the essentials of art-making. Rita Simon's classification of styles (1991, 1997) – Archaic Massive, Archaic Linear, Traditional Massive, Traditional Linear, as well as the transitions between them – is essentially a pattern-matching process. These patterns are comprised of certain combinations of 'lines, forms, colours, and tones' (Simon, 1997: 4) postulated to 'present four different ways of comprehending life, (p. 181). Schaverien (2000) is performing another type of pattern matching when she considers the formal components of art to assess whether an image is 'embodied' or 'diagrammatic'.

However, making a match by comparing it with the style of other drawings is just the beginning of a system for art therapy assessment. One must describe the pattern's attributes without including features of a particular drawing that may not be crucial to the pattern. Once the pattern has been put into words, it becomes possible to measure the components of the pattern and thus apply numbers. This then forms the basis for truly scientific research.

It is easy to demonstrate the capacity of art therapists to make a pattern match even though they may not be able to articulate the specific components. I asked naïve judges to assign PPATs to one of six diagnostic categories (Williams et al., 1996) and gave them only 15 seconds to make a decision. The results showed they could determine a diagnostic category by form alone and do so far better than by chance.

Advantages of focusing on global variables

We came to understand that the variables that interested us were the graphic equivalent of psychiatric symptoms. Our work thus far (Gantt and Tabone, 1998, 2003) shows that there are specific patterns of the formal, global variables in patient art, especially in the Axis I categories of schizophrenia, major depression, bipolar disorder, and the organic disorders. These four major disorders have been the most frequently studied and are the ones with the longest history, dating back 2000 years (Klerman, 1980; Lehmann, 1980; Lipowski, 1980).

Working with global variables culled from the literature and our clinical observations, we paired them with symptoms described in the *DSM-III* (American Psychiatric Association, 1980). For the four diagnoses above we developed 14 scales that we termed the Formal Elements Art Therapy Scale (FEATS). Five scales can apply to a variety of drawings: Prominence of Color, Implied Energy, Space, Integration, and Line Quality. Six more scales can be used with realistic drawings with recognizable subject matter: Realism, Developmental Level, Person, Logic, Details of Objects and Environment, and Color Fit. Two other scales, Perseveration and Rotation, come from the Bender-Gestalt Test. While most PPATs have high scores on these two scales (that is, *no* perseveration or rotation) these scales are especially useful in studying organic disorders. One scale, Problem Solving, is specific to the PPAT. This scale is unexpectedly proving to be an especially useful one in distinguishing one group from another (Gantt, 1990).

The variables can be assigned numbers, making it possible to use statistical tests. Each scale is constructed with a range from 0 to 5 with half-point increments. Thus, one can measure relatively small changes in a variable, increasing the utility of the FEATS for gauging therapeutic response.

Examples of PPATs from four major diagnostic categories

We collected the PPATs used in this chapter from patients in a psychiatric hospital during the first few days after admission; presumably, the drawings captured the symptoms at their peak.

Major depression

The general pattern for major depression is characterized by a relatively small amount of space, a lack of a three-dimensional environment, and a person drawn in a simple fashion or as a stick figure (see Plate 6, situated between pp. 100 and 101). This means lower FEATS scores on the scales for Space, Details of Objects and Environment, Person, Prominence of Color, and Implied Energy but higher scores on Logic, and mid-range scores on Problem Solving. It is easy to make the connection between these formal variables and the cardinal symptoms of depression, that is, loss of energy, depressed mood, and diminished ability to think or concentrate (American Psychiatric Association, 1994: 327). There are no extra details in the environment, such as ground lines or items other than a person, apple, and tree, and no Perseveration or Rotation. This drawing has only one color, dark green, (a score of 2 for Color Fit) and occupies less than 25 per cent of the page (score of 1 on the Space scale).

The term *depression* covers a large territory, ranging from 'dysthymia' to 'major depression severe with psychotic features'. This wide spectrum includes depressive moods brought on by or associated with grief or physical illness. Future research could examine the changes in PPATs in response to antidepressants as well as study the correlation of the degree of depression (as measured by independent assessments) with the FEATS scores.

Schizophrenia

The graphic equivalent of the positive symptoms, specifically, disorganized speech or behavior, are manifest in PPATs as relatively low scores on the scales for Logic, Integration, Color Fit, Problem Solving, and Realism. Material from hallucinations and delusions can appear as peculiar additions, such as the witch in Plate 7 (situated between pp. 100 and 101).

A problem in studying these PPATs is finding a reasonably sized sample of individuals with the correct diagnosis in order to make some useful generalizations. The diagnostic criteria for schizophrenia were considerably narrowed with the *DSM-III* because the earlier definitions were 'probably far too inclusive' (American Psychiatric Association, 1994: 273). Psychotic symptoms can be part of severe depression or mania, thus mimicking acute schizophrenia. The positive symptoms (such as hallucinations) and the negative symptoms (such as flattened affect and alogia) can manifest at different times in a person's life, leading to considerably different clinical presentations (American Psychiatric Association, 1994: 282). Furthermore, some apparently negative symptoms may be the result of factors such as side effects from medication or 'environmental understimulation' (American Psychiatric Association, 1994: 277). These symptoms could plausibly be displayed in PPATs as lower scores on the Implied Energy and Details of Objects and Environment scales.

In PPATs done by those with chronic schizophrenia, there is a depleted quality, consistent with the negative symptoms. For example, flat affect seems to be manifest as lower scores on the Prominence of Color scale and avolition seems associated with lower scores on the Implied Energy scale.

The varied course of schizophrenia and the fact that 'no single symptom is pathognomonic' of it (American Psychiatric Association, 1994: 274) suggests that longitudinal studies would be especially important in seeing how the illness influences art. Specific medications and changes in dosage will be important variables in both short- and long-term research.

The organic disorders

Often, a PPAT done by a person who has the early symptoms of a disorder such as Alzheimer's shows poor integration, poor line quality, and simplified forms. Sometimes, the person and the tree are fused making it impossible to make a rating on the Person scale. As the disease progresses, the PPAT becomes unrecognizable as such. Many PPATs done by people with advanced dementia merit a score a 0 or 1 on almost all FEATS scales because the variables cannot be distinguished from one another. Plate 8 (situated between pp. 100 and 101) shows moderately severe Perseveration. Something of the quality of 'treeness' is suggested and one might plausibly pick out details that indicate roots, trunk, branches, and apples, but this requires some effort from a rater. The color choice is related to the task (dark green) but the color is used for the entire picture so one cannot determine if the form on the left might have been intended to be the person. Instead, it appears to be a smaller version of the form on the right.

In the past, dementia implied a downhill course; in the current *DSM* dementing disorders 'may be progressive, static, or remitting' (American Psychiatric Association, 1994: 137). The PPATs collected over successive months or years from patients with Alzheimer's show increasingly less identifiable content. They can be visually 'busy' with considerable Perseveration (large numbers of dashes and dots) and extraneous marks.

Bipolar disorder

In PPATs done by people in a hypomanic state many of the FEATS scores are in the 4 to 5 range. The Details of Objects and Environment are excessive and sometimes inventive, although occasionally bizarre. The use of Space is generally a 5 as is Prominence of Color and Implied Energy. Not only is every inch of space filled, but often all the available colors are used. Plate 9 (situated between pp. 100 and 101) has a sky filled with pink, purple, and blue clouds in layers of orange, pink and turquoise. There are many apples and the artist expended considerable energy in drawing the top of the tree.

While Plate 9 is an example of hypomania, it does not represent the extent of the range of PPATs done by people with bipolar disorder. As the mania increases, a person may spend less time doing the PPATs but may add more bizarre or psychotic features. In the more florid stages of mania, it is more likely that a person will not put in many details. However, that same person may dash off a number of drawings in a short time.

Confounding variables

Art is an expression of many aspects of an individual and is influenced not only by age and mental status but cultural knowledge/ethnic group, artistic training, fine motor skills, attention span, creativity, color perception, vision, visuospatial capacities, and motivation. One confounding variable is artistic ability or formal art education (Carlson *et al.*, 1973; Cressen, 1975; Kaplan, 1991). A crucial question for future research is: does artistic ability mask symptoms in drawings and if so, to what degree?

Another confounding variable is that of intelligence. Lilienfeld *et al.* (2000) state: 'Global indexes [of overall quality in projective drawings] also tend to have moderate correlations with measures of intelligence, although we do not endorse them as substitutes for standard IQ measures' (p. 54). Controlling for intelligence, and for educational level, in studies of both adults and children is imperative.

Addressing problems raised by projective drawing research

Should the problems in projective drawing research deter us from using art in assessments? Not at all! As I see it, the difficulties are not due to a lack of information in drawings but to problems recognizing what kind of information it is. I agree with the criticisms leveled at previous studies. They are important but should not be the reason for discarding drawing as a means of assessment. I argue that we should revisit the underlying assumptions and rework them rather than discarding the whole enterprise. My suggestions are as follows:

1   Change the focus from personality disorders to the acute clinical disorders.
2   Investigate the use of color more thoroughly.
3   Study changes in drawings over time.
4   Use a different model for researching symbolism in art.
5   Refine art therapy rating systems so they are more reliable.

Change the focus from personality disorders to the acute clinical disorders

Although certain mental disorders have been described in similar ways over centuries, psychiatric diagnosis did not become truly systematic until the third edition of the *Diagnostic and Statistical Manual: DSM-III* (American Psychiatric Association, 1980). This was a crucial advance because this classification system distinguished the Axis I from the Axis II disorders. This made it possible to study the acute clinical disorders separately from the enduring and presumably lifelong personality disorders (American Psychiatric Association, 1987: 16). I cannot emphasize enough the importance of this division for it permits a focus on those disorders that have the greatest influence on artistic productions.

We have not seen any groupings of formal variables that seem sufficiently distinctive to separate the Axis I disorders from one another. This is also the case with Axis II disorders; investigators have had problems in reliably separating one from another. Some writers have suggested putting the personality disorders into 'clusters' because of the difficulty in making clear categories. The authors of the *DSM-IV* have cautioned:

> It should be noted that this clustering system, although useful in some research and educational situations has serious limitations and has not been consistently validated. Moreover, individuals frequently present with co-occurring Personality Disorders from different clusters.
>
> (American Psychiatric Association, 1994: 630)

We are convinced that the *pattern* of formal variables in the drawings of people with Axis I disorders is one that art therapists can recognize or identify, even though they may not be able to describe that pattern in so many words.

Investigate the use of color more thoroughly

Studying art without studying color seems inconceivable. The psychologists could not see any notable differences in color use since they usually restricted the drawing materials to pencils. The chromatic version of some projective drawings (Hammer, 1958b) is not commonly used. There are several dimensions worthy of study. The particular colors selected, the method of their application, and the amount of color can convey various moods independent of subject matter (Kreitler and Kreitler, 1972). Difficulty identifying and applying colors has implications for assessing those with Alzheimer's disease or with other organic brain disorders. If an individual has color blindness or a color weakness (Renfroe *et al.*, 1987), this will almost certainly be manifest in art.

Study changes in drawings over time

Because psychologists rarely collected a series of drawings over time, they seldom saw the drastic changes in drawings as a person recovered from an acute psychiatric episode. They incorrectly assumed that what appeared to be a drawing style was relatively static and, therefore, was an indication of personality *traits*. Art therapists who work in acute care psychiatric facilities can attest to the rapid and often predictable changes in art as a person is given medication or responds to the therapeutic milieu. Understanding that art is influenced by clinical state gives a particular advantage in being able to monitor changes.

In our outpatient trauma clinic (www.traumatherapy.us) we routinely administer a battery of assessments along with the PPAT as our pre- and post-treatment testing (Gantt and Tinnin, 2007). Another treatment we monitor with PPATs is electroconvulsive therapy (Gantt and Tabone, 2003). PPATs are easier to administer to confused patients than some other assessments such as the Beck Depression Inventory. In addition, we can use art to investigate changes in other conditions such as epilepsy (Anschel *et al.*, 2005), migraine (Vick and Sexton-Radek, 2005), frontotemporal dementia, cerebral vascular accidents, and various types of traumatic brain injury (http://weburbanist.com/2009/07/12/stroke-of-genius-abilities-borne-of-brain-damage/; http://www.abc.net.au/science/articles/2005/05/17/1370231.htm; http://www.abc.net.au/science/articles/2006/10/20/1769611.htm).

Use a different model for researching symbolism in art

Lilienfeld *et al.* (2000) criticize what they term the semantic associations in projective drawing research that underlie the 'sign approach' (p. 47). The assumption behind this is that particular details and the manner in which they are drawn can be interpreted as if those details had linguistic equivalents of psychological traits, for example, sharply pointed fingers being equated with hostility or aggressiveness. The problems with these 'dictionaries' that were developed following Freudian and Jungian theories are discussed in the FEATS manual. We stress that the utility of the FEATS scales is that the material we are measuring is not symbolic but 'of a different type and order of information' and that 'such material does not have multiple meanings' as do symbols (Gantt and Tabone, 1998: 53). Understanding symbolic material in art therapy requires other methods of study. It would be better to use models from anthropology, art history, and literary criticism (Gantt, 1986, 1998) that recognize and explain the one-to-many relationship between an element and its meanings than to use the sign approach.

Refine art therapy rating systems so they are more reliable

Strictly speaking, researchers must assess the reliability of a rating system each time it is used. For a variety of reasons, what may be reliable with one sample may not be with another. Several studies have demonstrated acceptable inter-rater reliability on most FEATS scales (Williams *et al.*, 1996; Lande *et al.*, 1997; Munley, 2002; Gussak, 2004; Anschel *et al.*, 2005). However, we question whether demonstrating test/retest reliability is necessary, given that we assume the Axis I disorders have a fluctuating course (especially when most people are given medication for these diagnoses).

Advantages of the FEATS and the PPAT

Art therapists seeing people with acute and severe psychiatric disorders are in a privileged position for collecting assessment material. The speed of collecting a PPAT is a distinct advantage because a short attention span is not a significant problem. Psychologists use instruments that require the examinee to focus for a longer time than it takes to get one drawing. Administering such tests is a waste of resources if the person being tested might not be able to follow instructions or be (temporarily) nonverbal. It is also easy to get a discharge drawing for comparison since relatively little time is required.

Limitations

While collecting a PPAT takes relatively little time, rating it takes longer in formal studies, especially if they involve large samples. The number of FEATS scales may be an impediment to those who do the ratings. The authors of one study (Lande *et al.*, 1997) did a factor analysis of the FEATS which resulted in three factors: activity, coherence, and complexity. After more research, we should be able to determine how we can reduce the number of scales or suggest which scales should be used in particular studies.

A major disadvantage of the PPAT is that one drawing is but a tiny sample of a person's behavior, thus severely limiting what is being assessed. A series of drawings (Ulman, 1975; Kramer and Schehr, 1983; Cohen *et al.*, 1988; Cox *et al.*, 2000) certainly gives more material. Therefore, those who use the PPAT should be modest as to the claims made about attributes of the artists.

Certain FEATS scales apply only to the PPAT or 'realistic' drawings. Other scales apply to drawings but not paintings. For example, there is a convention of leaving white space in the background of a drawing. This is not acceptable as a convention in painting unless it is a watercolor 'vignette'. Therefore, the Space scale can measure considerable differences between drawings but usually not paintings.

While the FEATS scales show promise in measuring differences among certain Axis I disorders in the acute phase, and also across the age span, they may not show statistically significant differences among other groups. The differences between drawings of a person who is in a manic episode and one who is in a major depressive episode can be considerable. However, the PPATs may show little measurable differences once the symptoms have remitted.

An important question about art assessments in general is whether the results will add anything to what we already know through more conventional means (Gantt, 2000). This question of incremental validity (Lilienfeld *et al.*, 2000) needs attention in future studies. Furthermore, in addition to being psychometrically sound, any assessment developed by art therapists, or music, or dance/movement therapists, needs to demonstrate its utility beyond its own field (Gantt, 2000).

Conclusion

Where does this leave us about art therapy assessment? We have a great deal of work to do before we can begin to claim that we have a sound, scientific approach. We may need to combine the PPAT and other drawings or to adapt the FEATS to other assessments. By understanding that the formal elements are the graphic equivalent of psychiatric symptoms, we can put numbers to drawings more easily and reliably.

This chapter made the case that art therapists have different assumptions and a different approach to art than do psychologists who use projective drawings. These differences demand that art therapists develop their own research models and methods in order to establish art as a scientifically sound means of assessment. Taking a fresh look at the drawings for what we can see *prior* to any interpretation or analysis appears to be the fundamental step to take.

References

American Psychiatric Association (1980) *Diagnostic and Statistical Manual of Mental Disorders: DSM-III*. Washington, DC: APA.

American Psychiatric Association (1987) *Diagnostic and Statistical Manual of Mental Disorders: DSM-III-R*. Washington, DC: APA.

American Psychiatric Association (1994) *Diagnostic and Statistical Manual of Mental Disorders: DSM-IV*. Washington, DC: APA.

Anschel, D. J., Dolce, S., Schwartzman, A. and Fisher, R. S. (2005) 'A blinded pilot study of artwork in a comprehensive epilepsy center population', *Epilepsy & Behavior*, 6 (2): 196–202.

Buck, J. (1947) 'The H-T-P, a projective device', *American Journal of Mental Deficiency*, 51: 606–610.

Burns, R. and Kaufman, S. (1970) *Kinetic Family Drawings*. New York: Brunner/Mazel.

Burns, R. and Kaufman, S. (1972) *Actions, Styles and Symbols in Kinetic Family Drawings*. New York: Brunner/Mazel.

Carlson, K., Quilan, D., Tucker, G. and Harrow, M. (1973) 'Body disturbance and sexual elaboration factors in figure drawings of schizophrenic patients', *Journal of Personality Assessment*, 37: 56–63.

Cohen, B., Hammer, J. and Singer, S. (1988) 'The Diagnostic Drawing Series: a systematic approach to art therapy evaluation and research', *Arts in Psychotherapy*, 15: 11–21.

Cox, C., Agell, G., Cohen, B. and Gantt, L. (2000) 'Are you assessing what I am assessing? Let's take a look!', *American Journal of Art Therapy*, 39: 48–67.

Cressen, R. (1975) 'Artistic quality of drawings and judges' evaluations of the DAP', *Journal of Personality Assessment*, 39: 132–137.

Di Leo, J. (1970) *Young Children and their Drawings*. New York: Brunner/Mazel.

Di Leo, J. (1973) *Children's Drawings as Diagnostic Aids*. New York: Brunner/Mazel.

Di Leo, J. (1977) *Child Development: Analysis and Synthesis*. New York: Brunner/Mazel.

Gantt, L. (1986) 'Systematic investigations of art works: some research models drawn from neighboring fields', *American Journal of Art Therapy*, 24 (4): 111–118.

Gantt, L. (1990) 'A validity study of the Formal Elements Art Therapy Scale (FEATS) for diagnostic information in patients' drawings'. Unpublished doctoral dissertation, University of Pittsburgh, Pittsburgh, PA.

Gantt, L. (1998) 'A discussion of art therapy as a science', *Art Therapy: Journal of the American Art Therapy Association*, 15 (1): 3–12.

Gantt, L. (2000) 'Assessments in the creative arts therapies: learning from each other', *Music Therapy Perspectives*, 18 (1): 41–46.

Gantt, L. (2001) 'The Formal Elements Art Therapy Scale: a measurement system for global variables in art', *Art Therapy: Journal of the American Art Therapy Association*, 18 (1): 51–56.

Gantt, L. (2004) 'The case for formal art therapy assessments', *Art Therapy: Journal of the American Art Therapy Association*, 21 (1): 18–29.

Gantt, L. and Tabone, C. (1998) *The Formal Elements Art Therapy Scale: The Rating Manual*. Morgantown, WV: Gargoyle Press.

Gantt, L. and Tabone, C. (2003) 'The Formal Elements Art Therapy Scale and Draw a Person Picking an Apple from a Tree', in C. Malchiodi (ed.) *Handbook of Art Therapy*, New York: Guilford Press.

Gantt, L. and Tinnin, L. (2007) 'Intensive trauma therapy of PTSD and dissociation: an outcome study', *Arts in Psychotherapy*, 34: 69–80.

Goodenough, F. (1926) *Measurement of Intelligence by Drawings*. New York: Harcourt, Brace, and World.

Goodman, R., Williams, K., Agell, G. and Gantt, L. (1998) 'Talk, talk, talk, when do we draw?', *American Journal of Art Therapy*, 37: 39–65.

Grove, W. M. (2000) *APA Division 12 (Clinical) Presidential Task Force 'Assessment for the Year 2000'. Report of the Task Force*. Washington, DC: American Psychological Association, Division 12 (Clinical Psychology).

Gussak, D. (2004) 'Art therapy with prison inmates: a pilot study', *Arts in Psychotherapy*, 31: 245–259.

Hammer, E. F. (1958a) *The Clinical Application of Projective Drawings*. Springfield, IL: Charles C. Thomas.

Hammer, E. F. (1958b) 'The chromatic H-T-P, a deeper personality-tapping technique', in E. F. Hammer (ed.) *The Clinical Application of Projective Drawings*. Springfield, IL: Charles C. Thomas.

Julliard, K. (1998) 'Outcomes research in health care: implications for art therapy', *Art Therapy: Journal of the American Art Therapy Association*, 15 (1): 13–21.

Kaplan, F. (1991) 'Drawing assessment and artistic skill', *Arts in Psychotherapy*, 18 (4): 347–352.

Kaplan, F. (2000) *Art, Science and Art Therapy: Repainting the Picture*. London: Jessica Kingsley Publishers.

Klerman, G. L. (1980) 'Overview of affective disorders', in H. I. Kaplan, A. M. Freedman and B. J. Sadock (eds) *Comprehensive Textbook of Psychiatry*, 3rd edn, Vol. 2. Baltimore, MD: Williams and Wilkins.

Kramer, E. (1979) *Childhood and Art Therapy*. New York: Schocken.

Kramer, E. and Schehr, J. (1983) 'An art therapy evaluation session for children', *American Journal of Art Therapy*, 23: 3–12.

Kreitler, H. and Kreitler, S. (1972) *Psychology of the Arts*. Durham, NC: Duke University Press.

Kwiatkowska, H. (1978) *Family Therapy and Evaluation Through Art*. Springfield, IL: Charles C. Thomas.

Lande, R. G., Howie, P. and Chang, A. (1997) 'The art of crime', *American Journal of Art Therapy*, 36 (1): 2–10.

Lehmann, H. (1980) 'Schizophrenia: History', in H. I. Kaplan, A. M. Freedman and B. J. Sadock (eds) *Comprehensive Textbook of Psychiatry*, 3rd edn, Vol. 2. Baltimore, MD: Williams and Wilkins.

Lehmann, H. and Risquez, F. (1953) 'The use of finger paintings in the clinical evaluation of psychotic conditions: a quantitative and qualitative approach', *Journal of Mental Science*, 99: 763–777.

Levy, B. and Ulman, E. (1967) 'Judging psychopathology from paintings', *Journal of Abnormal Psychology*, 72: 182–187.

Lilienfeld, S. O., Wood, J. M. and Garb, H. N. (2000) 'The scientific status of projective techniques', *Psychological Science in the Public Interest*, 1 (2): 27–66.

Lipowski, Z. (1980) 'Organic mental disorders: introduction and review of syndromes', in H. I. Kaplan, A. M. Freedman and B. J. Sadock (eds) *Comprehensive Textbook of Psychiatry*, 3rd edn, Vol. 2. Baltimore, MD: Williams and Wilkins.

Lombroso, C. (1888) *The Man of Genius*. London: W. Scott.

MacGregor, J. (1989) *The Discovery of the Art of the Insane*. Princeton, NJ: Princeton University Press.

Machover, K. (1949) *Personality Projection in the Drawing of the Human Figure*. Springfield, IL: Charles C. Thomas.

Munley, M. (2002) 'Comparing the PPAT drawings of boys with AD/HD and age-matched controls using the Formal Elements Art Therapy Scale', *Art Therapy: Journal of the American Art Therapy Association*, 19 (2): 69–76.

Naumburg, M. (1966) *Dynamically Oriented Art Therapy: Its Principles and Practice*. New York: Grune & Stratton.

Renfroe, J., Velek, M. and Marco, L. (1987) 'Dyschromatopsia in a psychiatric population', *Alabama Medicine*, 56 (20): 25–28.

Rubin, J. (1984) *Child Art Therapy*. New York: Van Nostrand Reinhold.

Schaverien, J. (2000) 'The triangular relationship and the aesthetic countertransference in analytical art psychotherapy', in A. Gilroy and G. McNeilly (eds) *The Changing Shape of Art Therapy: New Developments in Theory and Practice*. London: Jessica Kingsley Publishers.

Silver, R. (1982) *Stimulus Drawings and Techniques*. Mamaroneck, NY: Ablin Press.

Silver, R. (1988) *Draw-a-Story: Screening for Depression and Emotional Needs*. Mamaroneck, NY: Ablin Press.

Simon, R. (1991) *The Symbolism of Style*. London and New York: Routledge.

Simon, R. (1997) *Symbolic Images in Art as Therapy*. London and New York: Routledge.

Ulman, E. (1975) 'A new use of art in psychiatric diagnosis', in E. Ulman and P. Dachinger (eds) *Art Therapy in Theory and Practice*. New York: Schocken.

Ulman, E. and Levy, B. (1968) 'An experimental approach to the judgment of psychopathology from paintings', *Bulletin of Art Therapy*, 8: 3–12.

Ulman, E. and Levy, B. (1973) 'Art therapists as diagnosticians', *American Journal of Art Therapy*, 13: 35–38.

Ulman, E. and Levy, B. (1974) 'The effect of training on judging psychopathology from paintings', *American Journal of Art Therapy*, 14: 35–38.

Vick, R. and Sexton-Radek, K. (2005) 'Art and migraine: researching the relationship between artmaking and pain experience', *Art Therapy: Journal of the American Art Therapy Association*, 22 (4): 193–204.

Williams, K., Agell, G., Gantt, L. and Goodman, R. (1996) 'Art-based diagnosis: fact or fantasy?', *American Journal of Art Therapy*, 35 (1): 9–31.

Chapter 11

Positive art therapy assessment

Looking towards positive psychology for new directions in the art therapy evaluation process

Donna Betts

Introduction

'No important change takes place without measurement' (Clifton, 2003: xiii). Nonetheless, why should we, as mental health practitioners, assess? We do so in order to facilitate an 'optimal intervention' for our clients (Snyder *et al.*, 2006: 33). The process begins with referral questions, which provide information needed to structure an evaluation leading up to the formulation and implementation of a treatment plan. Assessment practice should strive to address individuals' mental health needs, to satisfy managed care restrictions, to comply with insurance requirements, to improve treatment effectiveness, to guide interventions, and to track treatment progress (Carlson and Geisinger, 2009). In addition, we assess in order to gather information about clients' behavior and aspects of personality (feelings, thoughts, motivations) so that we can help them to ameliorate their level of functioning, improve satisfaction with life, and establish coping mechanisms to deal with subsequent problems.

The reader of this book is likely aware of the long-standing debates about assessment in art therapy. Several authors have emphasized the need for assessment (Betts, 2006), while others have expressed concern that the 'reductive quantification of imagery' (Gilroy and Skaife, 1997: 60) inherent in formal evaluation serves to devalue clients and has little merit due to problems of validity and reliability. Many of us understand that attempts to identify meaning in a particular color or symbol in artwork are erroneous because this annihilates the 'overall Gestalt' of the image, thereby negating the context in which the image was created (Gantt and Tabone, 1998: 53). We endeavor to facilitate a process of personal growth for our clients, but in many settings we are also required to make formal evaluations about client strengths and potential psychopathology.

While the practice of formal evaluation in the field of art therapy continues to be the subject of much deliberation, practitioners generally agree that some form of assessment is necessary. According to Carlson and Geisinger (2009), many of the debating points bring forth unanswerable questions. What is indisputable, however, is that:

> It is the consensus of most mental health professionals, agency administrators, and insurance companies that regardless of the formality or structure, assessment – and reassessment at appropriate times – constitutes the core of good practice.
>
> (Gantt, 2004: 18)

To assess is to provide quality control. Despite their flaws, assessments are used because when making decisions about a client, even a small amount of information is better than none (Phelps, 2009). Furthermore, assessment is required course content for both UK-based art therapy training programs (endorsed by the Health Professions Council, a government organization), as well as American Art Therapy Association (AATA) approved art therapy education programs in the United States.

To clarify the use of terminology in this chapter, the art work that art therapists share with their colleagues can be gathered informally, in the case of art therapy *techniques*, or formally as with standardized art therapy *instruments*. These two different approaches of soliciting art work from clients for *evaluation* purposes may assist a treatment team in formulating a diagnosis, determine appropriateness for art therapy services, and help to formulate treatment goals. In this chapter, the terms *assessment*, *instrument*, *assessment instrument* and *tool* are used interchangeably.

The natural course of scientific progress involves the formation of two opposing camps that eventually unite (Groth-Marnat, 2000). The art therapy 'camps' with differing views regarding assessment could reconcile by addressing a few key areas, beginning with the way in which we conceive of the evaluation process in art therapy. In the present chapter, I invite the reader to reconceptualize the use of art therapy instrumentation by considering the necessity of the assessment process versus pure testing. I offer an opportunity to reflect on important implications of positive psychology approaches and provide direction for the establishment of positive art therapy assessment. I consider implications for educators and examine trends that will likely influence the future development and use of art therapy instruments.

I have deliberated the benefits and shortcomings of assessment in art therapy at length elsewhere (Betts, 2005, 2006). As you read the present chapter, I ask that you set the shortcomings aside and openly consider the concepts that are put forth here. The subsequent discussion establishes context for this chapter with a brief background of psychological assessment and historical foundations of art therapy assessment.

Foundations of art therapy assessment

A vast array of tests is available in North America for the purpose of evaluating individuals with developmental, cognitive, psychological, and/or behavioral disorders (Betts, 2005). Broadly defined, a test is:

a set of tasks designed to elicit or a scale to describe examinee behavior in a specified domain, or a system for collecting samples of an individual's work in a particular area. Coupled with the device is a scoring procedure that enables the examiner to quantify, evaluate, and interpret . . . behavior or work samples.

(American Educational Research Association, AERA, 1999: 25)

The Buros Institute of Mental Measurements, an American authority on assessment instruments, provides an online database that lists more than 3500 tests. Personality tests are defined as 'tests that measure individuals' ways of thinking, behaving, and functioning within family and society' (Buros Institute, Test Reviews Online, n.d.[a]; Betts, 2005). The American Psychological Association (n.d.[a]) and the British Psychological Society (BPS, 2009) share similar definitions for 'psychological assessment' or 'testing'. In Britain, the Psychological Testing Centre (PTC) at the BPS is the first point of contact for anyone who uses, takes or develops tests. Tests are also used in the National Health Service (BPS, 2009). In the United States, assessment tools should be administered by licensed psychologists, or students of psychology under supervision, according to ethical standards set for the by the American Psychological Association (2002).

In a hospital, day treatment facility, or in a school setting, psychologists often call upon the expertise of their treatment team, which can include art therapists, for input regarding clients. Sometimes art therapists are asked to show and discuss client art work, in order to elucidate client strengths, weaknesses, determine course of treatment, etc. Art therapists are adept at translating meaning in client art work for the benefit of their colleagues' improved understanding of clients. An integration of multiple sources of information derived from the art process allows the art therapist to evaluate and translate meaning in art work, producing a more comprehensive picture of the client. Such sources can include: client descriptions of art work, the art therapist's observations of the client during art-making, the therapist's subjective reaction to the work, combined with quantitative information derived from the rating of formal elements in the art.

Some of the techniques and assessments developed by art therapists have roots in personality instruments used by psychologists such as the House-Tree-Person (H-T-P) test (Buck, 1947) and the Goodenough-Harris Draw A Person (DAP) test (Harris, 1963; Betts, 2006). Hence, to validate a discussion about the applicability of art therapy assessment, it is important to consider the current status of personality assessment instruments. Ample data are provided in an extensive study by Camara et al. (2000). These authors set out to learn whether psychological assessments require more time than third parties are willing to reimburse in the era of managed care. The study, supported by the American Psychological Association, analyzed survey data from 179 clinical psychologists on their current uses of testing instruments. Camara et al. (2000) found that the popularity of projective techniques has persisted since 1969, especially the Rorschach (Rorschach, 1921), Thematic Apperception Test (TAT, Morgan and Murray, 1935), H-T-P and DAP which have all remained among the top ten. However, Human Figure Drawings (HFDs, Machover, 1949) decreased in ranking to 13. Although the data were gathered a decade ago, the study's primary investigators 'suspect that newer data (which we are attempting to gather) will probably reveal a continuing but possibly decreasing trend' in the use of projective tests (A. Puente and W. Camara, personal communication, 14 May 2009).

Also of note with regard to the popularity of personality assessments such as the H-T-P and the DAP is Groth-Marnat's rationale for removing his chapter on projective testing in the 2003 edition of his *Handbook of Psychological Assessment*. Groth-Marnat cited a decline in the use of projective drawings and questionable validity of projective drawing data as reasons for the removal of this content. The 2003 and 2009 versions of the *Handbook* include chapters on the Rorschach and the TAT, but the H-T-P and DAP sections were removed. Groth-Marnat (2009b) has put forth suggestions for improving the Rorschach, and other recent literature indicates improvements to this tool (Cassella and Viglione, 2009; Momenian-Schneider *et al.*, 2009; Sultan and Meyer, 2009), so the popularity of the Rorschach will likely persist.

Thus far, forecasts regarding the future of psychological drawing tests have not predicted their demise. However, if the use of drawing tests by psychologists maintains relevance but decreases in frequency of use, what are the implications for art therapy assessment? Art work created by a client provides a unique source of data. Furthermore, art therapy assessments provide a richer experience for the client than a simpler psychological pencil drawing test. With proper training, art therapists are better equipped to derive information about clients based on their art work than are other practitioners. We specialize in art media and we are therefore in a position to use our tools to their full capacity. Reconceptualizing the assessment process by de-emphasizing a testing approach provides justification for the use of standardized instruments in art therapy. This concept is elucidated in the next section.

Contextualization

Assessment should be understood as an evaluative process, incorporating tools that are used in the larger context of a process entailing triangulation of data from multiple sources. Groth-Marnat (2003) emphasized the distinction between using an assessment as a *test* versus an *instrument*. Tests are used merely to gather data, and the resulting descriptions of traits or ability are usually unrelated to the larger context of the individual's life and fail to address specific problems. Carlson and Geisinger (2009) cautioned that very few psychological tests are able to accurately identify a specific *Diagnostic and Statistical Manual of Mental Disorders (DSM)* (American Psychiatric Association, 2000) disorder. Conversely, most measures are useful to screen for symptoms. However, instruments for identification of all psychological diagnoses or every symptom do not exist. Furthermore, assessments are not useful in codifying more atypical, poorly differentiated cases, i.e. when a full picture of symptomatology is not available or when the duration of symptoms falls below the *DSM* requirements.

In the evaluation process, on the other hand, test scores represent only one source of data and as such are used to formulate hypotheses about the individual (Groth-Marnat, 2003). The larger context of the individual's life is considered and the generated hypotheses are used to help with problems experienced. In considering this larger context, we broaden our perspective of our clients and this provides justification for the use of assessments. In the art therapy evaluation process, when we conduct a Diagnostic Drawing Series (DDS, Cohen *et al.*, 1988) or a Person Picking an Apple from a Tree (PPAT) assessment (Gantt, 1990), for example, *how* we use the information derived from the resulting scores is vital. It is commonly understood that the dictionary approach – the interpretation of single signs or elements of a drawing – is not psychometrically accurate. So, when art therapy instruments place data in a broader perspective to enable 'problem solving and decision making' (Groth-Marnat, 2003: 3), they are being used to their fullest capacity and for the benefit of the client's well-being:

> When you as a clinician/art therapist ask the person to elaborate on the meaning that the eyes and other aspects of the drawings have for the client, then this interactive process creates meaning that is likely to be personally and therapeutically important . . . and it thus becomes both ipsatively valid as well as has potential therapeutic utility.
>
> (G. Groth-Marnat, personal communication, 19 May 2009)

Thus, focusing on the use of an instrument in the *context* of an evaluation session broadens the practitioner's perspective, enabling access to more information than could possibly be gleaned from the assignment of a score to a particular element in the drawing. Traditionally in the mental health arena there has been a focus on tracking outcomes in assessment rather than processes (Bornstein, 2009). However, as previously suggested, there is increasing recognition that assessment results should be interpreted 'within the context of the interpersonal milieu in which test data were obtained' (Bornstein, 2002: 60). Bornstein (2009) advocated for a process-based model for psycholgical assessment, which he termed the 'process dissociation' approach. It is defined as:

> A research strategy wherein subtle, naturally occurring influences on test scores (e.g., testee motivation or mood state) are used to illuminate underlying response processes. The process dissociation strategy reverses the usual procedure for dealing with potential test score confounds and requires adopting a kind of Zen attitude regarding these extraneous variables. Rather than attempting to minimize or eliminate test score confounds, the researcher leans into them, exploits them, and deliberately manipulates them to increase or decrease their impact and see how test results are affected.
>
> (Bornstein, 2009: 4)

By looking at clients' psychological processes (their motivations, mood states, etc.) as they respond to testing situations, it becomes easier to comprehend what an instrument actually measures, how it measures a given construct, and why resulting test scores are tied in to particular variables.

As art therapists we tend to be process oriented in our work – therefore, studying the process that a client undergoes in an evaluation session should be second nature to us. Many art therapists would welcome examination of processes as an augmentation and/or supplementation to the more objective, quantitative assessment outcome results that are generated through rating scales and other formal measures. There are some research-related challenges inherent in the process-oriented approach, however. Process is more difficult to examine empirically, because the investigator must 'operationalize unobservable psychological processes and hidden mental states' (Bornstein, 2009: 3). In addition, to study process, experimental treatment conditions are typically involved, which is more complex than crunching numbers generated by test scores.

Despite the challenges related to studying process, in clinical practice, employing assessment as a process and avoiding a pure testing approach enables us to provide more legitimate evaluation services. Furthermore, the way in which we structure the assessment process and interact with our clients impacts the quality of an evaluation. Do we consider our clients' strengths as well as weaknesses? The evaluation process has tended to look at problems and disabling conditions. In broadening our perspective to account for client strengths and the context in which we are assessing, we are much more likely to see the whole person. As such, positive psychology approaches to assessment provide a constructive framework for art therapists.

Looking to positive psychology

'Develop the strengths and manage the weaknesses.' This is the mantra of positive psychology, according to the movement's grandfather, Donald Clifton (2003: xiii). The goal of positive psychology, according to Clifton, is to study what is *right* with people, and 'to bring more balance to psychology' (2003: xiii). Thus, the movement's goal is not to split the field into 'negative' and 'positive' approaches, rather it is to place more emphasis on client strengths, and promote positive functioning (Snyder and Lopez, 2007).

Positive psychology is becoming globally recognized by art therapists. American authors Chilton and Wilkinson (2009) published their article 'Positive Art Therapy: Envisioning the Intersection of Art Therapy and Positive Psychology' in the *Australia and New Zealand Journal of Art Therapy*. They suggest the development of tools or modification of existing art therapy instruments to correspond to Peterson and Seligman's (2004) classification of strengths and virtues.

Psychologists who are actively engaged in positive approaches to assessment have determined that positive aspects of personality can be measured just as readily as negative aspects. Positive psychology calls for a balanced approach to assessment. It provides such advantages as realizing that the interviewer is invested in understanding the whole person, facilitating 'an alliance of trust and mutuality' (Snyder *et al.*, 2006: 42), and decreasing potential unease about the assessment process. Many of these approaches should be of interest to art therapists as we strive to improve the standards and quality of our own methods. In the positive psychology literature, integrating psychological reports is a recommended strategy. A well-integrated psychological report minimizes references to test results and maximizes descriptions about the individual and how the information derived from the assessment relates to his or her life (Groth-Marnat, 2009b). Integrated reports combine qualitative and quantitative data sources such as referral questions, interviews, records, observations, and a series of psychological tests. An integrated report is the 'blending' of all sources to derive a 'meaningful understanding of the client in the context of the client's life' (Groth-Marnat and Horvath, 2006: 78).

Snyder *et al.* (2006) advocated for a more balanced approach by emphasizing the inclusion of strengths and hope in client reports. Assessment data are a powerful force in people's lives, and this points to a need for responsible reporting. Despite the awareness of this responsibility, however, referral questions rarely focus on client strengths, centering instead on weaknesses. Snyder *et al.* (2006) suggested that, because people and their behaviors exist in many different contexts, clinicians should strive to understand clients' behaviors in response to different problems as well as their life situations: 'Attributing the source of all of a client's problems to the person biases clinicians and other professionals, hampering their abilities to assist clients effectively in achieving their goals' (Snyder *et al.*, 2006: 35). Thus, we should consider the extent to which a client alters his or her behavior in a given situation, or fails to do so, thereby assessing the client's environment. In this way, we would be increasing our ability to uncover the various sources of a client's difficulties.

Hope, according to Snyder's (1994) hope theory, is a cognitive variable that consists of three components: goals, agency, and pathways (Snyder *et al.*, 2006). Hope in this context is described as 'goal-directed thinking'. Most behavior is thought to center on the pursuit of goals, and people are seen as predominantly goal oriented. *Pathways thought* is 'the perceived capacity to produce routes to desired goals' and *agency* is 'the motivation to use those routes under both normal and impeded circumstances' (Snyder *et al.*, 2006: 37–38). The premise is that an individual can gain the best physical and mental health possible by motivating himself or herself to achieve goals. One's level of hope effectively predicts psychological adjustment, health outcomes, prevention, performance, and general coping style. Using hope theory in the interview and psychological report can provide useful information regarding pathways and agency thoughts related to the client's goals, which may prove significant in the process of therapy.

The assessor should be particular in selecting tests for acquiring information about a client (Snyder *et al.*, 2006). However, the best tests may not address client strengths, as there is a paucity of validated measures that provide both positive and negative information about a client's attributes. In addition, few tools exist to assess the strengths and weaknesses in the client's environment (home, work, etc.). Because further research is needed to address the deficiencies in psycho-logical assessment, clinicians in the meantime need to employ more tailored approaches.

Snyder *et al.* (2006) proposed a four-level matrix (based on a concept put forth by their colleague Beatrice Wright) for gathering diagnostic information about a client, to ensure that all relevant aspects are assessed. This matrix, used to structure the clinical interview, examines the client's 'inside' assets and weaknesses, and the assets and weaknesses of the client's environment. 'The presence of the matrix forces the diagnostician to look beyond the individual's shortcomings' (p. 37).

An art therapist could modify this matrix and request, for instance, that a client create art work reflecting each of the four quadrants. Alternately, a client could be asked to focus directly on his or her inside environment by making a picture about 'why you are here' (e.g. in the hospital). Other ideas for implementation of positive psychological assessment approaches in art therapy include: inviting the client to make art about a specific problem; developing or modifying existing tools to corre-spond to Peterson and Seligman's (2004) classification of strengths and virtues (Chilton and Wilkinson, 2009); and using art-based assessments specific to the criterion being measured, such as the Subjective Happiness Drawing (SHD, Betts *et al.*, 2010). In the positive psychology approach to assessment, practitioners aim to work collaboratively with the client (Snyder *et al.*, 2006).

Bornstein (2009) described the concept of therapeutic assessment, a method that considers the influence that both the assessor and assessee have on the outcome of a psychological test. This method emphasizes a collaborative approach to assessment that 'can have a positive impact on patient insight, adjustment, and therapeutic engagement' (Bornstein, 2009: 6). Therapeutic assessment approaches psychological testing as a way to help clients better understand themselves, find solutions to their problems, and facilitate positive changes (Finn, 2009). Therapeutic assessment encompasses techniques of collaborative assessment (Fischer, 2001), a method based in humanistic and human-science psychology, where the power differential between the assessor and client is diminished as much as possible in a team approach to understanding the client's problems and establishing new ways of thinking and being. Since the success of an intervention is dependent upon the quality of the client–therapist relationship, assessment techniques that will foster this relationship are advantageous (Martin *et al.*, 2000). In the art therapy literature, Dudley (2004) also emphasized the significance of the client–therapist relationship in the context of assessment and de-emphasized the traditional 'fact-finding' approach to evaluation. Rather, she suggested, the initial meeting with a prospective client is an important opportunity to examine the 'unfolding' of a relationship between the practitioner, the client, and the art (Dudley, 2004: 19). Similarly, Cohen and Cox's (1995) integrative method places import on integrating multiple sources of data to supplement formal evaluation of art work, to gain a more integrated and cohesive picture of the client.

This section delineated possible new directions for the art therapy evaluation process, borrowing ideas and approaches from positive psychology. Many of these ideas are avenues intuitive to art therapists but that have been articulated effectively in the positive psychology literature:

- integrating psychological reports by blending all sources of information about a client, thereby minimizing test results (Groth-Marnat, 2009b)
- including strengths and hope in client reports (Snyder *et al.*, 2006)
- being cautious about test selection (Snyder *et al.*, 2006)
- incorporating 'inside' and environmental assets and weaknesses in the clinic interview process (Snyder *et al.*, 2006)
- working collaboratively with the client (Snyder *et al.*, 2006; Bornstein, 2009)
- focusing on the relationship (Dudley, 2004).

Incorporating these positive psychology approaches to assessment addresses concerns about the use of instrumentation in art therapy. Art therapists could put these approaches into practice, and educators could introduce these concepts to students. Some ways in which positive psychology approaches can be applied in graduate art therapy assessment courses are subsequently described.

Positive art therapy assessment

Implications for educators

Cohen (2004) attributed a low level of interest in assessment among American art therapists in part to US-based graduate program faculty. Some art therapy educators seem to reject vital aspects of the scientific method that pertain to assessment, such as standardization and replicability, and may not understand or accept the importance of validity and reliability of tools, integral to evidence-based work. Since art therapy educators have a central role in helping shift perceptions of assessment in our field in general, they can relay to students the relevance of assessment, and provide a learning environment that inspires students to look at assessment as a positive means to gather information about clients. In this section I offer suggestions for implementing more broad-based and positive approaches to teaching assessment.

Based on the results of my dissertation research (Betts, 2005), I composed a syllabus for teaching art therapy assessment from a broad perspective. It is an ever-evolving document that I modify based on my research, professional experiences and developments in the mental health professions' approaches to assessment. I use my syllabus presently in teaching an assessment course to art therapy graduate students at the George Washington University. For the first few weeks of the course, my students study from the *Handbook of Psychological Assessment* (Groth-Marnat, 2009a), a comprehensive text that provides guidance on assessment and treatment planning vital to any mental health professional. My course content includes the concepts from positive psychology and related theories from the para-digms of therapeutic assessment and collaborative assessment described previ-ously. I emphasize the assessment process versus testing approach, and espouse both quantitative and qualitative approaches. Students are taught to be cautious about test selection (Snyder *et al.*, 2006), to work collaboratively with the client (Bornstein, 2009) and to focus on the relationship with the client (Dudley, 2004).

I teach a variety of art therapy techniques and instruments including: the Diagnostic Drawing Series (DDS) (Cohen *et al.*, 1988), the Person Picking an Apple from a Tree (PPAT) assessment (Gantt, 1990), and the Formal Elements Art Therapy Scale (FEATS) rating instrument (Gantt and Tabone, 1998), to name only a few. My students complete a project mid-semester, the 'Triangulation of the DDS'. They are expected to conduct a DDS on an adult client or a volunteer, and to integrate data derived from the following:

1   Interview data and behavioral observations made during the pre-assessment clinical interview and during the assessment process.
2   Interview data obtained from the post-assessment DDS Drawing Inquiry form (the subject's verbal responses to specific questions about the drawings).
3   Descriptive information derived from the CritCard (Anderson, 1997) method (described below) as applied to the Tree drawing (the interviewer's subjec-tive reactions to the art work guided by a series of questions).
4   Scores obtained from standardized, quantitative rating procedures, i.e. the DDS Rating Scale (a dichotomous/categorical rating system) used to rate the three drawings, as well as the FEATS (an interval system) used to rate the DDS Tree drawing.

Thus, students compose a broad perspective of the subject based on four different sources of information.

The CritCard method is a system for describing art work developed by art educator Tom Anderson (1997). Derived from the field of art criticism, this approach invites the viewer of art work to address three questions. In answering these questions, the viewer engages in the critical processes of description (what is it?), interpretation (what does it mean?), and evaluation (what is it worth?) (p. 21). Some examples of specific questions include: How does this (work of art) make you feel? Did the work address some significant human problem or need? Would you like to have it for your own? Art therapist Robin Tipple (2003) also advocated for a descriptive approach to the assessment process. He drew from the work of Michael Baxandall (1985), an art historian who offered interpretive and descriptive ways of looking at art work. This evaluation process on the part of the art therapist, although subjective, is important because it invites the therapist to become acquainted with the art work more intimately, which has implications for the therapist–client relationship. To take this approach one step further, the thera-pist can replicate the client's work, a technique which has been found to increase empathy (Moon, 1999).

The DDS triangulation project provides a broad-based perspective in teaching the importance of considering multiple sources of data when assessing a client's mental state, current functioning and environmental influences, in keeping with positive psychology approaches. I also teach my students that different assessments are applicable for identifying specific psychological states, personal challenges, strengths, or types of pathology, because instruments should be tailored to the reason for the client's referral and pertain to specific referral questions (Carlson and Geisinger, 2009). To draw from a few examples in art therapy, the DDS has been shown to effectively discriminate between a variety of diagnostic groups when an experienced rater is used, such as: psychosis, schizoaffective disorder and alcoholism (B. Cohen, personal communication, 28 May 2009).

To name a few other instruments, the Bird's Nest Drawing (BND, Kaiser, 1993) has demonstrated success in revealing problems (or absence of problems) with attachment. An assessment that seeks to measure the strengths of an individual with a developmental and/or communication disorder is the Face Stimulus Assessment (FSA, Betts, 2003). The PPAT (Gantt, 1990) is often able to ascertain whether a client has depression, mania, organic brain disorder, or psychosis. The Silver Drawing Test (SDT, Silver and Lavin, 1977) is adept at examining potential cognitive impairment. Each of these assessments can pertain to specific referral questions or be tailored to identify a client's unique strengths and challenges.

To summarize, I teach positive psychology approaches to assessment in my course and a balance of qualitative and quantitative methods. I provide context for the purpose of assessments (i.e. treatment planning, diagnostic indicators, identifying client strengths), and teach the benefits and drawbacks of the tools. Next I offer a review of literature that includes predictions for the future of assessment practices. These are relevant for art therapists and provide avenues for potential new directions in our own evaluation processes and methods of teaching assessment.

Looking to the future

Likely trends in the future of psychological evaluation can provide beneficial insights for art therapists, as we often work in concert with psychologists and other mental health professionals, and these trends will therefore likely impact our assessment approaches. Psychology must continue to meet the demands of managed health care in the United States (Groth-Marnat, 2003). Managed health care places time constraints on practitioners, so that assessment practices need to be time efficient and cost effective.

Groth-Marnat (2003) also predicted the need to make accommodations for distance health care delivery, and computerized assessment is one solution. Camara et al. (2000) found that both neuropsychologists and clinical psychologists infrequently use computer-based testing, and the most common use of computers was found to be in the realm of test scoring. Authors including Kim et al. (2006) and Mattson (2009) have explored the computerized scoring of art therapy instruments with some interesting results. This is an area that is likely to grow.

Kamphaus *et al.* (2000) set out to identify major trends that will probably impact the future of psychological testing with children. In examining the literature, the authors found that clinicians are using a wider variety of instruments, and behavior rating scales are considerably more popular than tests such as the DAP and the HTP in child assessment. Three trends were cited: school-based psychological evaluation is expected to grow; intelligence testing will become more abbreviated; and use of child behavior rating scales will continue to increase. Groth-Marnat (2009b) put forth predictions for what he hopes may be expected in the realm of assessment by the year 2050:

> a fully integrated assessment system using a combination of artificial intelligence, interactive virtual/reality hologram, physiological monitors, massive interlinked Internet norms, branching strategies, analysis of the genome, and in session as well as time series measures.
>
> (Groth-Marnat, 2009b: 309)

Keeping up to date with trends in psychology will benefit art therapists as we strive to improve our assessments and work to maintain their relevance. This will be a challenge, given implications from the art therapy assessment research. However, some of these problems, discussed forthwith, can be overcome.

Results of a meta-analysis of art therapy assessment and rating instruments research revealed that flaws are numerous and that much work has yet to be done (Betts, 2005). The lack of research in this area means that we cannot yet use our tools with confidence that they will give us sufficient information about our clients or measure process of change. Thus, there is much room for improvement in our approaches to assessment research. Standardization of instruments is vital. Valid and reliable instruments help to generate research emphasizing 'the honesty, believability, expertise, and integrity' of mental health professions (Fraenkel and Wallen, 2000: 165).

Establishing large collections of normative drawings would help us to identify indicators that do not fit into the 'norm'. Bucciarelli (2007) collected over one hundred PPATs from a normative sample of college students. A few art therapists have made a concerted effort to develop norms for children (Silver, 2003; Deaver, 2009; Levick, 2009). Additional normative studies on art therapy are needed, to establish baselines for data comparison.

Solid research on patient groups will also improve the validity of art therapy assessments. To be more useful clinically, assessments should focus on examining how art changes with psychological state (Gantt and Tabone, 1998). Furthermore: 'There are a number of diagnoses that have not been sufficiently studied, and many that have co-morbid pathology reflected in the art (eating disorders, for instance) that complicate the findings' (B. Cohen, personal communication, 28 May 2009). Although it is difficult to isolate many psychiatric diagnoses, as previously discussed (Carlson and Geisinger, 2009), large-scale studies may be able to identify some trends in art work.

Art therapists assess their clients both formally and informally. If we conceive of the evaluation process as an approach for getting to know our clients so that we can intelligently inform the path that treatment will take, then our work is beneficial. In 2005 I concluded that objective measures such as standardized assessment procedures (formalized assessment tools and rating manuals, portfolio evaluation, behavioral checklists) represent an optimal approach to assessment, when combined with subjective approaches (the client's interpretation of his or her art work and the therapist's subjective responses).

In this chapter, I have explored the ways in which we can reconceptualize assessment by broadening our perspective on the application of our tools. Looking to positive psychology, I offered new directions that art therapists may pursue in evaluating our clients. I emphasized the relevance of staying current with advances in psychological assessment, since our work is often integral to a treatment team comprised of psychologists and other mental health professionals. Whether you practice art therapy in the United Kingdom, the United States, Canada, or elsewhere, I hope you will find value in the positive art therapy assessment process.

References

American Educational Research Association (AERA, 1999) *Standards for Educational and Psychological Testing.* Washington, DC: American Educational Research Association.

American Psychiatric Association (2000) *Diagnostic and Statistical Manual of Mental Disorders: DSM-IV-TR.* Washington, DC: American Psychiatric Association.

American Psychological Association (n.d.[a]). *Psychological Assessment.* Retrieved 5 April 2010 from http://www.apa.org/research/action/glossary.aspx.

American Psychological Association (2002) *The Ethical Principles of Psychologists and Code of Conduct.* Washington, DC: American Psychological Association.

Anderson, T. (1997) 'A model for art criticism: talking with kids about art', *School Arts*, September: 21–24.

Baxandall, M. (1985) *Patterns of Intention: On the Historical Explanation of Pictures.* New Haven, CT: Yale University Press.

Betts, D. J. (2003) 'Developing a projective drawing test: experiences with the Face Stimulus Assessment (FSA)', *Art Therapy: Journal of the American Art Therapy Association*, 20 (2): 77–82.

Betts, D. J. (2005) 'A systematic analysis of art therapy assessment and rating instrument literature'. Doctoral dissertation, Florida State University, Tallahassee. Published online at http://www.art-therapy.us/assessment.htm.

Betts, D. J. (2006) 'Art therapy assessments and rating instruments: do they measure up?', *Arts in Psychotherapy*, 33 (5): 371–472.

Betts, D., Chilton, G. and Wilkinson, R. (2010) 'The Subjective Happiness Drawing (SHD)'. Unpublished paper.

Bornstein, R. F. (2002) 'A process dissociation approach to objective–projective test score interrelationships', *Journal of Personality Assessment*, 78 (1): 47–68.

Bornstein, R. F. (2009) 'Heisenberg, Kandinsky, and the heteromethod convergence problem: lessons from within and beyond psychology', *Journal of Personality Assessment*, 91 (1): 1–8.

British Psychological Society (2009, 12, 8) 'Psychological testing'. Retrieved 5 April 2010 from http://www.psychtesting.org.uk/about-psych-test/about-psych-test_home.cfm.

Bucciarelli, A. (2007) 'Normative study of the PPAT assessment on a sample of college students'. Unpublished master's thesis, Florida State University, Tallahassee.

Buck, J. N. (1947) 'The H-T-P, a projective device', *American Journal of Mental Deficiency*, 51: 606–610.

Buros Institute (n.d.[a]) 'Test reviews online'. Retrieved 23 November 2009 from http://buros.unl.edu/buros/jsp/category.html.

Camara, W. J., Nathan, J. S. and Puente, A. E. (2000) 'Psychological test usage: implications in professional psychology'. *Professional Psychology: Research and Practice*, 31 (2): 41–154.

Carlson, J. F. and Geisinger, K. F. (2009) 'Psychological diagnostic testing: addressing challenges in clinical applications of testing', in R. P. Phelps (ed.) *Correcting Fallacies about Educational and Psychological Testing*. Washington, DC: American Psychological Association.

Cassella, M. J. and Viglione, D. J. (2009) 'The Rorschach texture response: a construct validation study using attachment theory', *Journal of Personality Assessment*, 91 (6): 601–610.

Chilton, G. and Wilkinson, R. (2009) 'Positive art therapy: envisioning the intersection of art therapy and positive psychology', *Australia and New Zealand Journal of Art Therapy*, 4 (1): 27–35.

Clifton, D. (2003) 'Foreword', in S. J. Lopez and C. R. Snyder (eds) *Positive Psychological Assessment: A Handbook of Models and Measures*. Washington, DC: American Psychological Association.

Cohen, B. M. (2004) 'Foreword', in S. Brooke *Tools of the Trade: A Therapist's Guide to Art Therapy Assessments*, 2nd edn. Springfield, IL: Charles C. Thomas.

Cohen, B. M. and Cox, C. T. (1995) *Telling Without Talking: Art as a Window into the World of Multiple Personality*. New York: Norton.

Cohen, B. M., Hammer, J. S. and Singer, S. (1988) 'The Diagnostic Drawing Series: a systematic approach to art therapy evaluation and research', *Arts in Psychotherapy*, 15 (1): 11–21.

Deaver, S. P. (2009) 'A normative study of children's drawings: preliminary research findings', *Art Therapy: Journal of the American Art Therapy Association*, 26 (1): 4–11.

Dudley, J. (2004) 'Art psychotherapy and the use of psychiatric diagnosis', *Inscape*, 9 (1): 14–25.

Finn, S. E. (2009) 'How is therapeutic assessment different from other types of psychological assessment?' Retrieved 5 April 2010 from http://therapeuticassessment.com/about.html.

Fischer, C. T. (2001) 'Collaborative exploration as an approach to personality assessment', in K. J. Schneider, J. F. T. Bugenthal and J. F. Pierson (eds) *The Handbook of Humanistic Psychology: Leading Edges in Theory, Research and Practice*. Thousand Oaks, CA: Sage.

Fraenkel, J. R. and Wallen, N. E. (2000) *How to Design and Evaluate Research in Education*, 4th edn. New York: McGraw-Hill.

Gantt, L. (1990) 'A validity study of the Formal Elements Art Therapy Scale (FEATS) for diagnostic information in patients' drawings'. Unpublished doctoral dissertation, University of Pittsburgh, Pittsburgh, PA.

Gantt, L. (2004) 'The case for formal art therapy assessments', *Art Therapy: Journal of the American Art Therapy Association*, 21 (1): 18–29.

Gantt, L. and Tabone, C. (1998) *The Formal Elements Art Therapy Scale: The Rating Manual*. Morgantown, WV: Gargoyle Press.

Gilroy, A. and Skaife, S. (1997) 'Taking the pulse of American art therapy: a report on the 27th annual conference of the American Art Therapy Association, November 13–17, 1996, Philadelphia', *Inscape*, 2 (2): 57–64.

Groth-Marnat, G. (2000) 'Visions of clinical assessment: then, now, and a brief history of the future', *Journal of Clinical Psychology*, 56 (3), 349–365.

Groth-Marnat, G. (2003) *Handbook of Psychological Assessment*, 4th edn. New York: Wiley.

Groth-Marnat, G. (2009a) *Handbook of Psychological Assessment*, 5th edn. New York: Wiley.

Groth-Marnat, G. (2009b). 'The five assessment issues you meet when you go to heaven', *Journal of Personality Assessment*, 91 (4): 303–310.

Groth-Marnat, G. and Horvath, L. S. (2006) 'The psychological report: a review of current controversies', *Journal of Clinical Psychology*, 62 (1): 73–81.

Harris, D. B. (1963) *Children's Drawings as Measures of Intellectual Maturity: A Revision and Extension of the Goodenough Draw-A-Man Test*. Oxford: Harcourt, Brace.

Kaiser, D. (1993) 'Attachment organization as manifested in a drawing task'. Unpublished master's thesis, Eastern Virginia Medical School, Norfolk, VA.

Kamphaus, R. W., Petoskey, M. D. and Rowe, E. W. (2000) 'Current trends in psychological testing of children', *Professional Psychology: Research and Practice*, 31 (2): 155–164.

Kim, S., Ryu, H., Hwang, J. and Kim, M. S. (2006) 'An expert system approach to art psychotherapy', *Arts in Psychotherapy*, 33 (1): 59–75.

Levick, M. F. (2009) *The Levick Emotional and Cognitive Art Therapy Assessment: A Normative Study*. Boca Raton, FL: Myra F. Levick Books.

Machover, K. (1949) *Personality Projection in the Drawing of the Human Figure*. Springfield, IL: Charles C. Thomas.

Martin, D. J., Garske, J. P. and Davis, M. K. (2000) 'Relation of the therapeutic alliance with outcome and other variables: a meta-analytic review', *Journal of Consulting and Clinical Psychology*, 68 (3): 438–450.

Mattson, D. (2009) 'Accessible image analysis for art assessment', *Arts in Psychotherapy*, 36 (4): 208–213.

Momenian-Schneider, S. H., Brabender, V. M. and Nath, S. R. (2009) 'Psychophysiological reactions to the response phase of the Rorschach and 16PF', *Journal of Personality Assessment*, 91 (5): 494–496.

Moon, B. (1999) 'The tears make me paint: the role of responsive artmaking in adolescent art therapy', *Art Therapy: Journal of the American Art Therapy Association*, 16 (2): 78–82.

Morgan, C. D. and Murray, H. H. (1935) 'A method for investigating fantasies: the Thematic Apperception Test', *Archives of Neurology and Psychiatry*, 34: 289–306.

Peterson, C. and Seligman, M. E. P. (2004) *Character Strengths and Virtues: A Handbook and Classification*. Oxford: American Psychological Association/Oxford University Press.

Phelps, R. (ed.) (2009) *Correcting Fallacies about Educational and Psychological Testing*. Washington, DC: American Psychological Association.

Rorschach, H. (1921) *Psychodiagnostik*. Bern: Bircher.

Silver, R. (2003) 'Cultural differences and similarities in responses to the Silver Drawing Test in the USA, Brazil, Russia, Estonia, Thailand, and Australia', *Art Therapy: Journal of the American Art Therapy Association*, 20 (1): 16–20.

Silver, R. and Lavin, C. (1977) 'The role of art in developing and evaluating cognitive skills', *Journal of Learning Disabilities*, 10 (7): 416–424.

Snyder, C. R. (1994) *The Psychology of Hope: You Can Get There From Here*. New York: Free Press.

Snyder, C. R. and Lopez, S. J. (2007) *Positive Psychology: The Scientific and Practical Explorations of Human Strengths*. Thousand Oaks, CA: Sage.

Snyder, C. R., Ritschel, L. A., Rand, K. L. and Berg, C. J. (2006) 'Balancing psychological assessments: including strengths and hope in client reports', *Journal of Clinical Psychology*, 62 (1): 33–46.

Sultan, S. and Meyer, G. J. (2009) 'Does productivity impact the stability of Rorschach scores?', *Journal of Personality Assessment*, 91 (5), 480–493.

Tipple, R. (2003) 'The interpretation of children's artwork in a paediatric disability setting', *Inscape* 8 (2): 48–59.

Concluding remarks

Andrea Gilroy, Robin Tipple and Christopher Brown

This book shows art therapists to be engaged in a heterogeneity of assessment practices. There is variety of theoretical approach, attitude and desire present in the writing. On the one hand there is a wish to develop formal assessment processes and evaluative techniques; this is accompanied by a desire to demonstrate the validity of research findings that relate to the use of assessment tools, for objectivity perhaps. On the other hand there is a wish to privilege subjectivity and aesthetic understandings, intuition and the full use of empathic imagination. The discourses that frame these different practices are driven by agendas from systemic, institutional and professional arenas. Whilst editing we noticed the repetition of themes and issues that these discourses evoked and wanted to know more about them. Consequently, we decided to ask our contributors some questions. We received an illuminating series of replies and what follows brings together our contributors' responses and our thoughts about the topics we encountered.

During one of our editorial meetings we became aware of the absence of the direct voice of clients in this book. We found ourselves talking about our own experiences of being assessed, whether for therapy or for the treatment of physical problems. We talked about how vulnerable we felt, how relieved we were when hope was offered that a treatment could help us feel better and how we just wanted to get through the assessment and on with the treatment. The complexities and ethics of client consultation made it too late to include in this volume, so we asked our contributors about their own experiences of being assessed and how they imagined their clients responded to the art therapy assessment they had.

The general view was that clients found art therapy assessment a difficult, anxiety-provoking encounter, one that was frequently influenced by negative experiences of mental health services. Contributors reported clients wondering if they would be taken seriously, feeling angry at having to wait for treatment, resentment at being positioned as dependent and helpless and 'having to repeat their story over and over'. Contributors' personal experiences mirrored those of their clients and ours as well. There were feelings of being judged, scrutinised and sometimes frustrated by the assessing therapist: 'I remember . . . getting very angry at the dismissive way I felt we were being treated.' Assessment encounters with fellow professionals made these art therapists determined not to make their clients feel the same way.

Thankfully not everyone's experiences of assessment were negative. There were occasions when contributors had been 'very reassured by being taken seriously and listened to' in an assessment, and of course there were 'the pleasurable aspects of another's attention; that the therapist's gaze might at times really be benign!'

However, and as noted in the Introduction, institutions place considerable demands and constraints on the assessment practices of art therapists, whether the work is with children or with adults. Systemic and institutional needs exert pressure on the function of art therapy assessment and on the practice developed in the assessment itself. For example, when treatment is funded according to diagnosis, whether through insurance or state provision, a diagnostically oriented assessment may be required. The art therapist may also be obliged to think carefully about matching clients to therapeutic resources; treatment options can be both limited and determined by the particular philosophy or treatment approach of the team. The art therapist's availability, waiting lists, suitable space for different kinds of work, therapeutic approach, tools, techniques, criteria and desires in relation to both assessment and therapy all play a role here. Similarly, the client's pathology, capacities for expression, social relating and ego strength, their hope, pain, sense of entitlement and refusal, all influence their ability to engage with the institution and what it and the art therapist have to offer. Private practitioners are not exempt from institutional pressures, being influenced by their professional referral networks, which may be linked to insurance companies or the organisation where they trained.

The worlds of the therapist and the client should interact positively in an art therapy assessment, although the encounter may be weighted towards the needs of one or other person in the assessment dyad. Institutions may require both evaluation and a 'gate-keeping' function to be performed by the art therapist. A relationship with the client also has to be fostered, not one of subordination but rather one where some solidarity is achieved and hope of change generated. It is a situation where there needs to be some shared reality, but it is also one where a decision has to be made. This leads some art therapists to emphasise the centrality of the patient, endeavouring to create a mutuality of purpose within the encounter (McNiff, Chapter 5; Liebmann, Report 6), whereas others seek to develop criteria against which they can make decisions about whether or not to offer art therapy, based on their patients' responses to them, to making art, and to particular tasks (Etherington, Report 1; Loumeau-May, Report 7; Marshall-Tierney, Chapter 7; Thomas and Cody, Chapter 8; Levick, Chapter 9).

The institutional and assessment needs meet when the therapist has to make a judgement and decide whether or not to offer art therapy. We asked our contributors about this 'gate-keeping' function: how did they determine whether or not a client was suitable for art therapy? One said 'everyone is suitable' but another remarked:

> I don't think there is any point in an assessment unless the therapist has the confidence and authority to say either yes or no to the client. Why put the client through the anxiety of 'assessment' if you're just going to say yes to everyone?

This related to our initial impression: that art therapists rarely said 'no' to a client. However, contributors' responses identified clear criteria for unsuitability: clients could be over compliant or looking for an art class or a 'magic potion'; they could be non-compliant and refuse to engage with art materials or be too unwell, aggressive, or likely continue their misuse of illicit drugs or alcohol; clients could also be considered to require too high a level of support from the team to be in art therapy. Some contributors spoke about excluding clients in the absence of a specific 'art therapy "task"' and how 'there must be a "purpose" as the organisation expects this'. Not everyone was comfortable with this, feeling caught by institutional limitations, having to conduct their assessments in the context of the available time and resources.

Despite the different practices described in the chapters and reports, an underlying consistency emerged in contributors' responses to our question about exactly what it is that makes someone suitable for art therapy. There was agreement that the client should be 'psychologically minded'; be willing to address feelings that might be difficult and have a sense of personal agency in relation to their problems. There was also the client's motivation to change coupled with a willingness to engage with the therapist, factors that mirrored the criteria outlined by Ghaffari and Caparrotta (2004) that indicate suitability for psychotherapy. They make a useful distinction between generic factors that indicate suitability for a psychological intervention (motivation to change and the capacity for a therapeutic relationship) and specialist factors that indicate suitability for a particular model of therapy. Art therapy is certainly a particular kind of intervention, suitability for which can be indicated by generic factors but can also be determined by whether or not the person can make use of art materials and can link art-making to their personal experiences. However, suitability for a particular model of art therapy might hinge on the theoretical concepts and techniques used to make a formulation, that is, how the art therapist understands their client and the therapeutic value of art-making.

Having said 'yes' to suitability, what then? When different kinds of art therapy services were available it seemed that contributors operated differently. Some simply discussed with their clients if they would prefer a slow, open group, or studio-based art therapy, while others considered links between the identified problems and the recommended intervention, the latter being more prevalent when working with children who may have less say in adult decision making. These factors demand a qualitative judgement on the part of the therapist, and where the client's motivation might be missing or at a premium some flexibility may be required (Saotome, Report 5). Sometimes the assessment requires time so that therapist and client alike can see if art therapy 'suits' the individual (McCulloch, Report 3).

The assessment enterprise is founded on a meeting of two people in which, usually, there is an experience of being in relationship to another and an engagement with making art. Here it is worth noting that art therapists do not always require their clients to use art materials in assessments (Brown, Chapter 2; Leibmann, Report 6). Nonetheless, several contributors remarked on the importance of the clients' interest in art-making, linked specifically to an understanding of what this entailed in art therapy, that is, how it differed from art classes. Was art therapy actually what the client wanted? As one contributor said, could the client 'use them [art materials] over a significant portion of the session . . . [and] . . . trust me enough in order to have a conversation about themselves?' Authors outlined different ways of helping this engagement to happen as well as describing different approaches to the art object. For example: McNiff (Chapter 5) emphasises gesture in his exploration of creativity; Gantt (Chapter 10) stresses the formal elements in the art object; Case (Chapter 4) approaches the image through the countertransference; Henley (Chapter 3) highlights the aesthetic quality in a visual communication; and Tipple (Chapter 6) engages with art-making through the frame of social semiotics. Generally speaking, our authors' methods could be clustered into techniques that either promote trust and facilitate creative expression or seek to reach beneath the surface of appearance in order to construct a picture of the client's intrapsychic world. These methods are not mutually exclusive but they do access different kinds of data upon which different kinds of formulation – aesthetic, dynamic and diagnostic – can be made. How art therapists position themselves in relation to aesthetic discourses in particular seems to influence the development of assessment techniques and this, in our view, is a neglected debate.

Art therapists' theoretical orientation in their assessments can be located at any point on a continuum from belief in the healing power of art to the use of psychoanalytic ideas about the unconscious. Here it is interesting to note contributors' responses to our question about engagement with unconscious processes in their assessments. Although some chapters and reports emphasise the use of tools and techniques for diagnostic purposes, all our contributors were either aware of or worked with unconscious processes, 'even though unconscious material is slippery'. Several agreed with one contributor who said, 'It's always there in the thinking about what's going on even if not used directly in interactions with patients.' There was some agreement that the unconscious, along with transference and countertransference phenomena, was significant in art therapy assessments. As one contributor remarked:

> I am keenly aware whenever I administer a formal assessment of the potential transference experienced by the client . . . more often than not, I have found a desire (conscious or unconscious) to please on the part of the client. . . . Conversely, I have also found, at times, a more rebellious nature revealed by the individual who is asked to complete an assessment. My ability to correctly identify the source of the client's transference, whether consciously or unconsciously expressed . . . is another potentially valuable source of diagnostic information about that individual.

Art therapists also position themselves in a variety of ways with regard to the therapeutic relationship and the institution. Within this diversity there is a tension between processes that validate subjective and aesthetic understandings and those that favour rationality and objectivity, such that they can be endorsed as scientific. Those therapists more concerned with subjectivity and symbolic representation interest themselves in the meaning of emotional experiences and the construction of relationships, whereas those who aim to achieve objectivity often utilise formal, replicable, art-based instruments. The development of these instruments reflects both the need to address diagnosis, develop treatments and services linked to diagnoses and to evaluate the clinical and economic effectiveness that is inherent to health care systems that require rapid throughput, symptom reduction and measurable outcomes. This aspect of the modern workplace has led to political tension and to art therapists who take a psychodynamic approach to assessment coming into conflict with the institutions in which they work.

Fonagy (2009) describes some of the dichotomies between psychodynamic and empirical approaches. He suggests that empirical studies generate objective, quantitative data whereas psychodynamic inquiry produces subjective, first-person data. The challenge is to link the two in a systematic way 'yet to be specified' in order to generate a 'science of experience' (Northoff and Heinzel, 2006). This suggests the possibility of a synthesis of the dialectic, which resonates throughout the art therapy assessments described in this book, where number and description support and challenge each other. However, can we be confident that disparate discourses, for example, the psychoanalytical and the neurological, reflect an underlying shared reality about the object of inquiry?

The tension between 'sitting beside' a client and a more distant calculation in art therapy assessments may lessen as research develops. Research requires the clear identification of a question or topic for investigation, a methodology, subjects or respondents – in this instance, clients who belong to a certain population – and an equally clear treatment approach. Identifying different 'conditions' in an art therapy assessment and thus the particularities of the therapist's task, as Richardson (2004) suggests in relation to assessment for psychotherapy, is both a necessary and helpful part of contemporary evidence-based practice (EBP).

Our view is therefore a pragmatic one: the research-informed and diagnostically driven basis of EBP, coupled with diminishing resources and diagnostically determined treatment frameworks in mental health care, now requires art therapists to integrate a more diagnostic approach to assessment without losing or diluting their empathic response to the individual. Art therapy assessment in contemporary clinical settings is not always going to be a comfortable experience for client or therapist. Global economic pressures, coupled with political ideologies that position clients as consumers, gives rise to increased expectations but art therapists' ability to meet them declines. Demands to categorise people into diagnostic care packages that have treatment plans and associated costs attached to them may not allow space for therapists to think about understanding the person. This difficulty has to be addressed within art therapy assessments if practitioners are to maintain both their integrity and their position in the marketplace.

References

Fonagy, P. (2009) 'Postscript', *Psychoanalytic Psychotherapy*, 23 (3): 276–280.

Ghaffari, K. and Caparrotta, L. (2004) *The Function of Assessment Within Psychological Therapies*. London: Karnac Books.

Northoff, G. and Heinzel, A. (2006) 'First-person neuroscience: a new methodological approach for linking mental and neuronal states', *Philosophy, Ethics and Humanities in Medicine*, 1 (1): E3.

Richardson, P. (2004) 'Foreword', in K. Ghaffari and L. Caparrotta, *The Function of Assessment Within Psychological Therapies*. London: Karnac Books.

Index